Lexis Ludens

American University Studies

Series VII
Theology and Religion

Vol. 105

PETER LANG
New York · San Francisco · Bern
Frankfurt am Main · Paris · London

Anthony J. Petrotta

Lexis Ludens

Wordplay and the Book of Micah

PETER LANG
New York · San Francisco · Bern
Frankfurt am Main · Paris · London

Library of Congress Cataloging-in-Publication Data

Petrotta, Anthony J.
   Lexis Ludens : wordplay and the book of Micah /
Anthony J. Petrotta.
      p. cm. — (American university studies. Series VII,
Theology and religion ; vol. 105)
      Includes bibliographical references and index.
      1. Play on words.   2. Bible. O.T. Micah — Criticism,
interpretation, etc.   I. Title.   II. Series.
P304.P4   1991   224'.93066 — dc20   91-16769
ISBN 0-8204-1539-1   CIP
ISSN 0740-0446

Die Deutsche Bibliothek-CIP-Einheitsaufnahme

Petrotta, Anthony J.:
Lexis Ludens : wordplay and the book of Micah /
Anthony J. Petrotta. — New York; Berlin; Bern;
Frankfurt/M.; Paris; Wien: Lang, 1991
   (American university studies : Ser. 7, Theology and
religion ; Vol. 105)
   ISBN 0-8204-1539-1
NE: American university studies / 07

CONTENTS

Preface

This study, a revision of my doctoral dissertation at the University of Sheffield, grew out of a dissatisfaction with what commentators were saying regarding wordplay. Precious little was said besides its presence in the text. This dissatisfaction led me to read about wordplay in disciplines other than biblical studies, especially literary criticism and linguistics, where the comments focused on the function that wordplay serves in a passage, a notion that coincided with my feelings and interests.

Many people deserve thanks for the completion of any book. I wish to thank Professor D.J.A. Clines for working around my teaching responsibilities at Sterling College, and especially for his persistent questions that helped give shape and focus to this project, and his, sometimes, off-hand comments that sparked my thinking, and Dr. Heidi Burns of Peter Lang Publishing, Inc. for her encouragement and faith in the project. I also wish to thank my colleague Professor Dorothy Behnke for commenting on two drafts of this research project—a deed that goes well beyond collegial duties—and for her love of "grammar"; my friend and colleague Dr. Steven Fratt; and the staff at Sterling College library, especially Kay Kennedy for obtaining materials that even the Wizard of Oz would have had trouble locating. Thanks are also due Bruce, Keith Jarrett, U2, and 10,000 Maniacs for musical interludes during the writing of this project.

One's family always pays the steepest price in completing a work of this proportion. My love goes to Brian and Jenna, who have little enthusiasm for reading this work at this point in their lives. Jenna did read Micah, and, evidently, decided that my adding nearly 200 pages to the original story would not come up to the level of Judy Blume; Brian quite simply would rather read "Calvin and Hobbes" than Calvin's commentaries.

This research project, however, is dedicated to my wife, Janet, who laughs a lot ... but not always at my jokes.

Abbreviations

The abbreviations follow those in the Society of Biblical Literature, *Member's Handbook* (1980). The following abbreviations do not appear in the *Member's Handbook*.

CJ	*Classical Journal*
AUMLA	*Australian Universities Modern Language Association*
RestQ	*Restoration Quarterly*
BRev	*Bible Review*
NLH	*New Literary History*
PMLA	*Proceedings of the Modern Language Association*
AJS	*American Journal of Sociology*

PART ONE
THE UNIVERSE OF WORDPLAY

Surely we ought to move in the opposite direction from such moral earnestness, stressing not words as duty but words as play.

R.A. Lanham, *Style: An Anti-Textbook*

INTRODUCTION
PARONOMASIA UNBOUND

If puns can be found working thus in the writings of declared enemies, they may well be presumed to lurk everywhere.

J. Culler, "The Call of the Phoneme"

The study of wordplay is not at the forefront of biblical studies; indeed, the last full-scale monograph on the subject was Immanuel Casanowicz' doctoral dissertation at Johns Hopkins published in 1894.[1] Paronomasia is not a central issue, yet instances of paronomasia are found throughout the canonical and extra-canonical literature of biblical times. The pervasiveness and perdurability[2] of the pun are attested inter-lingually and intra-lingually. Like a meddlesome mother-in-law, wordplay is, by design or default, never far from the action.

THE PERPETUITY AND PERMEATION OF WORDPLAY

The perpetuity, or perdurability, of wordplay is indicated by those scholars who recognize and locate wordplay in the authors of antiquity: the actual use of the trope[3] by authors whose literary works date to earlier epochs, especially, perhaps, significant literary epochs of antiquity. E.S. McCartney furnishes plentiful examples of wordplay in Western, Classical authors ranging from Euripides and Aristophanes in Greece to Plautus and Cicero in Rome.[4] He cites examples not only from orations and plays, but also from histories, philosophies, and gravestones as well. Moreover, philosophers discuss wordplay in treatments of poetics and rhetoric. Plato and Aristotle argue about the relative merits of various σχήματα τῆς λέξεως in their writings. The figures based on the similarity of their sounds are not viewed for their own sake, but as elements delineating structure.[5] Thus wordplay, often called παρονομασία by the Greeks and *annominatio* (also spelled, *admoninatio* or anglicized as *agnominatio*) by the Latins, was practised and commented upon, not always with approval,[6] in the early stages of Western literature.

Western literature, however, does not hold an exclusive claim to wordplay. Wordplay also occurs in the classical literature of the East: the ancient Near East, India, and the Orient. W.G.E. Watson finds examples of assonance, alliteration, wordplay, and even rhyme—a trope not usually well-attested or widely used in Semitic languages—in Ugaritic and Akkadian (as well as Hebrew),[7] L. Peeters provides a few examples from Egypt,[8] and R.H. Blyth gives examples from Sanskrit, Chinese, and Japanese literature.[9]

A later example, though still within the classical tradition of its culture, from yet another locale, is provided by J. Huizinga. He records that the inhabitants of an East Indian archipelago engage in a "form of ceremonial antiphony." Huizinga says that

> what constitutes the formal poetic element is the assonance which, by repeating the same word or a variation of it, links thesis to antithesis. The purely poetic element consists in allusion, the sudden bright idea, the pun or simply in the sound of the words themselves, where sense may be completely lost. Such a form of poetry can only be described and understood in terms of play, though it obeys a nice system of prosodic rules.[10]

Thus diverse ancient cultures reflect a tradition of engaging in various forms of wordplay.

The second pointer to the antiquity and enduring quality of wordplay is the frequency of its occurrence in "timeless" myths—creation and judgment (death and eschatology). Huizinga speaks of the play element in Hindu and Scandinavian creation stories.[11] R. Frank discusses the Old English practice of playing *weard* (God) and *word* (word) off one another as the poets conflate Gen 1: 1 and John 1: 1 to show that God created heaven (*rodor*) and earth (*rod*) through his son.[12]

Is it any accident that before creation there was *tohu wabohu* (תהו ובהו)? Or that Genesis begins *bᵉreshit bara'* (ברשית ברא)?[13] Casanowicz cites the study of E. Nestle, *Die israelitischen Eigennamen*, who finds fifty-one etymological explanations of proper names in Genesis, which amounts to about half of the etymological explanations found in the whole of the Hebrew Scriptures.[14] In the beginning was the pun, as C.J. Ackerley writes in a slightly different context.[15]

Not only does wordplay exist at the Beginning, but also at the End, both death and eschatology. McCartney report examples of puns on gravestones in Greece and Rome. One such example suggests at least a degree of happiness resulting from the death of a spouse: *Solvit vota sua laetus cum coniuge Care* . McCartney reports twenty inscriptions punning on Felix, Felicula, and Felicitas.

In the Gospel of John, wordplays and puns abound throughout the narrative when Jesus stands on trial for his life before Pilate (John 18: 28-9: 15). One example is the question of Jesus' kingship: Pilate, Jesus, and the soldiers proclaim Jesus' kingship, each with different meanings and motivations; but the Jews, over whom he is to exercise his kingship (John 1: 49), do not proclaim Jesus as King . A more interesting example because of its complexity is found in John 19:13, ἐκάθισεν ἐπὶ βήματος: is καθίζειν intransitive, Pilate sitting down on the "throne" ("He [Pilate] sat upon the throne") or transitive, Jesus sitting on it ("He [Pilate] sat [him, Jesus] upon the throne")? C.K. Barrett concludes his examination by saying, "We may suppose then that John meant that Pilate did in fact sit on the βῆμα, but that for those with eyes to see behind this human scene appeared the Son of man, to whom all judgment has been committed (5: 22), seated upon his throne."[16] Not all commentators accept this understanding,[17] but it is highly suggestive and illustrates a use of wordplay that is often overlooked— play on the syntax as well as sound and meaning.

Wordplays are also prevalent in OT texts concerning death; indeed an unnatural amount of wordplay occurs in the laments of the OT. One such example, germane to our study of wordplay in Micah, is the lament of David over Saul and Jonathan in 2 Sam 1: 18-27,[18] and again in 2 Sam 3: 33-34 where David laments over Abner's death: "Should Abner (*'abner* ; אבנר) die as a fool (*nabal* ; נבל) dies?" (RSV).

Not only the death of a person, but the death of Time itself gets caught in wordplays. In his study of Early English verse, Frank cites examples from both *Genesis* and *Daniel* that show "ironic contrast" and "verbal pyrotechnics" in visions of hell and eschatology. A brief example from *Daniel* will suffice: *Fyr on feondas for fyren daedum* (Fire on the enemies for their wicked deeds).[19] The notorious instance of numerology or *gematria* in the Apocalypse with "666" (Rev 13:18) is a biblical example of wordplay being used in an eschatological setting.

Thus, thanatology—"'Let punners consider how hard it is to die jesting, when death is so hard in digesting'"[20]— and eschatology—"one of the advantages of nuclear warfare is that all men are cremated equal"[21]—cannot escape the punster's sting.

The preceding discussion of the perdurability of wordplay also indicates something of its permeation, or pervasiveness: from chaos, through creation, to consummation; *Urzeit und Endzeit* , and all that lies between. In English Literature, for instance, wordplay is present in Chaucer, Shakespeare, James Joyce, and Dr. Seuss. Wordplay travels not only vertically through time, but also horizontally between borders of cultures, authors, and genres. Time and genre neither contain nor control wordplay.

Statistics also supply support for the pervasiveness of wordplay. McCartney finds 330 puns in his study of wordplay covering only personal names in classical languages. Further support for the ubiquity of wordplay comes from Casanowicz, who charts the occurrences of the trope in the Bible: every book in the Hebrew Bible except Obadiah contains identifiable paronomasia. The "historical" books contain the fewest number of puns per page, 0.36, whereas the prophets have 1.22 and the poetical books 1.40. At the low end are Leviticus, Numbers, and Ezra; the high end includes Joel (the highest with 3.25), Micah, Habbakuk, Zephaniah, and Nahum.

Statistics, of course, are of relative value, and these no less than others. Casanowicz' chart is in need of augmentation and correction,[22] and consequently his listings are questionable. For example, Casanowicz claims that Obadiah contains the lowest percentage of wordplay per page (0.00). Surely the brevity of the book accounts, at least in part, for this figure. If the author had used paronomasia twice, it would be listed among the highest! Similarly, C.J. Fordyce supplements McCartney's statistics.[23]

Statistics, nevertheless, miss the point that reading is more than an echo, and that the limits of wordplay are difficult to set; statistics miss the qualitative aspects in favor of quantification. Statistics do show that wordplay is not uncommon. Wordplay is perpetual and permeates all facets of literature.

THE STUDY OF WORDPLAY

The purpose of the present study is to examine this pervasive and perdurable figure of speech as it occurs in the book of Micah. However, a problem arises as soon as one begins to read the literature regarding wordplay: an uncertainty is exhibited over the role wordplay plays in composition, the method of study, and even its very nature. At one extreme is the recent *On Puns* whose subtitle, "The Foundation of Letters" indicates the considerable weight the essayists give wordplay.[24] At the other extreme are those who suggest that wordplay is of popular origin and dismiss it as "mere literary embellishment," as, for example, G.R. Driver.[25] Is wordplay foundational or cosmetic?

Part One of the present study focuses on the nature of wordplay, especially as it relates to "play" more so than "word." That is, this study views wordplay from a theory of humor more than a theory of language.[26]

In the light of the contrariety regarding wordplay as mentioned above, an examination of the scholarly approaches to the trope is in order. Chapter One reviews wordplay as studied by biblical and literary critics. The influential works of Casanowicz in biblical studies and Mahood in literary studies form the basis of the comparison. Some overlap exists, but a fundamental difference of approach is identified: biblical critics, as evidenced in the literature specifically addressing wordplay, focus their attention on sound rather than sense, list examples more so than discuss the occurrences of the trope within given pericopes, and speak of wordplay as ornamentation not rhetoric.

The following chapters of Part One present an argument for the importance of wordplay in composition, but not for its preeminence; these chapters lead to a discussion of how wordplay works within a theory of humor. That is, wordplay is a sophisticated linguistic and literary endeavor, sometimes subtle, sometimes obvious, that often fulfils important aesthetic and affective functions in a passage; rather than being foundational for composition and thought, wordplay stands alongside other linguistic and literary factors that make communication possible. The affective function of wordplay is seen when the communication is disrupted by an alternative and incongruous reading of the utterance that turns out to be "logical." Thus, chapter Two argues that a particular kind of linguistic collocation—one sign displays both identity and difference with another sign—works with formal aspects of composition, which may occasion "cognitive development" (the exploration of meaning). Chapter Three explores the kind of ambiguity that arises when these similarities (identity and difference) of signs come together. The ambiguity involved in wordplay is not simply due to the polysemous nature of words nor to uncertainty or ambivalence, but occurs where two meanings are *not* excluded by the context. Chapter Four discusses the formal relationships of wordplay, relationships that affect a reader cognitively. Chapter Five concludes the more theoretical issues surrounding wordplay by suggesting that the ambiguous phonological, semantic and syntactical relationships in wordplay may have an affective consequence alongside the cognitive— wordplay is often humorous. Chapters Two through Five defend the argument that wordplay is truly rhetorical, part of the persuasive angle of a text.

Part Two of this study shows how the theoretical understanding of wordplay argued for in Part One is supported by evidence from the text of Micah, and how this way of viewing wordplay enriches the understanding of various passages. Since biblical critics have traditionally focused on sound to the exclusion of other aspects of wordplay, Chapter Six shows that wordplay is not all of one type, but takes a variety of forms from etymological plays to plays involving the connotation of terms. Chapter Seven focuses on the formal aspects of wordplay in composition and some of the cognitive effects a reader is invited to share or explore, especially "reversals" brought about by God's words or actions in response to those who pervert justice and yet "lean upon the Lord and say, 'No harm will come to us.'" Chapter Eight rounds out the study by showing the ludic effect of wordplay, the neglected side of wordplay, especially in biblical studies.

In the conclusion of Part Two, I suggest that wordplay involves the "infinite plasticity" of sounds, words, syntax, and, therefore, the critic should be alert to the ambiguities in a text, ambiguities that result in both greater understanding and greater pleasure in reading the text.

The overall purpose is to show that the study of wordplay by biblical critics has been too narrowly carried out, and by examining the trope in the book of Micah we see the variety in both form and function of this much maligned figure.

MATTERS OF DEFINITION

In the opening paragraph of this introduction, I used "wordplay," "paronomasia," and "pun" interchangeably. The terms are often used interchangeably or used as if the referent were clear. Some terms are general terms necessary for study and for communicating ideas to others without the burden of precision; we assume that the audience knows what is meant by the terms we use. In biblical studies, "eschatology" and "midrash" often fall into this category. Paronomasia, for biblical critics, functions similarly: it covers a multitude of significations.

This assumption that the reader knows the meaning of paronomasia (pun and wordplay) is reflected in much of the literature on wordplay by biblical scholars. Neither A. Guillaume[27] nor G.R. Driver defines wordplay. J.M. Sasson's definition is so broad that it fits into this category as well: "Paronomasia is the term employed by ancient Greek commentators when referring to rhetoric devices designed to engage the attention of an audience."[28]

Others interchange the terms. J.J. Glück uses wordplay, pun, and paronomasia in the first page of his article;[29] J.H. Charlesworth says, "The Odist loved to create paronomasia. His plays on words ...";[30] and M. Black similarly says that paronomasia is "not only the pun but word-play generally, the opposition and juxtaposition of similar sounding words."[31]

We see that a certain indeterminacy, which is neither new nor unusual in discussions of rhetoric, governs the use of the terms "paronomasia," "pun," and "wordplay" in biblical studies.[32] Dictionary definitions show a similar overlap, but also introduce overlooked aspects of the terms.

The *Oxford English Dictionary* defines "paronomasia" as "a playing upon words which sound alike, a word-play, a pun." If we turn to "word-play" we find, "A playing or trifling with words; the use of words merely or mainly for the purpose of producing a rhetorical or fantastic effect ... or humorous effect by similarity of sound with different meaning; a pun." And of "pun" it says, "The use of a word in such a way as to suggest two or more meanings or different associations... so as to produce a humorous effect; a play upon words."

Webster's *Third International* plays less of a circle game than *OED* but similarly shows an overlap of meaning. Paronomasia is "a play upon words in which the same word is used in different senses or words similar in sound are set in opposition so as to give antithetical force." Wordplay is "verbal wit based on the peculiarities of words ... a pun is a form of wordplay." The pun is the "humorous use of a word is such a way to suggest different meanings or applications ... a play upon words."

The more recent *Random House Dictionary* (2d ed., unabridged) offers this distinction for the three terms: Paronomasia is either the use of different senses of a word or the use of words that sound similar in order to achieve "a special effect, as humor or dual meaning." Wordplay is a "clever repartee; verbal wit." A pun comes about in the humorous use of a word to suggest either different meanings or applications.[33]

Some distinctions are made in these sets of definitions, but overlap of meaning remains. In contradistinction to the definitions of biblical scholars, emphasis is placed on the humorous effect of the collocation of words—wordplay is "witty."

What observations can we make concerning these terms? "Wordplay," we can see, is a transparent combination of common terms, which, until recently, was either not connected or connected with a hyphen; i.e., "word play" or "word-play."

Paronomasia is like wordplay; it is transparent, being a combination of παρά "by the side of," and ὀνομασία "naming"; hence, παρονομάζειν: "to alter slightly in naming." In classical usage, paronomasia usually refers to words in proximity that differ only slightly in form and have a different meaning.

The lineage of "pun" serves less to draw lines of descent, and more lines of dissent. L. Spitzer seeks to establish the etymology of "pun" by relating it to derivatives of *poindre* , "to sting." By the addition of suffixes, he comes up with *poindrillon*, by which he posits "pundigrion" as a "theoretically possible" approximation in English.[34] Spitzer cites Dryden, who says that the pun is a "clipped" word from "punnet" and "pundigrion" ("punnet" also being a derivative of *poindre* —*poignette* , according to Spitzer). Redfern, which reminds us of *OED* ("of uncertain origin"), is a more practical guide: "The genealogy of the word for pun in both English and French is highly dubious, which befits this trope which many consider illegitimate."[35] Like Melchizedek, its patrimony is uncertain, and the tribute paid to etymological speculation yields too little dividend to be pursued much further than noting these possibilities.

Uncertainty exists etymologically (with respect to "pun") and a circularity of sorts exists in the common usage of these terms. Nevertheless, I want to introduce a helpful distinction between the three terms that allows us to use "wordplay," "paronomasia," and "pun" with more precision while taking into account etymology and common usage.

"Wordplay" is best suited as the comprehensive term.[36] Better might be "playing with words"—for the various ways the device is employed all involve some sort of *lexis ludens* —but the simpler "wordplay" has an appealing concision and introduces no new terms with which to contend. "Pun" will refer to those aspects of wordplay that highlight the semantic elements, a use that is reflected in its application in linguistic studies. "Paronomasia" can then be reserved for the more phonological plays that occur, a usage in accord with its etymology and traditional employment (words with slightly different forms in close proximity).

These distinctions between wordplay, pun, and paronomasia will allow further classifications of the diverse kinds of wordplays that an author has at his or her disposal. Introduction of "classifications" leads to the first topic of enquiry: How have critics understood the workings of wordplay?

ONE
HISTORICAL BEARINGS AND CONCEPTUAL OPTIONS

'Unlike children, puns should be heard, not seen.'

Redfern, *Puns* [1]

Literary language [is not] ... an occasional ornament of the writer's art: [it is] his art.

Ahl, *Metaformations*

Wordplay is found in every genre, language, and period, yet attitudes vary towards this ubiquitous trope, attitudes which result in different conceptions of its nature, the method of study or presentation, and the role it plays in the passage. While differences exist, in biblical studies a particular pattern has come to dominate the discussions: that is, the chief feature of wordplay is sound, the method of presentation is classifying or listing, and the role is "literary embellishment." This conception and approach to wordplay derives largely from the seminal study by Casanowicz.

In contradistinction to biblical studies, the characteristics of literary-critical studies of wordplay are not sound but meaning, not listing examples but discourse about the passage or line where the wordplay occurs, and not "embellishment" but various functions from structuring to pathos. This approach to the study of wordplay is best illustrated by M. Mahood's classic study of wordplay in the plays and sonnets of Shakespeare.

The following discussion will examine each pattern in turn, starting first, however, with terminological considerations since they differ from my approach and set up the problem as I see it.

DISTINCTIONS IN TERMINOLOGY

In defining wordplay, we saw that a certain indeterminacy and interchangeability exists, especially in the definitions by Black, Glück, and

Sasson. Distinctions, however, are attempted. Casanowicz says that "in paronomasia, the physical side of language, its phonetic material, is employed as a means of style"; other tropes are used to bring out the "psychical" side of language, "*i.e.* with the effect brought about by the special signification, or grammatical and logical relation, of a word or clause."[2]   Further in the essay he says that "plays upon word" involve both sound and meaning; he designates these plays upon words as "sense-paronomasia" in contradistinction to the "sound-paronomasia," the physical side of language mentioned above. Casanowicz clarifies the distinction between the two when he says, "Sound-paronomasia is a spontaneous outgrowth of the genius of language, or, at least, engendered by instinct and natural law; sense-paronomasia is rather an artificial offspring of the former."[3]   (To put it in our terminology, paronomasia is a natural result of language, while puns are imposed upon language usage.)

The situation in literary studies is not unlike what we find in biblical studies with its reluctance to define wordplay. Mahood offers no definition and she admits that it is not easy to fix the frontiers of wordplay. In her preface, however, she does mention "homonymic puns" and "semantic wordplays," but does not define or sufficiently qualify either category other than to mention her indebtedness to experts for the "pronunciation" of homonymic puns and "disentangling the meanings" of semantic wordplays.[4]

Thus a distinction between wordplays based on sound and those based on sense is common in much of the literature on wordplay. However, this common distinction does not become an organizing principle in many of the literary studies but does in the biblical studies. More importantly, the fuzzy boundaries between these two sides of wordplay are duly noted in literary studies, and the focus of attention is on semantic considerations that accompany the sounds even in those literary studies that deal predominantly with paronomasia.[5]

The fuzzy boundary between paronomasia and pun—the distinction between the "physical" and "psychical" sides of language (Casanowicz)—is easily illustrated; and, as will become clear through this study, confining these two aspects of wordplay to a too specific enclosure is artificial and simplistic. One biblical example of the intertwining of sound and sense will suffice to show that such a distinction is not easily supported. Isa 28: 10 reads:

כִּי צַו לָצָו צַו לָצָו
קַו לָקָו קַו לָקָו
זְעֵיר שָׁם זְעֵיר שָׁם

Admittedly the lines are difficult, but the traditional interpretation—"precept upon precept, line upon line; here a little, there a little" (cf. AV)—has not been suitably or convincingly replaced by an alternative suggestion. H. Wildberger,[6] R.E. Clements,[7] and O. Kaiser[8] cite with some degree of approval the suggestion that the words reflect a teaching situation, perhaps especially that of children learning the alphabet (an interpretation that goes back at least to Ibn Ezra, although not often noted). This interpretation gains credence from v 9 where the question is asked to whom knowledge will be taught, and accords with the echoing effect of the text. Whether the words are onomatopoeic, alphabetical (צו and קו being designations of the letters), or the more traditional pedagogical, sound and sense cross betwixt and between as the author uses his art to create an effect and deliver a message.[9] Sound and sense co-mingle; separation is neither necessary nor advantageous.

Excursus: Wordplay as "Soundplay."

The conception of wordplay as "similar sounding words" is a chord that Casanowicz, among others, strikes. Holladay goes so far as to define wordplay by sound: "By 'word-play' I mean any likeness of sound between two words or phrases whether it is deliberate punning on names, or assonance of any sort."[10] Such a reduction of wordplay to soundplay requires examination.

The link between sound and wordplay is interesting and perplexing, especially when one is examining the biblical text where the language is not spoken by any living community.[11] Indeed, the problem is not confined to sound elements of "dead" languages. Without some pronunciation guide, even a familiar language could pose problems. For example, in the hymn, "Hope and Aspiration," we find these "rhymes":

My heart is weak and poor Until it master *find* ;
It has no spring of action sure—It varies with the *wind* ;
It cannot freely move Till Thou hast wrought its *chain* ;
Enslave it with Thy matchless love, And deathless it shall *reign.*

"Find" and "wind"[12] "look" as if they rhyme, but they do not in contemporary pronunciation, whereas "chain" and "reign" do not appear to rhyme, yet they do.

The example shows that the permutations are almost inexhaustible for what may or may not constitute a sound relation, whether that relation be rhyme, alliteration, assonance, or some other device, and that an intimate knowledge of the language is essential for establishing such a relation. Moreover, cognizance of approximate and pseudo-relations is a relevant factor to consider, as well as the development of a language over time and the dialects or regional pronunciation.

These considerations are complicated in an ancient language such as Hebrew where scholars differ over how to reconstruct the sound of the "dead" language: Holladay suggests that we reconstruct the phonological correspondences of David's time through comparative phonetics, while Watson suggests that the Masoretes, in the absence of other guides, must be viewed as reliable. So which guide cuts the truest path, comparative phonetics or tradition?

The problem and the need for caution in determining the sound of biblical Hebrew is recognized by all, and the use of whatever evidence is available is how biblical critics generally proceed in practice. At the same time, we must suspect any results that rely primarily on so tenuous a position as sound in a dead language—the mere fact of an unvocalized text for several centuries necessitates some ambiguity.[13]

A less obvious but related issue crops up: What makes a line "euphonious"? Is rhyme more pleasing than alliteration? Are gutturals less aesthetic than laryngals? Frank avers that phonological repetition is affective: "Phonological recurrence, the repetition of similar words linking related things, imparts a ritualistic, almost litany-like quality to Old Testament events described … [and] manages to convey the sense of an underlying order and purpose to the flux of divine history."[14] Not every sound recurrence, however, produces this "ritualistic" or pleasing effect. Watson, in a note, quotes Culler as saying, "We have only the crudest idea of what makes a line euphonious or successful and of how phonological modulations from one line to another contribute to the effects of a poem."[15]

I would suggest that what makes these phonological modulations effective is the ability or tendency to think associatively or analogically—*how* that works is a much more complicated issue.[16] The associations of sound patterns are complex, but, perhaps never autonomous. They contribute to the meaning of a literary work on various levels, not simply the oral/aural level.

Moreover, the analogical or associative thinking does not stop with sound, but extends to sense as well. For example, A. Berlin argues that "word-pairs" are not produced as much from a fixed semantic stock that poets could draw from, as from normal, but complex, associations that speakers —and writers— experience linguistically.[17] Phonetic patterning and sense (image)-bonding, it seems, work interdependently or reciprocally as well as analogically. We delight in the cadences of sound marching along a sentence and the resulting uniformity of meaning. If this is the case, can we, then, ever speak merely of "similar *sounding* words"?

The cause or causes of phonological indeterminacy, whether because of the problem of reconstructing the original oral/aural effect or because we simply cannot predict what makes a line euphonious, suggests that equating wordplay with soundplay is hazardous. The hazard of sound denotation and sound euphony is especially true with Classical Hebrew texts where a necessary transformation of the predominantly oral/aural pattern into a more graphic representation is a natural result from the absence of a community speaking Hebrew as an everyday language. The printed page, whether produced by scribe or press, introduces an element in addition to sound.

Sounds are not autonomous but heteronomous, not only with respect to sense but also script. The sounds we utter are transcribed graphically as signs in texts, and therefore the graphic representation becomes part of the play as well;[18] that is, this representation can either be another source of play alongside the utterance, or suggest other plays that were not part of any supposed original oral utterance.

R.D. Roberts, who argues that poetry is still essentially oral, reports several experiments with more "graphic" representation of poems in English, some dating back to medieval times and others associated with poets noted primarily for the "sound" of their poetry (e.g., Dylan Thomas).[19] However, Roberts maintains that such poems continue to be enjoyed for the sound itself once the initial impact of the graphic representation wears off, though exceptions, such as Lewis Carroll's "Cat and Mouse" exist. A further, deceptively simple example, is e.e. cummings' "Leaf":

l(a

le
af
fa

ll

s)
one
l

iness

Examples are readily available that show that not all "wordplays" can be taken aurally in the same way that not all poems can be read aurally. The children's riddle "half of eight is nothing" is solved if represented graphically. "Eight" written as "8" "solves" the riddle (half of 8 = o).

We also find graphic "plays" in the Masorah in such things as suspended letters, e.g., מֹנַשֶּׁה (Judg 18: 30); large letters, e.g.,שְׁמַע ישׂראל יהוה אלהינו יהוה אחָד (Deut 6: 4); and especially in the תקרי אל, e.g., at Exod 32: 16, "Do not read חרות ("engraved"), but read חֵ(ר)וּת ("liberty")." A homiletic point is made in all these examples: The suspended *nun* might reflect an editor's desire to distance "Moses" from the idolatrous practices of his heirs,[20] and the enlarged letters of Deut 6: 4 are perhaps a warning for precision in reading the *shema'* .[21] The wordplay on חרות is meant to show that true liberty is found in the observance of *Torah*.[22]

Thus plays may exist on any of the many levels of linguistic competence—phonological, morphological, lexical, and graphic—and constructing plays at any level of communication or composition is possible. Furthermore, the phonological utterances and lexical representations form words that are further constructed in such a way as to form sentences, and paragraphs, and even larger structures. The medium will produce its own plays, whether they be oral, written, typewritten (opposite fingers—e.g., "k" for "d"—or missed keys), or from computers (computerese, computer logic, or computer generated graphics).

Too many antinomies exist to define this trope predominantly in terms of sound; wordplay cannot be reduced to soundplay.

The preoccupation with sound that dominates many of the discussions of wordplay in the Bible, in addition to erecting practical obstacles, has been a hindrance to seeing wordplay in a number of different contexts that involve primarily semantics, but extends to orthographical and syntactical plays. Moreover, the focus on phonetics often results in aesthetic depreciation, as evidenced in numerous remarks about wordplay (e.g., Casanowicz, Driver), and misses other functions of play in the overall utterance. Sound, sense, and syntax are not independent, but interdependent and work within the discourse.

Before we examine the widespread "depreciation" of wordplay in biblical studies, especially as it relates to its role in the composition (whether oral or written), examination of the method of study or presentation is in order since, I feel, both the conception of wordplay as soundplay and the listing of examples contributes to the view that wordplay is little more than literary embellishment. Thus, how do biblical critics examine or present their examination of wordplays? How do literary critics approach this trope? Do the differences produce practical consequences?

CLASSIFICATIONS OF WORDPLAY

Rather than offering a formal definition of pun, paronomasia, and wordplay, many scholars are content to define it by example—we know it if we see it, even if we cannot name it. Since nearly all who study the trope resort to some form of cataloguing for their examples, perhaps the best way to understand wordplay is through classifying examples. While cataloguing is necessary and helpful, it easily leads, however, to "pigeon-holing"; and, therefore, together with seeing wordplay as soundplay, it is often assigned a superficial role for the figure to play in the composition. The trope is named but not explained.

Casanowicz classifies wordplay as *sound* - and *sense* -paronomasia. He further subdivides sound-paronomasia into alliteration, assonance, and rhyme, whereas sense-paronomasia entails antanaclasis, homonyms, a change of the voice of the verb, a juxtaposition of a simplex and a compound (or two compounds of the same stem), or a change of letters within a word.[23] He makes these distinctions when he speaks of wordplay generally; however, when he turns to paronomasia in the Hebrew Scriptures, he simply arranges them alphabetically.

Others in the field of biblical studies follow the basic two-fold classification of sound and sense. For example, Charlesworth says that wordplays are either paronomastic, which includes repetition, double entendre, and double entente (the former, for Charlesworth, means similar sounding words with different meanings, while the latter refers to two different meanings of the same word), or assonantic.[24] Driver, to his credit, differs in his approach being neither as simple or as formal as Casanowicz. He mentions assonance, equivocal plays (double entendre) and plays upon names, but he also includes *gematria* (the use of numerical equivalents of words to produce a covert meaning) and *notrikon* (letters of a word used as an acronymic abbreviation for other words or phrases).

The mention of *gematria* and *notrikon* introduces a point about wordplays in the Bible that does not figure prominently in studies of wordplay outside biblical studies, and provides the basis for the somewhat novel approach to classifying wordplays not by sound and sense, but by what Sasson calls "visual" wordplays.

Sasson's classification, as novel and comprehensive as it is, however, is still not complete.[25] If one's object is to "pigeon-hole" wordplays, then being exhaustive becomes important; however, the very completeness of the project makes it unwieldy for general acceptance, and impractical for a study of the trope in individual books or of a particular author's style.

Moreover, the basic distinction that Sasson makes between "visual" and "oral" is, I think, as misguided and misleading as the more usual sound and sense distinction. Is anastrophe any less aural than antanaclasis or farrago? Would we fail to recognize parasonancy simply by reading a text? Although the usual "sound" and "sense" distinction has a degree of artificiality about it as well, these categories are generally recognized and accepted, even across disciplines. At the very least, Sasson should add a third category, "sense," and make appropriate adjustments for where the examples belong.

My major objection is not to quibble over the finer points of taxonomy; rather, those who "postal-clerk" the trope as the sole or primary manner of presentation create the false impression that if one simply "plugs" the wordplay in the correct socket, then they have said something significant taxonomically about the trope or its use. Moreover, this over-attention to taxonomy itself obscures features inherent in wordplay and creates distinctions where overlapping is more common. Pigeon-holing flattens our view so that we lose sight of the tropes orientation to the text.

The stricture of over-attention to taxonomy is best illustrated by appeal to the approach by literary critics, who often employ the distinction between sound and sense, and spell out the various "typologies" that exist, but these distinctions seldom become organizing principles. Rather, the varied roles that wordplay works in the composition are discussed in theory and practice: structure and balance, exploration of semantic range and associations, and revelation of character and "mental processes" are among the options encountered. Moreover, reference to the "verbal wit" or humor of the author in question is invariably mentioned.

WORKING WITH WORDPLAY: MAHOOD ON SHAKESPEARE

In her classic study of Shakespeare's wordplay, Mahood spends precious little time on classifications. Indeed, she claims that one must be wary of nomenclature: "... every godfather can give a name."[26]

The seriousness of wordplay is seen in the many ways Shakespeare, as poet, dramatist, and dramatic-poet, employs wordplay to achieve certain ends. Moreover, Mahood contends that Shakespeare's imagination works through the plays he makes with "verbal meanings"—an indication of what Mahood considers wordplay. The poetry works through puns: Shakespeare has the characters pun because the situation calls for it, or uses puns to clarify the particular view of life Shakespeare wishes to present.

Mahood introduces one formal feature of wordplay not often cited. she contends that wordplay can exist even when the word is not present: "Sometimes a word, the various meanings of which offer the poet a range of images, itself remains unexpressed."[27] These "unspoken" puns, which she claims may be conscious or not, abound in Shakespeare. For example, In *Henry IV* part 2, Hal, a tennis-court keeper, says:

> for it is a low ebbe of Linnen with thee, when thou kept'st not *Racket* there, as thou hast not done a great while, because the rest of thy *Low Countries* , have made a *shift* to eate up thy *Holland* : and God knows whether those that *bal* out the ruines of thy linnen shal inherite his kingdom: but the Midwives say, the children are not in the *fault* whereupon the world increases, and kindreds are mightily strengthened (II. ii. 22-31).[28]

The puns on "racket," "ball," and "fault" are evident, but Mahood argues that the "quibbles" in "shift" and "Holland" are sustained by an unspoken pun on "piece-maker," "which gives rise to the echo of the Beatitudes in 'shall inherit his kingdom.' "[29]

The notion of "unspoken" puns is not as farfetched as it may appear. A possible example of an unspoken pun in the Bible is found in 2 Sam 24 where David purchases a threshing floor from "Araunah," a Jebusite. David proceeds to build an altar and the plagues are averted by the sacrifices made there. "Araunah" (ארונה) calls to mind the ark of the covenant (ארון), though the ark is not mentioned in the narrative, and, as J. Rosenberg observes, 2 Sam ends where 1 Sam begins "with a stable and functioning shrine."[30]

But formal features are only interesting to Mahood as they relate to the broader meaning(s) of the play. Near the end of her introductory chapter, Mahood remarks: "The vital wordplay in Shakespeare's writings is that between the characters and their creator, between the primary meanings of words in the context of a person's speech and their secondary meanings as part of the play's underlying pattern of thought."[31] However, it is "not the elusive mind of the playwright" that is important, as if a psychological study of the author or detecting authorial intention were necessary to unravel the (word)play. Rather, the wordplays—the words and the drama—weave the meaning of the play.

Shakespeare reveals character through wordplay; these revelations can be as sinister as they are funny. Mahood contends that most often the "attacker shields himself behind" the innocuous meaning of the word, while the aggressive meaning "is the blade that strikes home."[32] One example comes from the scene in *Macbeth* where MacDuff uses ambiguity to rouse Malcolm:

Bleed, bleed poore Country,
Great Tyrrany, lay thou thy basis sure,
For goodnesse dare not check thee: wear thou thy wrongs,
the Title, is affear'd   (IV. iii. 31-34).

"Affeared" means "assured, confirmed" whereas the thrust of MacDuff's words lies in Malcolm's fear to claim the Scottish throne.

"Funny" wordplays work in a similar way to the sinister ones: the underlying themes of the play are brought out and character is revealed. Shakespearean "wisecracks" are not intrusive but often contrast the "simpletons, who are at the mercy of words they do not fully understand, and the sophisticated wits, who show their mastery of words by ringing all possible changes on their meanings."[33]

Shakespeare uses wordplay on occasion to produce an ironic interplay between audience, character, and creator: "It may be anticipatory or retrospective, may imply a difference of values between what the speaker is allowed to say for himself and what the writer and his audience think, or it may simply intensify or widen the speaker's meaning to give it significance beyond the moment of speech."[34]

An interesting, though unspectacular, instance of wordplay as a vehicle for differences of values lies in the reply of Antonio to Shylock's account of how Jacob's flocks multiplied. He says, "This was a venture sir that Jacob serv'd for." "Venture" means both "a course the outcome of which is uncertain" and "a commercial enterprise." Antonio's ventures as a merchant come under the same scrutiny as Shylock's money-lending, and, therefore, a faint light is reflected on the conduct of the Gentiles, at least temporarily, before Shakespeare continues with the iniquities of the Jews.[35]

Mahood says in the concluding paragraph of her chapter, "The Fatal Cleopatra": "A poet makes his discovery of poetic truth only through an exploration of the meaning of words."[36] And this, it appears, is her "definition" of wordplay: exploring verbal associations in order to discover some truth beyond their ostensive reference.

Wordplay, then, is often subtle, diverse, and fluid. Classification easily becomes an end in itself for those who study wordplay by listing examples with little comment on their semantic and structural significance in the pericope; much of the dynamism of the device is lost. Reversing the proverbial feline problem: cataloguing kills the curiosity.

THE SPECTRUM OF WORDPLAY

I want to suggest an alternative model for classifying wordplay, one less dependent upon categorical distinctions and more dependent upon the linguistic features of words—the parts and purposes of words and their relationships to each other. An appropriate metaphor for this model is a continuum since linguistic features, though distinct, are also related.[37] However, continuum suggests something that one can easily represent graphically on a page (something I would caution against), so perhaps spectrum is a more appropriate metaphor, especially since the prismatic effect of wordplay comes to mind: as the author and reader turn the sounds, senses, and syntax of the utterance, different refractions become visible/audible.

The definitions we offered in the introductory comments form the basis for the following classification (recognizing that these classifications are relative to each other and to other figures). "Wordplay" is the comprehensive term since it conveys the idea that words are put to use without implications of how that use is realized—wordplay comes in diverse forms. "Pun" corresponds to the common "sense" distinction that is often advocated, and "paronomasia" fulfils the "sound" distinction. A third general category, dubbed "sequencing"[38] for lack of a comprehensive term, seems necessary since language is more than sound and sense, and wordplays invoke all aspects of language usage. This category corresponds roughly to syntax, either generated by syntactical considerations (e.g., parallelism, hyberbaton) or affecting syntax (e.g., acrostics, *gematria*).

A pun may be formed by a single term that carries two meanings (syllepsis[39]); a single term repeated in the same sense (repetition); a single term repeated with a different sense (antanaclasis); two terms similar in sound but dissimilar in meaning or morphology (homonymy; paronym[40]); two terms whose meanings overlap or contrast (synonym; antonym); and two terms fused into one (portmanteau).

Paronomasia includes alliteration (repeating consonant clusters, usually near the beginning of a word); assonance (repetition of vowel sounds); consonance (consonant clusters at the end the words); and rhyme. Metathesis produces anagrammatical plays (a "chiasm" of phonemes), and onomatopoeia is formed by sound imitative lexemes.

Under the "sequencing" category, we find hyperbaton (disruption of normal word order); anaphora (identical words beginning subsequent clauses); gradatio (words forming a "ladder" effect—A-B, B-C, C-D); chiasm (inversion of words); and parallelism. This category also includes *gematria* , *notrikon* , and acrostics.

The controlling metaphor for the wordplay is a spectrum, however, so the categories are not inveterate, but protean. Sound, sense, and syntax intermingle as, for example, in onomatopoeia, paronyms, or anaphora. Moreover, an intermingling of the structures that generate the figures takes place: Paronomasia depends upon proximity, a condition which is analogous to the syntactical plays where placement of the words forms the locus of the wordplay; puns rely less on placement and more on (semantic) relationships between words, but is similar to paronomasia where phonemic relationships determine the play; and syntactic plays, while based upon placement, also depend upon semantic relationships in many instances, as, for example, with gradatio, chiasm, or parallelism.

Spectrum also carries with it the possibility that the categories can be extended further: tongue-twisters are a kind of paronomasia; metaphor is a type of pun; and crosswords can be viewed as an extension of our third category. Moreover, the borders of wordplay itself, as an enveloping category, are no more easy to set than the distinctions between paronomasia, pun, and syntactical plays—wordplay moves in the direction of irony, allegory, and the like.

The following figure is not an attempt at graphic representation, but may be useful for organizing the various manifestations of wordplay.

WORDPLAY				
Paronomasia	*Pun*		*Sequencing*	
Alliteration	Syllipsis	Homonyn	Hyperbaton	
Assonance	Repetition	Paronym	Anaphora	Acrostics
Consonance	Antanaclasis	Synonym	Graditio	Gematria
Rhyme		Antonym	Chiasm	Notrikon
Anagram	Portmanteau		Parallelism	
Onomatopeia				

In offering this organizational chart I want to underscore two points: (1) The formation of wordplays is diverse, and thus simplicity of terminology is helpful (the more transparent the better). (2) The terminology is a descriptive tool that should not obscure what happens in a text—wordplays are both a technique and an art.

Having provided an alternative model for classifying wordplays, one based on their linguistic relationships, I can now return to the question of how biblical scholars relate wordplay to the composition itself: What role does wordplay fulfil in a text?

WORDPLAY, ORIGINALITY, AND ORNAMENTATION

The conception of wordplay as soundplay and the presentation of its study in lists of examples by biblical critics is often accompanied by the notion that wordplay is popular in origin and is used to "hook" the audience through embellishment. Casanowicz contends that the figures of speech based on the similarities of sound originate in "popular poetry and proverbs" and antedate the "rise of any regular literature."[41] These figures pass into literature and if "judiciously employed, and subordinated to the higher ends of speech . . , can be made to give tone and colour to an entire passage."[42] Casanowicz' sentiments are echoed by Driver who begins his essay by saying that playing upon words "may well be colloquial in origin," but very early on were employed as "literary embellishments."[43]

Casanowicz carries the "higher ends of speech" notion further when he says that plays upon words "are more frequent and easily formed in languages in proportion as they are less original and poor in words."[44] Driver again makes a similar point:

Such double uses of a word as these [he is speaking primarily of prepositions used in different senses within one verse, but not exclusively since the preceding paragraphs deal with double entendre], however, are at bottom due as much to the poverty of the language as to any desire to make a point by playing on a word and are therefore in all probability devoid of significance.[45]

F. Ahl encounters a similar attitude by Classicists. Wordplay, he says, is "messy" and Classicism prides itself on orderliness: "The idea that a 'serious' Greek or Roman poet might be creating a texture of wordplays, regularly intending more than one meaning, is dismissed as 'unthinkable.'"[46] He goes on to say, "The plural, latent, paradoxical, or contradictory often seems primitive or degenerate."[47]

Excursus: Neither Degenerate Nor Noble.

In recent years an opposite approach is adopted where wordplay is not only accepted as legitimate but is embraced as a true child of language usage. Indeed, Ahl's treatment of Ovid is a product of this shift in thinking about wordplay and the recent volume edited by J. Culler, *On Puns* , brings together essays that argue for the supremacy of the pun in composition and thought.

With respect to our study, this view of wordplay comes mostly by way of the examination of rabbinic texts. The Christian approach to the text, so S.A. Handelman argues, is to incarnate the word: "For the Christian, the fact that language involves the absence of its referent is an unbearable circumlocution ... Jesus, as the word-become-flesh, redeems language, returns substance to the shadows, collapses the text, time, history, and the distance between man and God. And absolute presence means the end of language, the text, the law."[48] In contrast to the Christian view, the rabbinic tradition "based itself on the principles of multiple meanings and endless interpretability, maintaining that interpretation and text were not only inseparable, but that interpretation—as opposed to incarnation—was the central divine act."[49]

However, from the Christian perspective and as a counter to Handelman, one should note Frank's study of Old English scriptural verse in which she argues that wordplay flourished precisely because God acts or is incarnated in Word(s).[50]

Wordplay, it would seem, is not inherently degenerate nor ennobled, but is simply part of language usage generally, Christian, Jewish, or otherwise.

The conception that paronomasia is popular and has "primitive" roots leads some critics to contend that the role of wordplay is to "hook" the audience or elicit a sense of satisfaction through embellishment—paronomasia titillates the curiosity of the audience.

Casanowicz observes that wordplay's "primary object and immediate effect is simply to attract the ear";[51] on three occasions Driver calls wordplay a "literary embellishment";[52] Sasson says that wordplay engages "the attention of the audience";[53] Glück, though more affirming but still with the audience reaction in the forefront of his thought, says that paronomasia is "no pun, but an integral part of the elevated diction of the Bible."[54]

Not unlike the attitude that wordplay is mere literary embellishment is the supposition that wordplay is (simply) a mnemonic device. Black suggests that the "appropriate and modulated sound ... beauty of the sentiment or the passion out of which the thought arose ... " is an aid to memory, among other things.[55]

The attention paid to paronomasia as popular, primitive, and "rhetorical" (more specifically, when considered simply as a trope, i.e., "ornamental") to the exclusion of other features of the device causes wordplay to lose much of its power. T. Rajan, playing off a quote from Paul de Man, says, "Considered as a system of tropes ... rhetoric is self-consuming, but considered as persuasion it can still be performative."[56] Rhetoric is not *mere* rhetoric—with connotations of simplicity and inferiority—but an essential aspect of the persuasive function of speech or writing or argumentation.[57]

Little justification is offered for seeing wordplay solely, or strictly, in terms of ornamentation and the like. These value-laden statements concerning the "originality" and suitability of language and wordplay,[58] like all such statements, reveal more about Casanowicz and the others than about the nature of wordplay itself. This attitude is little more than cultural chauvinism, and, like any chauvinism, cannot stand up to liberalism or self-examination.

More importantly, wordplay viewed simply as a trope causes oversight of important features of the device. Some authors, like Driver, overlook evidence in their own examples that suggest other functions for paronomasia than simply, or exclusively, literary embellishment.

For example, the double use of מן in successive words in Isa 53: 8, מעצר וממשפט, is due to the "poverty of language" and probably "devoid of significance," Driver says.[59] He may well be correct in his assessment of the passage; however, if we view the text from another perspective, other possibilities emerge. The text is not unambiguous; עצר is translated in other texts as "restraint, coercion." By employing the same preposition before both משפט and עצר, the author may be indicating some connection: no (מן, "without") "protection" is tantamount to saying no ("without") "justice." Alternatively, if עצר is taken as "oppression; coercion," then the preposition is best rendered as "by" (instrumentally)—"by coercion andwithout justice." Thus, the wordplay is properly an instance of antanaclasis, which suggests a subtle linguistic manoeuvre. The result is a momentary shuffle or quick step; the unity divided and then restored.

Possible support for the view that מִן is used not because of the "poverty" of the language is found in the expression לקח + the preposition ב expressing "take by ... " as in לקחתי בחזקה, "I take by force." An option is available for the author and it is not inescapably necessary to employ the single preposition. At the least, we can say that the verse deserves closer attention and that Driver's conclusion is not the only one to draw; he has not sufficiently explored the role or function of the preposition in the context.

Another example, Gen 2: 23 (the play between אִיש and אשה), functions, for Driver, to "fix it in the memory of the hearer," rather than being simply a literary embellishment. Driver does say that the "assonance" emphasizes the "essential connection" between the man and the woman, but the resemblance between the two terms is "purely superficial."[60] However, is it not this superficial lexical correspondence, granted a "popular" and not a true etymology in modern linguistic terms and practices, that allows the author of Gen 2: 23 to to show the essential unity of Man and Woman? In other words, by exploiting the correspondences of the two words, the author expresses what he considers a more important unity, the correspondence between the sexes.

These examples merely suggest that scholars are potentially overlooking the heart—the functions—of wordplay by preoccupation with the outward appearances.

CONCLUSIONS

The foregoing discussion sets forth a dichotomy in approaching wordplay, and like all such dichotomies, this one has a built-in superficiality to it—what we encounter in practice is seldom servile to our icons of theory. However, focusing on these two central texts (Casanowicz and Mahood) proves helpful in organizing our thoughts towards wordplay. Casanowicz, with his central metaphor that wordplay is "primitive" and "popular" represents the reticence that many show towards the trope, the feeling that jingling words together is reserved for poets and prophets, and not for clear communication. If Casanowicz is the anthropologist examining an aboriginal culture and seeking, almost in vain, to find some reflection of contemporary culture, then Mahood is the explorer trekking through paths that hint of treasures perhaps long buried. Wordplay for her, is not a jingle to arouse interest, but a field for gleaning. Of course poets and prophets use wordplay, for simple truths cannot be put simply.

Casanowicz is correct to single out sound as a distinguishing mark of wordplay, yet that mark has a meaning (sense) in relation to other marks (syntax). Similarly, examples are necessary to organize our thoughts regarding wordplay, but unless the enterprise of organizing is part of a larger taxonomic framework—unless we also get a glimpse of the function of that particular form in relation to other forms or other functions—then the taxonomy only fulfils some need to pigeon-hole, but not explain. Finally, some speak of "embellishment" as if logic suffices when in fact it is more often rhetoric that brings us to reason regarding an opposing or unexamined position.

We cannot, however, simply substitute Mahood for Casanowicz, as if the dichotomy gives us only these alternatives to wordplay. Even if our sympathies lie more with Mahood than with Casanowicz—as mine do—we must be wary of imposing foreign categories or being anachronistic. Studying Shakespeare is not the same as studying Second Isaiah. This caution is especially true since biblical scholars do not have a rhetorical handbook or a philosophical treatise on language contemporaneous to the authors of the Bible, as is the case with Shakespeare.

At the very least, the dichotomy between those in biblical studies and those in literary studies shows that classification easily erects borders on essentially fluid terrain; theoretical issues, as important as they are, must not obscure what actually happens in a text where specifics rather than generalities determine the outcome. While it is true that theoretical issues may obscure what actually happens in a text, this survey of the approaches and attitudes towards wordplay by biblical and literary critics indicates a diversity that is not easily resolved. The following chapters form an argument for what I consider to be essential for understanding the workings of wordplay. Though theoretical, the discussion always has an eye on the *workings* of wordplay, what we find in a text and how we can discuss what we find.

TWO
THE MEANING OF WORDPLAY

Wordplayers sense that they tread on very basic territory: meaning, communication, the nature of reality itself.

Redfern, Puns

With the background material thus far provided, a provisional statement, at least, about wordplay can now be made. In the ensuing chapters, the justification for this conception will be undertaken.

I want to suggest that wordplay is a *sophisticated linguistic and literary endeavor that collates sound, sense, and syntax in such a way as to exploit similarities and create ambiguities in an effort to suggest relationships, both cognitive and affective, that go beyond the ostensive reference of the individual phonological, semantic, and syntactical units* .

This chapter will show that wordplay is a sophisticated[1] linguistic endeavor. In order to accomplish this task, studies by linguists who have attempted to identify the nature of wordplay and its linguistic role will be examined. Two such studies in particular—L.G. Heller, "Toward a General Typology of the Pun" and J. Brown, "Eight Types of Puns"—will show the similarities as well as the limitations of a linguistic approach. Specifically, these studies uncover the formal aspects of the linguistic collocations that form wordplays; however, in identifying the particular manifestations of the general formula, clarity becomes diversity, if not confusion.

Heller and Brown advance the discussion by pressing beyond these formal aspects to suggest that wordplays explore "meaning," which in turn speaks to our understanding of cognitive development, a supposition supported by the examination of a third study—L.G. Kelly, "Punning and the Linguistic Sign."

"Exploration of meaning" will lead us to two studies that touch on this feature of wordplay as it relates to the Bible—L. Peeters, "Pour une interprétation du jeu de mots" and A.R. Ceresko's study of מצא. However, exploration of meaning in the biblical texts seems limited to the meaning of words and not the meaning of meaning, at least to the extent that we find this latter idea located in more recent literary texts and suggested by current literary and linguistic studies.

TYPES AND CONTEXTS: WORDPLAY AND LINGUISTS

L.G. Heller offers a general typology of the pun, noting the lack of formal analysis of the trope.[2] He suggests that a number of "more respectable" literary genres—"including allegory, the mystery, and the detective story"—share the same structural pattern at a deep level as the pun (though he does not specify what this pattern is[3]). Heller notes in passing that beyond these structural concerns the nature of reasoning itself is touched upon by the pun.[4] Thus the oft repeated, but little heeded, disparaging remarks about puns (which Heller acknowledges) may not be entirely justified; this low form of wit may have important consequences or insights into how we think.[5]

Heller's general typology is that "a single manifesting mark signals more than one conceptual function."[6] The "manifesting mark" is often, but not always, a single word that represents, at some level, two distinct concepts. However, this general typology is complicated by various patterns, the particular instances of the phenomenon, that make up the type.

Heller represents the typology graphically as two concepts coming together in a single mark:

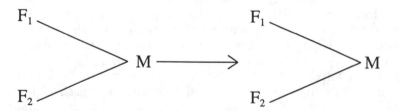

F_1 and F_2 = functions (concepts); M = manifesting mark (word, or that which signals different concepts).

The disparate patterns are mapped with broken lines and strike-throughs to indicate the combinations that are not realized until the entire line or passage is read:

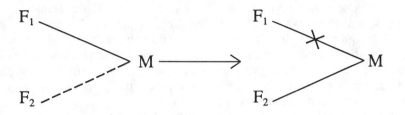

F$_2$ can be a solid line, as in the general typology, or a broken line, where F$_2$ is not realized until the second structure is introduced. F$_1$ in the second sequence can be a solid line, as in the first sequence, or scored out by the second manifesting mark. Permutations arise from the various combinations of solid and broken lines, or strike-throughs.

Heller gives two illustrations that will help clarify both the type and the tokens:

The doctor fell into the well
And brake his collar bone.
He should have tended the sick
And left the well alone.

The manifesting mark "well" signals both "a place for collecting water" and "healthy people." This example follows the general typology pattern where two concepts are realized in a single mark (word).

The permutations possible from the general typological pattern are illustrated by a quote from James Joyce: "Come forth, Lazarus! And he came fifth and lost his job."

The mark "forth" usually signals direction, but it is phonetically similar to "fourth" which signals a sequence. With the introduction of a second manifesting mark, "fifth," the reader is forced to reinterpret the initial mark. In the first sequence, the F$_2$ (sequential function) is broken, representing a potential direction (at least phonologically), but not a semantic correlation, whereas F$_1$ (direction function) in the second sequence is scored out since the context necessitates rejection of the F$_1$ as a potential meaning. The second mark necessitates a reprocessing of the first mark. In effect, one meaning is written over another.

The second study, by J. Brown,[7] reinforces the notion that puns show two disparate meanings in a single sign and that the context permits both meanings.[8] Brown, however, introduces a new element in the discussion—recognition of a syntactical element alongside the phonological and lexical. Brown classifies puns into two groups corresponding to the relationship between the syntactical assertion of a sentence (syntax) and the overall sense of the sentence (sense). Brown's appeal to syntax is not quite the same as the one I proposed under the rubric of "sequencing," but it does indicate that the meaning of the wordplay stands in relation to the other elements in the sentence, even though it is usually the semantic element that triggers the pun. Nevertheless, considering elements other than sense permits finding relationships on the levels of phonology and syntax, something that Brown downplays.

Brown's eight types of puns are structured around these two groups, syntax and sense, with four permutations to each group. Group I puns are those where the syntax is identical to (literal to) the sense. Group II puns are more complex and introduce an additional metaphoric factor: syntax is metaphoric to the sense of the sentence. The four permutations correspond to a situation where the word meaning is literal to both syntax and sense, metaphoric to both, literal to one and metaphoric to the other, in either direction.

A few examples cited by Brown will help clarify the classification. A line from *Romeo and Juliet* illustrates the first group, third class, i.e., literal to the sense of the sentence, but one meaning metaphorical to the syntax. Juliet says: "And learn me how to lose a winning match" (III. ii. 12). Brown says that "winning" in the sense of "victorious" cannot be literal to the syntax since one does not lose a victorious match. However, "winning" as "appealing" is literal to the syntax. Both meanings are literal to the overall meaning of the sentence.

An example of the second, more complex type is found in Milton's second Hobson poem. The complexity of this example is furthered by being of the fourth class—metaphoric to both sense and syntax.

> Obedient to the moon he spent his date
> In Cours reciprocal, and had his fate
> Linkt to the mutual flowing of the Seas,
> Yet (strange to think) his wain was his increase.

By making a pun on "cours reciprocal"—the meaning "wane" is equated to one phase of Hobson's professional activity—Milton prepares the reader through the comparison to the moon's phases, for the second pun, on "wain." Brown says that "his wain was his increase" is metaphoric to the sense (the sense being that his trips were a source of money and satisfaction); "wagon" for "wain" is literal to the syntax, but the meaning "wane" is metaphoric for the trips to London and back.

Brown concludes his study by saying:

> But the fundamental accomplishment of the pun—the definition of context-linking and the resultant expansion of the total context—is visible in all pun occurrences, is perhaps to be found in all literary language-use. This achievement marks the pun as an

important symbolic phenomenon, identifies it as a fundamental structured symbol form possessing literary power and significance.[9]

Thus Brown is very similar to Heller: in a particular collocation of sense, sound, and syntax; wordplay pushes beyond linguistic accomplishment to a cognitive accomplishment, the exploration of symbol and sign.

The structure of a pun, then, centers on a single lexical item that manifests multiple meanings in a given context. However, by the end of each article one is left with the disparity of ways that wordplay manifests itself rather than a simple or complete formula. Brown says that "further analysis of the pun leads into more and more complicated aspects of language-use,"[10] and Heller posits eleven criteria that serve the general typology and suggests that other criteria will surface as more examples are examined.[11] In each case, the general typology tends to fade among the ranks.

A third study supports the general structure of the pun as argued by Heller and Brown. L.G. Kelly offers "collocations" and "catalysts" (critical collocates that "crystallize" meaning in much the same way that certain chemicals act as catalysts in chemical reactions) rather than manifesting marks (Heller) or metaphoric assertions (Brown) for his identification of the structure of puns.[12] Although Kelly's nomenclature differs, what is designated is similar: an element within the sentence requires a "second look"; a double meaning is realized and one or the other meaning comes to the forefront (but both are evident).

Kelly's broader aim, however, is to show that this analysis of pun "enriches" the two major positions in linguistic theory on meaning—meaning found in the sign itself (once the rather arbitrary decision is made that this sign signifies this meaning) or meaning dependent upon the social-contextual situation. Kelly suggests that the pun shows the interplay between these two extremes.

Thus, Kelly is less concerned with the structure of wordplay and more concerned with the implications for meaning with a pun since under normal circumstances the context eliminates optional meanings. Kelly is quick to point out that puns are not entirely anomalous: "It would seem that we are not describing an abnormal process, but a normal process with abnormal features."[13] A pun is not aberrant, but contributes to how we conceive of the meaning of lexical signs, a feature suggested by Heller and Brown as well.

WORDPLAY AND THE "MYSTERY" OF LANGUAGE

L. Peeters argues for a similar connection between wordplay and the nature of meaning, but his examples include biblical ones to illustrate the connection.[14] Peeters' observations need to be put in the larger context of his approach to wordplay. He does not begin by defining wordplay, classifying wordplay, or citing studies of wordplay. Rather, Peeters begins by linking wordplay to language and humor. Communication depends on the correct usage of signs, yet wordplay goes against the conventions of language.[15] This point is important for Peeters because he cites Henri Bergson's theory of humor in support. For Bergson, the essence of humor is the flouting of mechanism, a social mockery of inflexibility. It is no accident either that Freud is cited in a footnote by Peeters. Both Freud and Bergson hold to a "relief" theory of humor: humor results from the release of energy one feels when, as Freud puts it, the "censor" is outwitted. Wordplay produces this mockery of mechanism on a linguistic level by going against the conventions of language.

Peeters maintains that recognizing and employing wordplay can be a source of either "anguish" or "liberty." Employment of wordplay shows the inherent strictures of meaning as one searches for a word to express a sentiment. But also, wordplay is liberating when one breaks through the strictures to new meanings.

Rather than classifying wordplay, Peeters uses three general categories of language usage. The first is "low level," where the focus is on the text and the language employed and not on ideas per se. Peeters says that this category is employed frequently in the Bible, especially by the prophets (but he cites no examples). His example is a poem by the poet A. Gryphius:[16]

Nacht mehr denn lichte Nacht! Nacht lichter als der tag
Nacht heller als dies Sonn' in der das licht geboren
Das Gott der licht im licht wohnhaftig ihm erkoren:
O Nacht die alle Nacht' und Tage trotzen mag!

This example of low level language usage is what I term paronomasia, with its emphasis on the phonological correspondences. No balancing of meanings is evident, but the repetition of *cht* in both "Nacht" and "licht," the liquid-nasal sound (*l* and *n*), and the rhyme between "geboren" and "erkoren" are obvious and call attention to themselves.

The second category Peeters proposes is "expression," a more profound level of language use. In this category, the conventions and function of language are played off one another. Wordplay is a way of critiquing the fundamental imperfections of language.

As an example of this category, Peeters cites Isa 28: 10 and 13 where the drunken priests and prophets accuse Isaiah of babbling (צו לצו צו לצו קו לקו קו לקו זעיר שם זעיר שם), and this accusation is turned against them by Yahweh (v 13). Wordplay is used to parody language—language of others and language itself.[17]

The third category moves beyond expression to "knowledge" (*connaissance*). Here the author investigates the nature of words and the world beyond the word. There is something beyond the text; a problem of correspondence and of getting "behind" language. Wordplay is an exploration of the secrets of reality and the mystery of creation.

As examples of this category, Peeters cites the poems of the French Surrealist Robert Desnos and briefly discusses Ezek 7: 7; 8: 2; and 15: 36, where, Peeters maintains, the biblical author breaks the barriers of meaning to new meanings in order to express his sentiment.

Thus Peeters pushes the reader to consider what wordplay is about with respect to language. His study suggests that wordplay is serious play. As play, it can be little more than "mere" play, the clever combining of consonants. As "serious" play, wordplay pushes conceptual constraints; a new truth or a new way of looking at things may emerge from the exploration of language.

No doubt such works as *Finnegan's Wake* (to which Peeters refers), the poetry of Robert Desnos or Max Jacob (A. Thau[18]), and the philosophy of Nietzsche and Derrida reflect both anguish and liberty in their play with words. However, to what extent this semantic and epistemological approach to language is particularly modern is not addressed by Peeters.

If we examine the examples from Ezekiel that Peeters cites, we find that they do not support his supposition, at least in the sense that he argues, or to the extent that he wishes to show. Peeters argues that צפירה in Ezek 7: 7 is a new term created to express the apocalyptic event envisioned. The term is elsewhere employed only in Isa 28: 5, and there the sense "garland" or "crown" is fitting (a meaning inappropriate to Ezekiel). Several suggestions are offered for the meaning of the term;[19] however, from the context, something like "doom" is expected. The passages in Isaiah and Ezekiel share an eschatological outlook ("in that day"), but in Isaiah the Lord will be a "crown" for the remnant of the people, whereas in Ezekiel the צפירה will come "upon" (אליך) the people; not joy but panic is envisioned.

To say that a term is difficult is one thing, especially with the limited literary corpus we possess from Hebrew antiquity, but it is quite another thing to suggest that an author is breaking the bonds of language to express an otherwise inexpressible sentiment. It may be true that Ezekiel is extending a metaphor or using an existing metaphor in a creative way—which supports the view that wordplay involves linguistic innovation and exploration, as Peeters argues—however, to ground this in the ontology of language is a much more difficult step, and one that Peeters has not established. Ezekiel may simply be intensifying or extending the meaning of an existing term, not creating a neologism or breaking the barriers of meaning in language.

The same could be said of Ezek 16: 36, where נחשת ("copper" elsewhere in the OT) is used in, perhaps, the sense of menstruation or sexual desire. However, נחשת in Ezekiel may reflect an entirely different root. Greenberg cites the Akkadian *nahšati*, "morbid genital outflow (of a woman)," from *nḫš*, "to be abundant, overflowing." The author may not be extending the meaning of "copper" at all; he may simply be using an uncommon term or loan term. This usage is, of course, noteworthy, but not exactly supporting Peeters' argument that Ezekiel is exploring the mystery of language.

It is clear that meanings of words are explored in certain biblical wordplays even if the meaning of meaning is not—the examples from biblical literature are not as self-consciously reflective of their role in creating meaning as those from more contemporary authors are. A fine example of exploring meaning and its limitations is suggested by A.R. Ceresko in his analysis of מצא in Qoheleth. Ceresko says, "In expressing diverse activities ... with a single word (מצא), [the Israelite sages] are implying a connecting web among those activities ... The reader or listener is invited to probe that pattern further."[20] He continues: "Despite his skill in the use of language in his rigorous search (Qoh 12: 9-10) he cannot find (מצא) the answer; in honestly admitting such, he marks the boundaries for human wisdom behind which one dare not attempt to reach (מצא) in order to grasp (מצא) the fruit of the tree of knowledge of good and bad."[21]

In other words, the author and the audience probe the limits of meaning, which, in this case, are shown by probing the various meanings of מצא, but they do not "break the bounds of meaning," with the implications of anarchy or autonomy that the phrase entails.

CONCLUSIONS

In examining the studies of Heller, Brown, and Kelly in linguistics, and Peeters and Ceresko in biblical studies, we see that wordplay signals multiple possibilities of meaning, which may become vehicles for exploring meanings of words and relationships between words. Wordplay is latent in language use, but not an aberration of its use. With respect to the Bible, the notion of the exploration of the meaning of language itself seems anachronistic, or not sufficiently supported by the examples cited; we do not find an unequivocal distrust of language, as we find in some recent writings. However, in either case, whether exploring the meaning of words or the meaning of meaning, the employment and recognition of wordplay in a text is a linguistic endeavor that requires some order of abstraction and hence displays a sophistication beyond "mere ornamentation."

THREE
WORDPLAY AND AMBIGUITY

> Fruitful Ambiguity, that popular *deus ex machina* of the contemporary critical scene.
>
> Nowottny, *Language Poets Use*

In the previous chapter I have argued that wordplay is a sophisticated linguistic endeavor; wordplayers and their audience explore the meanings of words and sometimes even explore how words mean. This conception of wordplay goes against the tendency in biblical studies to portray the figure as "popular" and "literary," at best. Little is expected of this trope, certainly not, as Casanowicz so pointedly claims, "lofty transformations of meaning."[1]

In this chapter I will further support my contention that wordplay is a sophisticated linguistic and literary enterprise by examining the similarities and differences that arise in the particular collocations of sound, sense, and syntax that we designate wordplay. The inherent contiguities of sound and the polysemous nature of words are exploited in wordplay rather than circumvented. This observation regarding wordplay follows from the linguistic studies examined in the previous chapter, especially their focus on ambiguity of an element within the sentence/utterance, and the corresponding reflection required both to create and recognize such ambiguity.

Baum says, "Similarity of sound makes two different words momentarily one. But in all these forms the meaning of the word is paramount. Further, since ambiguity is prevalent in nearly all language, *it is necessary to examine the kind of ambiguity in a pun*."[2] What does it mean when we say that wordplay involves the ambiguous use of words? I will answer that question by looking at ambiguity with respect to biblical studies (where we find very little reflection on what "ambiguity" means for exegesis), what ambiguity entails (two readings *not* being excluded), and how it works (a polyvalent word is found in a context that does delimit the meaning(s) of the word).

AMBIGUITY AND BIBLICAL STUDIES

The recognition that wordplay involves ambiguity is prevalent in some of the more recent studies done by biblical critics. Watson defines wordplay as "lexical ambiguity"; this, he says, is "simply a way of saying that words can be polyvalent."[3]   A certain irony exists in this definition of wordplay since wordplay is included in the chapter "Sound in Hebrew Poetry." Subsuming wordplay under "sound" echoes—and perpetuates—the myth of "soundplay" that so dominates the discussion of wordplay in biblical studies. More importantly, wordplay is less an issue of the *existence* of polyvalency, as the *exploitation* and *recognition* of the polyvalency of words.

In "normal" discourse, ambiguity is avoided by authors and rendered distinct by the audience. In wordplay, however, an author, usually purposefully,[4] uses words in such as way as to draw attention to the overlapping sounds and sense—synonymy, homonymy, and paronymy. Similarity also implies difference and therefore antonymy can be added to the other terms.   Cohesion and disjunction are revealed and concealed in the employment of wordplay.

Watson's study of wordplay is dependent upon a chapter on ambiguity in *Semantics: An Introduction to the Science of Meaning* by S. Ullmann. Ullmann argues that linguistic ambiguity takes three forms: phonetic, grammatical, and lexical.   Lexical ambiguity is the most important because of the inherent polyvalency of words. Ambiguity, whether phonetic, grammatical, or lexical, is almost always resolved by context. On the "problem" of ambiguity, Ullmann remarks: "What is astonishing is not that the machine occasionally breaks down, but that it breaks down so rarely."[5] He further states that both polysemy and homonymy are "prolific sources of puns."[6] Kelly makes similar observations about the language of the pun and the context eliminating most instances of ambiguity. Kelly says, "The peculiarity of the pun is that more than one meaning survives."[7]

Watson is not the only biblical scholar to mention or allude to ambiguity in reference to wordplay. Guillaume says that double entendre creates suspense until the significance of the word is shown.[8] Driver says that the OT "affords numerous instances of the use of a word in an equivocal sense or senses."[9] Glück says that paronomasia involves ambiguity, then describes what he means: "The use of a word in such a manner as to imply a meaning and draw an image other than the one expected in the context, or in addition to it as a secondary or tertiary idea."[10] Sasson talks of an "aura of ambiguity" which excites the curiosity of the audience and invites a search for meanings not readily apparent.[11]

Lip service is paid to the ambiguity of wordplay; but, with the exception of Watson, and, to a lesser extent, Glück, little reflection is given to this aspect of the trope. For example, Driver records an interesting example of ambiguity. In Exod 5: 18 Pharaoh replies to Moses' and Aaron's objection regarding the plight of the Israelites whose workload has just been increased: לכו עבדו. Driver says that the words may be rendered, "Go, work" or "Go, serve (i.e., worship [God]"), and then comments: "Possibly the best translation of these words is 'go and do what you must,' leaving the precise meaning put upon the frustrated king's angry outburst an open question."[12]   Leaving the words an open question is appealing, but if, as Driver rightly says, the words are an "angry outburst," then the question is not really open: the sense, "Go, work" seems most appropriate. However, the words are pregnant with meaning and Pharaoh, who seems oblivious to the ambiguity of his words, becomes entrapped by them; he is telling them to get back to work, but the words can equally be contrued as "go and serve," which is how the "audience" is to take them. The ambiguity of the wordplay suggests that simple words turn out not so simple and meanings require more than one reading.[13]

The point remains—critics work diligently to resolve any sense of ambiguity within a text. The question also remains—What *kind* of ambiguity are we talking about with respect to wordplay?

AMBIDEXTROUS AMBIGUITY

The juxtaposition of "curiosity" and "search for meanings" in Sasson seems odd: one trivial, the other nearly metaphysical. Sister Miriam-Joseph says: "Although the ordinary function of words is to mirror thought, there are occasions when words are employed to veil meaning rather than to reveal it openly. Consequently, the figures of deliberate obscurity—enigma, noema, and schematismus—depend on notation."[14] In other words, wordplay is a dexterous speech-act that conceals through verbal slight of hand what it ostensively reveals. Language used in such a way as to reveal and veil meaning requires some degree of conceptual abstraction, not simply "curiosity."

Of biblical scholars, Charlesworth seems to catch the linguistic sophistication of wordplay most readily. Charlesworth calls the wordplays in the *Odes of Solomon* "paronomasia" and classifies the tropes as repetition, double entendre (similar sounding words that have different meanings), and double entente (the same word used with two different meanings). "Desirable" features of repetition result: "Subtle differences of meaning appear, and the idea is seen from more than one perspective."[15]   More pointedly, with double entente, for which the author of the *Odes Sol.* has a particular penchant, ambiguity may arise "under [the author's] genius."   Double entente shows the "inseparable double aspect of a theological subtlety";[16] both interpretations or meanings of the word are necessary to express a complex theological idea (often these ideas concern the revelation of the Messiah).

An example of double entente (also double entendre and alliteration) is found in Ode 11: 15. The Syriac reads:

w 'tbsmt nšmty
bryḥh bsymh dmryh

One translator renders this:

And my nostrils had the pleasure
of the pleasant odour of the Lord.

Nšmh is ambiguous, however, and can mean "breath, spirit, living being,"
or, in later literature, even "soul"; thus Charlesworth offers this translation:

And my spirit was refreshed
By the pleasant fragrance of the Lord.

The first translation appeals to the senses, while Charlesworth's suggests
the renewing of the spirit by the Lord; both readings have linguistic support.
Linguistic dexterity creates an image of the sensuality of spirituality for the
author of the *Odes Sol.*

The move of some translators, then, to opt for one reading over the other
reduces the effect of a text that does not exclude either reading—and indeed, may
be attempting both.

Wherein lies ambiguity and what does it accomplish? Kelly distinguishes
between inherent ambiguity, which lies in the sign itself and can be discovered
through semantic analysis, and functional ambiguity, which lies in the context or
collocation of signs. He finds it "difficult to see" how context, however, can
generate two unrelated meanings for a single sign.[17]

In a similar fashion, Thau says, "Unlike metaphor, however, the pun
cannot be said to be ambiguous; it cannot be said to be obscure." She goes on to
say, nevertheless, that, "the only possible ambiguity is the momentary balancing
of possible meanings as one becomes aware of the pun. The pun's effect is
derived from the recognition of its multiple meanings as equally applicable to a
particular context. The text's control of interpretation is complete."[18] Baum
carries the gist of Thau's statement a step further to the point that he says the
opposite of Kelly. Baum says that unless the context is such that it permits doubt,
then "there is no ambiguity and no pun."[19]

In the literature on ambiguity generally, we find a similar indeterminacy
regarding ambiguity. Linguist D.A. Cruse says that ambiguity arises because of
multiple semantic uses of a single word form that does not have a grammatically
different function.[20] Thus, the classic example, "We finally reached the bank,"
can mean either a place to safeguard one's money or the side of a river. "Bank"
is lexically ambiguous; nothing in the lexical formation or grammatical function
distinguishes between the possible senses. At the other extreme, W. Empson, in
his masterful study of ambiguity, is more expansive, focusing on ambiguity as the

"manysidedness" of language: "[Ambiguity is] any verbal nuance, however slight, which gives room for alternative reactions to the same piece of language."[21] Is, then, ambiguity in the sign or a product of the sign's function in the discourse?

At the outset we can dispense with two misconceptions about ambiguity: ambiguity is not the same as complexity nor is it the same as uncertainty. Complexity simply requires a more careful reading, while uncertainty implies that a text is somehow incomplete or that one's reading lacks some necessary component.

W. Nowottny in *The Language Poets Use* addresses the use of ambiguity by poets. Her purpose is to provide a moderating position between the extremes of denying that ambiguity has a place in literary composition, that is, that all we can contend with is lexical ambiguity, and losing a clear sense of the distinctiveness of ambiguity, that is, that ambiguity means any source of "uncertainties" in a text (her foil here is Empson). Nowottny's observations clarify the ambiguity of "ambiguity," at least with respect to wordplay.

Nowottny does not deny lexical ambiguity; indeed, when we "dispense with the support of a particular context, [language's] potential ambiguity becomes apparent."[22] Nowottny also does not deny the insights of Empson that ambiguity may result from a poet's evading or transcending unequivocal assertions, and is associated with such concepts as "ambivalence, tension, paradox and irony," as well as metaphor.[23] These insights, however, create a very broad understanding of ambiguity that allows a poet to "declare our own inchoate and complex experience in a verbal form to which 'every bosom returns an echo.'"[24]

Nowottny addresses the complexity of the problem with ambiguity, but wants to focus on a narrower aspect rather than become embroiled in the effects of the manysidedness of ambiguity (Empson). She avers that it is "more realistic" to "hold that the meaning of a locution is what is left in, *what is not excluded* , by the context of the locution."[25] She terms this kind of ambiguity "extraloquial," because the locution has "more in it, not less": "Having more meanings than one is the result of not entering into the full commitment of unequivocal assertion; to use an extralocution ... is to decline citizenship in that kingdom of single-eyed men to which language (as ordinarily used) aspires."[26] Thus an author puts into the context of the locution only that which will not exclude "meaning-potential" of a lexical item. It is less the manysidedness of language and more the creation of a context that is not exclusive of "verbalities" (from vocabulary) or values (from culture)—the meaning-potential of a word, as both sign and context.

What this approach to ambiguity means with respect to wordplay is this: an obvious pun, which is generally not ambiguous in a lexical sense (the "reader" knows which meaning is present, unlike "bank" where, without further clues, one cannot judge between possible meanings), may still be ambiguous in the sense that two meaning-potentials are present because a single context does not exclude either meaning from view. On the other hand, the reader who stops short of the task of teasing out the meanings of a subtle pun, that is, a reader who actualizes only one meaning, does not thereby disambiguate the pun itself; he or she simply misses the meaning-potentials in the discourse. The text as word and context remain determinative rather than simply the author's lexical choice or the reader's competence.

Kelly, then, is correct in affirming a distinction between inherent (lexical) and functional (contextual) ambiguity, but errs by failing to see that context, by not excluding meaning-potential, *may* perpetuate the ambiguity, not resolve it. In the case of the pun, "resolution" of the ambiguity often comes only when the intended pun is recognized. Recall a previous example we used:

> The doctor fell into the well
> and brake his collar bone.
> He should have tended the sick
> and left the well alone.

The two sentences read separately pose little difficulty in meaning (the second sentence is odd, but not ambiguous). Taken together, "well" is ambiguous in the sense that one lexical item has more than one semantic use and does not have a separate grammatical function (Cruse); one is forced to reread the "poem" to sort out the meanings of "well." The ambiguity is never fully resolved by the context; indeed, the context causes the echo. We are given just enough information both to cause the ambiguity and locate its source. Thus, the context, together with a lexical item that signals (at least) two "opposing" truth values— meanings opposite only within a particular discourse. Both word and context create the possibility for the pun effect, then, usually, "resolves" the source of ambiguity, but not the ambiguity itself. In other words, the word is not simply indeterminate; both senses must be possible. In the case of the lexically ambiguous "bank," the context should resolve the ambiguity by showing either one meaning or the other as appropriate.

In the example from Exod 5: 18, both senses are appropriate depending on whether one wants to see the situation from Pharoah's perspective or from God's, and the reader is invited to explore the irony, in this case, between the two senses, or, in the case of the *Odes of Solomon* example, the relationship between the senses.

As Baum says: "In the true pun, however, there is first a recognition of two or more possibilities, and a rapid balancing between them; then the pleasure of finding that either will fit; and finally the increased pleasure of seeing that both will fit."[27] The two meanings, however, remain distinct. A. Hamori says that once you have despaired of seeing two meanings, and you had been deceived by the word, then the recognition comes that this newly gained thing is a capital, a benefit from the economy of words.[28]

CONCLUSIONS

To say that a word or passage is ambiguous does not mean that language is necessarily or inherently anarchic. Both the author, in supplying directional clues, and the reader, in exercising the option to disambiguate a word by "supplying" information deemed appropriate, have some control with respect to the text. Authors and readers fade away or move on; the text remains.

The task of this chapter has not been to resolve ambiguity, only to clarify the ambiguity wordplay requires. We saw in the previous chapter that in the general typology of the pun a single mark may signal more than one conceptual function. In this chapter we have explored that "more than one conceptual function." We have argued that ambiguity manifests itself as both a linguistic and a literary device; words are polyvalent, as Ullmann and Cruse suggest, but a given context either delimits or exploits the polyvalency, as Nowottny argues. This use of words and context "engages" the audience, not superficially, but subtlely. Thus, even if wordplay does not create "lofty transformations of meaning" (Casanowicz), it does allow for crafty equivocations.

This chapter has led us to another aspect of wordplay that needs examination and explication. Ambiguity raises the possibility of a special kind of relationship between text and reader, an affective relationship: the overlapping of sound, sense, and syntax results in a reader's finding "pleasure" (Baum) in the economy of words (Hamori), where two meaning-potentials fit a single context.

However, before exploring the affective relationship ("pleasure") that wordplay may create, examination of other relationships, mainly cognitive, as indicated by the conception of wordplay outlined above, require examination. Moreover, examination of these cognitive relationships will lead us back to consider the affective nature of wordplay.

FOUR
THE RELATIONSHIPS OF WORDPLAY

Wordplay suits those convinced that rational argument suffices.

Redfern, *Puns*

Is wordplay simply an exercise in ingenuity for an author and a momentary pleasure at recognition of such ingenuity for the reader, much as others have seen wordplay as a bringing together of similar sounds for the purpose of embellishment? I have suggested that wordplay creates relationships beyond the ostensive reference of the particular sound, sense, and syntactical units. In this chapter these relationships will be examined first by looking at the "ostensive" relationships, and then by looking at the relationships that readers either find or create in the act of reading a text.

OSTENSIVE REFERENCES

Wordplays form relationships that go beyond ostensive reference, but what are these ostensive references? Four relationships between the text and the trope emerge in studies of wordplay: historical information; textual criticism; emphasis; and lexicography.

HISTORICAL INFORMATION

Driver comes to the conclusion that the study of wordplay is significant for the exegete. He does so after several pages of disparaging remarks such as: "These freakish forms [e.g., צאינה for צאנה, conforming to ראינה in Qoh 3: 11], however, are surely not the work of the original authors [why? are "original" authors not creative in this regard?] but mere Rabbinic fancies, for which readers or commentators, scribes or copyists, must be held responsible."[1]   His concluding paragraph is worth quoting in full:

> In conclusion, playing on words is an important practice to which sufficient attention has hardly been paid. It seems to have begun merely as a literary device to embellish or add point to a story, *but it clearly comes to serve an entirely different end, namely that of imparting esoteric information to interested readers.* As such it deserves careful attention; for it may well reveal secrets of historical importance to the interested enquirer.[2]

This "esoteric information" comes chiefly through *gematria* and *notrikon*, and late in the literature (Driver cites several examples from the Dead Sea Scrolls). For example, Driver refers to the case of "Nebuchadnezzar" in Daniel, where it is written *plene* only in Dan 1: 1 and elsewhere *defective* . He rejects the explanation that the first instance is Hebrew whereas the rest are Aramaic; rather, the shorter form has the numerical value 423, the same as "Antiochus Epiphanes."

As interesting as it is to find such historical information, does it deserve any more "careful attention" than the millennium of non-esoteric wordplay prior to the time of the post-exilic or intertestamental community? Does Second Isaiah's use of wordplay lead to the employment of the trope for embedding historical information during a period of crises and occupation? If the primary benefit of studying wordplay is to acquire (esoteric) historical information, then it seems of rather restricted use, especially since most wordplays have more mundane matters in view, and thus not really deserving "careful attention." Nevertheless, a wordplay may yield historical information, as Driver avers.

TEXTUAL CRITICISM

A more practical outcome of studying wordplay, to which Driver happily makes passing reference earlier in the essay, is for purposes of textual criticism. As Sasson suggests, "An appreciation of paronomasia allows scholars to reconstruct or interpret certain OT passages,"[3] and reports Gen 9: 6b as an example.   The reconstructed text reads כי בדמות אלהים עשה את־האדם (MT: כי בצלם אלהים עשה את־האדם).   The pun is between דמות ("likeness"), and אדם ("man"), as well as a play on דם ("blood") in Gen 9: 6a.

This use of the trope is readily accepted by critics in all disciplines. Mahood cites an emended line from *Twelfth Night* .   "Coole my nature" is best emended to "curl my nature" on the basis of the contrast with "art" in the previous line. This, Mahood argues, is proved right as another scholar recognized the pun on "tongues" ("tongs"; i.e., curling tongs).[4] The dialogue reads:

An. What is purquoy? Do, or not do? I would I had bestowed that time in the tongues, that I have in fencing dancing, and beare-bayting: O Had I but followed the Arts.

To. Then hadst thou had an excellent head of haire.

An. Why, would that have mended my haire?

To. Past question, for thou seest it will not coole [emended to "curl"] my nature (I. iii. 98-107).

Thus, the critic can sometimes find help in untangling a textual problem by recognizing a wordplay. However, a caution needs to be raised at this point. Wordplay, admittedly having some mnemonic function, would tend to be preserved, which means that conservation is a counter-force to reconstruction with respect to wordplay. Moreover, the "witty" aspect of wordplay reinforces the conserving element; an editor is unlikely to alter such a trope.

In both the Shakespearean and Gen 9: 6 examples, the textual critic may be moving beyond reconstruction to creation—the "reconstructed" wordplay results from the mind of the scholar, much as Driver's "Rabbinic fancies" above were attributed to "commentators, scribes, and copyists," and not the "original" author. The critic, in an attempt to "restore" a wordplay, could be creating a more effective wordplay than the author.

We come full circle when we recognize that a wordplay too subtle is easily missed once the pun effect is lost or overlooked and thus could become corrupted in the handing down of texts (oral or written). Wordplay, then, is of great assistance to textual criticism, though one must be able to sort out which path the text has taken—corruption or conservation.

EMPHASIS

Casanowicz says that "these syntactically co-ordinated words ... are combined by the sound to give an idea greater emphasis and solemnity, or merely more fulness."[5] The observation that paronomasia functions as a mnemonic device is very similar to seeing it used for emphasis. These sound-links are less likely in normal discourse; thus, when they occur, they are more likely to call attention to themselves and fix in the mind their presence.

P.P. Saydon argues that studies in the psychology of language indicate that we often find a corresponding intensity of form accompanying an intensity of feeling.[6] Thus in Mic 4: 10 גחי, in the sense of "throwing oneself down with pain" (cf. its Arabic root) in connection with חולי forms an "emphatic assonant expression denoting the intensity of the impending calamity."[7]

LEXICOGRAPHY

Guillaume says that paronomasia is of "great value" for exegesis and lexicography: "It throws light on words that are obscure, and it shows that the Hebrew vocabulary was much larger than is commonly supposed."[8] Chisholm makes a similar point: "In each of the examples recognition of wordplay contributes to a fuller exegetical and theological understanding of the passage and thereby enhances interpretation of the prophetic message."[9]

Guillaume cites an interesting example in the story of the birth of Perez and Zerah by Tamar in Gen 38: 27-30. The first child's hand emerges and a scarlet thread is tied to it by the midwife, who says, "This one came out first." However, the infant withdraws and the second child comes out first, to which the midwife remarks: מה־פרצת עליך, "What a breach you have made for yourself" (RSV), and the child is called "Perez (פרץ)."

Guillaume contends that "breach" may not be the real import of what the midwife says. The passage deals with tribal matters, especially the line of David who descended from Perez. Guillaume links פרץ with the Arabic *prt* "excess." Another meaning of the Arabic cognate is "he came first, preceded," and "ascendency, predominance." Guillaume suggests the meaning of the midwife's words as, "How have you arrived first. Priority is yours." Zerah is to be explained by Arabic *zrh* , "He moved from one place to another." In his concluding remarks, Guillaume notes that the first use of פרץ could still be translated as, "How have you burst forth," while the second could carry the idea of priority. He further remarks on how difficult these distinctions between homonyms are to determine. Since antanaclasis is a regular feature of wordplay, Guillaume's suggestion of a double sense for a single word in succeeding lines is not far-fetched, and becomes an interesting and enlightening possibility.

Wordplay can contribute to lexicography, but wordplay is equally as likely to exploit a false philological connection. Eilberg-Schwartz cites a fanciful example of Rabbinic exegesis: the word "heaven" (שמים) is a contraction of "fire" (אש) and "water" (מים), a contraction that signifies the composition of the heavens (*Gen. Rab.* 4: 7).[10] Yet recognition that authors themselves, and not just (rabbinic) redactors, often use "popular" etymologies is as important for understanding a passage as "true" lexicographical information. The famous case of the creation of Man (איש) and Woman (אשה) in Gen 2: 23 is such an example. Driver says that the "assonance" between the terms emphasizes the "essential connection" between the man and the woman, but the resemblance is "purely superficial."[11] However, is it not this superficial lexical correspondence, granted "popular" and not a true etymology in modern linguistic terms and practices, that allows the author to show the essential unity of Man and Woman? In other words, by exploiting the correspondences of the two words, the author expresses what he considers a more important unity, the correspondence between the sexes.

Wordplay, then, may enhance our knowledge of the words within a passage, whether these analogies are "popular" or based on true lexical correspondences.

COGNITIVE RELATIONSHIPS

These "ostensive" references are manifested by the linguistic item itself and require little abstraction on the part of the reader or critic. I want to suggest that these particular collocations of sound, sense, and syntax are supportive and interactive with other meaning-levels in a given discourse and that these formal relations of language produce relationships on a cognitive and perhaps even emotional level.

These cognitive effects come about by certain structural relationships of apposition or opposition. The particular relationship may be one of similarity, correlation, progression, contrast, contradiction, reversal, and similar associations that bring either coherence or interruption to the passage. Wordplay is open-ended in structural pattern just as it is open-ended in form. These relationships are abstracted from the particular linguistic collocations, just as native speakers make abstractions of semantic relations (e.g., idiom, metaphor or symbolism) and general syntactical or compositional patterns (e.g., parallelism, meter, and rhyme). A few examples will help illustrate what I have in mind.

COHERENCE
Mahood argues that wordplay can illumine various aspects of a passage or larger structure (in her case, a play). Words can be intensified in meaning or widened, depending on the context and purpose of the author; wordplay can also be anticipatory (and therefore also retrospective) of other words, phrases, or ideas in a work, and as such, can bring coherence to the passage. Such an example is actually provided by Guillaume, though he himself does not draw attention to this benefit of studying the trope.

Anticipation/Retrospection . The cursing of Canaan and the blessing on Shem and Japheth in Gen 9: 25-7 illustrate the coherence that wordplay brings to a pericope by introducing a word in the narrative that is later used to make a significant point. With respect to Shem, the text reads, "Blessed be Yahweh, the God of Shem." Guillaume notes the "double entente" since שם אלהי can mean "God of Shem" or "Glorious God." Guillaume concludes: "So it follows that Shem will share in the glory of the God whose name he bears."[12] For Japheth, there is a "simple" etymological pun, a play on his name—"may God enlarge Japheth (יפת אלהים ליפת)."

The wordplay on Ham is unexpected. Rather than a curse on Ham, the offender, the curse falls on Canaan, the son. Guillaume enquires of the motivation of this shift. First, since the curse was to follow the descendants of Ham, "it made no difference to posterity whether the father or his son began the mischief!" Second, and perhaps more importantly, "Canaan" provides better material for a pun than "Ham"; "Canaan had to be written, and not Ham, because the oracle demanded a name with an unhappy entail."[13] Since כנע suggests "he was humble," it follows that Canaan would be subject to his brethren.

The shift is unexpected in not cursing Ham, but the reader has been prepared for this in vv 18 and 22 where the author introduces Canaan. These verses are often seen as explanatory glosses, but they could equally be a deliberate "foreshadowing" of what is to follow; "Such a theory [that vv. 18 and 22 are glosses] presupposes that a later editor thought that a mistake had been made; but it does scant justice to the writer's intelligence, and fails to recognize the importance of paronomasia, which constitutes the prophetic and ominous nature of the patriarch's words."[14] The reader retreats to the earlier words in recognition of what the author (or editor) has cleverly and carefully done; the destiny of the descendants of Noah is explicated, and coherence is brought about, by the use of paronomasia and pun.

Progression . In Jer 3: 1-4: 2 various forms of שוב, "turn," are used to link the pericope together. Will a divorced wife who marries another man "turn" (ישוב) back to her former husband? Neither will the harlot Israel "turn" (שוב) back to the Lord (3: 1). The Lord asks Jeremiah if he saw what the "faithless" (משבה) Israel did, how she did not "return" (תשוב) to the Lord but continued to play the harlot, just as Judah is now doing as well (3: 6-11; cf. 3: 19-20). Jeremiah is then told to proclaim שובה משבה ישראל, "Return, O Faithless Israel" (3: 12; cf. 3: 14, 22). All this talk of "turning," "returning," and "turning away" culminates in 4: 1-2 where if Israel will "turn" (תשוב), it is to the Lord that they should "return" (תשוב) by cutting off their idolatrous practices and living their lives justly and in righteousness. The forms and nuances of שוב return again and again throughout the passage until everything turns out right by true repentance.

INTERRUPTION

Watson, cognizant of many of these pattern or functions of wordplay, provides several examples of how wordplay causes dissonance in a passage. Three uses in particular are worth noting.[15]

Reversal . An expression of reversal can be achieved by the use of wordplay. Watson cites the play between בוש שוש and שוב שו in Ps 6: 11:

יבשו ויבהלו מאד	Exceedingly confused and dismayed,
כל איבי	all my enemies
ישבו יבשו רגע	shall turn away, suddenly confused.

The play is between יבש and ישבו, an "anagrammatical" (or chiastic, ABA', relation).

An example might also be seen in Phil 2: 3 and 7. At 2: 3 Paul warns not to act out of "empty opinion" (κενοδοξίαν) as those who demand their own way; rather have the attitude of Christ, who "emptied" himself (ἐαυτόν ἐκένωσεν) and did not insist on his rightful place (2: 6). The proper attitude is not empty conceit, but emptying self.

Deception . Wordplay can be used to show that appearances can be deceptive. Watson cites Ps 5: 10:

כי אין בפיהו נכונה	For there is nothing trusty in any mouth,
קרבם הוות	Their *inwards* are words,
קבר־פתוח גרונם	an open *grave* their throat,
לשונם יחליקון	their tongue is *glib*.

The smooth words of the enemies are deceptive for they are really an open grave. Watson says that the "inherent ambiguity" of wordplay is well-suited for this use.

Disparate ideas . Two disparate things or ideas can play off one another or be equated even as their sound plays. Watson cites an example from Sirach 4: 11:

חכמות למדה בניה	Wisdom teaches her *sons,*
ותעיד לכל מבינים בה	and cherishes all *who understand* her.

A wise son (בן) is equated with understanding (מבין).

CONCLUSIONS

These relationships that wordplay form give further support to our contention that wordplay is not mere aural ornamentation, but involves subtleties, whether of phonological and semantic associations or of serving various functions within the pericope. I have grouped these rhetorical functions as coherence and interruption. One could as easily have opted for: associative or contrastive; compressive or expansive; or revealing and concealing for the various ways that apposition and opposition manifest themselves in wordplay.

The precise terminology one adopts for these relationships is less important than conceptualizing wordplay as more than ornamentation or embellishment. Wordplay provides a depth and variety of language use that encourages experimentation and exploration by author/text and audience in form and structure in relation to content. Wordplay serves ideological purposes and persuasion rather than neutrality and logic—or ornate speech.

Sister Miriam-Joseph says of Shakespeare and his Age that wordplay "was not merely an elegance of style and a display of wit; it was also a means of emphasis and an instrument of persuasion. An argument might be conducted from step to step ... by a series of puns. The genius of the language encouraged them."[16] Vickers takes persuasion a step further by linking rhetorical figures with psychological and emotional reactions and responses,[17] a point made on the cognitive level by Nowottny but potentially applicable to an emotional response as well: "A passage may be so devised as to make the reader himself experience the kind of mental event the poet's language describes; the poet constructs a highly-organized structure of forms, which makes the reader himself leap at the truth the poet sees."[18]

One example of paronomasia used "persuasively" (either cognitive or emotive) is found again in Philippians where the author employs various forms and nuances of meaning of πᾶς in 1: 3 and 4. Paul thanks God in "all" (πάσῃ) remembrance of them; he "always" (πάντοτε) in "every" (πάσῃ) prayer prays for "all" (πάντων) of them. The repetition reinforces the all-inclusiveness and consistency of Paul's prayers, and further invites the reader to make an abstraction regarding this boundless concern Paul has for each one of his audience, collectively.

Vickers calls figures of speech "pockets of energy" and concludes, "A figure always has a function."[19] The cognitive effects are more easily identified than the affective; however, one affective result of wordplay is identifiable: wordplay's role as humor. How this aspect of wordplay works and how humor is conceived is the subject of the next chapter, and the direction that this particular study of wordplay has been heading.

FIVE
THE HUMOR OF WORDPLAY

'You told me a hundred times, Uncle Willie. Words with a 'k' in it are funny.'

Ben, *The Sunshine Boys*

In the previous chapter I argued that wordplay produces relationships beyond the ostensive reference of the sounds, sense, and syntax of the word, line, or passage. The reader takes these linguistic collocations and abstracts patterns of similarities and differences. By the end of the chapter I was prepared to argue that wordplay may do more than elicit cognitive responses, that an affective side of wordplay exists alongside the cognitive.

The problem of arguing for affective elements in literary compositions is that readers do not always act predictably. To argue that a certain literary technique or semantic unit will produce a particular emotional or psychological result is difficult, perhaps even impossible to argue for convincingly since so many exceptions can be marshalled against such psychological or emotional appeals. One may be able to construct an argument that an author intends to create a particular affective response, but the approach adopted in this study consciously avoids authorial intent, insofar as that avoidance is possible and necessary. Moreover, such an argument must appeal to some biographical or psychological information concerning the author, a rather dangerous argument without the presence of an author or diary to verify such claims, as is the case with most biblical passages.

Nevertheless, at least one affective response is possible to argue for on the basis of the text itself and the structure of the linguistic collocations. Enough research has been done on humor to suggest that when readers are given a particular kind of literary and linguistic context, a humorous response on their part is possible. Moreover, the counter examples where an individual does not find the particular collocation "funny" can be explained by the same theory that allows for one to argue that the assertion is humorous in the first place. To state it briefly at this point, language used dissonantly allows for humor; failure to see the dissonance or disambiguating the dissonance too slowly will nullify any possibility for humor.

This chapter will show why and how humor results from incongruities of sound, sense, and syntax, by examining theories of humor and "humorous language." However, comments on the humor of wordplay are often lacking because of certain prevalent attitudes towards the trope.

FAMILIAR STRANGERS

Terms such as "wit," "humor," and "pleasure" occur in the literature regarding wordplay from the dictionary definitions to the complicated linguistic explanations of wordplay—with the notable exception of comments by biblical critics. For example, Mahood, drawing upon Freud, speaks of the tendentious puns in Shakespeare that "please speaker and hearer because they act as a safety valve for these anti-social instincts" and the revelation of character that results from contrasting "simpletons, who are at the mercy of words they do not fully understand, and the sophisticated wits, who show their mastery of words by ringing all possible changes on their meanings."[1]

Verbal wit not only reveals character but thought itself. Thau says, "Sound and word play serve these ends [that logic and appearances become unfamiliar] since familiar words, suddenly strangers, become the instrument whereby the reader renews his perceptions and assumptions concerning language and reality."[2] Similarly, Ackerley says: "As a figure of speech, the pun combines the extremes of both the rational and irrational ... This lowest form of wit may well be the basis of all communication ... By treating 'differences' as if they were the 'same' the pun overcomes those differences, creating meaning, so that the *Word* or *Logos* is possible."[3] The following example, a stream of consciousness on the etymology of "gas" before the death of Beckett's character, "Murphy," is an "irrational" meditation that comes together as a coherent unit through the author's use of allusion, paronomasia, etymology, and other devices:

> Could it be the same word as Chaos? Chaos was yawn. But then cretin was Christian. Chaos would do, it might not be right but it was pleasant, for him henceforward gas would be chaos, and chaos gas. It could make you yawn, warm, laugh, cry, cease to suffer, live a little longer, die a little sooner. What could it not do? Gas. Could it turn a neurotic into a psychotic? No. Only God could do that. Let there be heaven in the midst of the waters, let it divide the waters

from the waters. The Chaos and the Waters Facilities Act. The Chaos, Light, and Coke Co. Hell. Heaven. Helen. Celia.[4]

What is evident in the "gas" example is the sheer "playfulness" of the language and ideas; the juxtaposition of the sacred and the mundane.

In biblical studies this recognition of play is rare. Casanowicz points out that "comedy chiefly made use of it [the ambiguous interpretation of words] as a means of γελίον,"[5] but he is speaking of Classical authors not biblical ones, and cites "riddles and puzzles" or distortions of syllables and pronunciations as premier examples of this jocular use of wordplay. His discussion of "humor" is brief, limited to two paragraphs; however, this attention to the humorous element of wordplay is more than his followers have devoted to it.[6] Peeters, who is not a biblical critic but who writes citing examples from the Bible, discusses wordplay and humor in a similarly brief manner, but for Peeters the connection is essential: "Quel est l'effet produit par le jeu de mots? Le premier effet se présentant a l'esprit est l'effet comique."[7]

An excellent example of the familiar becoming "strangers"—of playfulness even in a tendentious situation—is found in Isaiah's famous wordplay: "He looked for justice (למשפט), but behold! bloodshed (משׂפח); for righteousness (לצדקה), but behold! a cry (צעקה)." Phonetically and syntactically, the two opposing terms are linked, but logically "justice" and "righteousness," and "bloodshed" and "cry" belong together. The reader is confronted by an effective but almost irrational collocation where phonetics unite and semantics separate. (Since this wordplay is so familiar, the element of surprise, which is essential for finding something funny, is missing.)

The reason why the humor of wordplay lies largely unexplored is, in part, attributable to the mixed attitudes towards the trope.[8] Addison, in his remarks on the history of the pun, notes that great authors used the trope, but, since they were the start of a great age of writing, they "were destitute of all Rules and Arts of Criticism, and for that Reason, though thye excell later Writers in Greatness of Genius, they fall short of them in Accuracy and Correctness."[9] Ahl observes that, "Many scholars find such 'jingles' [anagrams and etymologies] distasteful and not only fail to recognize them but sometimes seem to emend texts to eliminate them."[10]

One frequently encounters statements such as, "The pun is the lowest form of wit" (to which Glück cites, "The bun is the lowest form of wheat," and we rightly groan), "The harlot of the Arts," and "That pestilent cosmetic" for descriptions of wordplay. Peeters cites a "typical" definition of wordplay, "Une phrase où l'on abuse de la ressemblance du son des mots," and retorts, "En effet, pourquoi employer le verb *abuser* et non pas *user* ?"[11] Dr Johnson is reported to have said, "A man who will make a pun will pick a pocket." [Is the conjunction of "man" and "make," and of "pun," "pick" and "pocket" intentional? Does Johnson's use of alliteration persuade us to believe that a punster picks sound and sense much as a pickpocket lifts a purse?]

Remarks such as the foregoing—with perhaps a smidgen of humor in themselves—reveal why it is that many who ponder the pun feel compelled to offer some justification for their enterprise. The reader may recall Heller's attempt to link wordplay with "more respectable" genres and with the "nature of reasoning itself."[12] We find that those who study this trope of questionable origin swiftly and easily become defensive.

A marvellous apologetic for the pun is Pope's "God's Revenge Against Punning" in which he shows various calamities which befell certain punsters who incurred the wrath of God for "the Corruption of our Language, and therein of the Word of God translated into our Language; which certainly every sober Christian must Tremble at."[13] One example will suffice to show the extreme personal danger of punning:

> "The Right Honourable _____ (but it is not safe to insert the Name of an eminent Nobleman in this Paper, yet I will venture to say that such a one has been seen; which is all we can say, considering the largeness of his Sleeves:) This young Nobleman was not only a flagitious Punster himself, but was accessory to the Punning of others, by Consent, by Provocation, by Connivance, and by Defence of the Evil committed; for which the Lord mercifully spared his Neck, but as a Mark of Reprobation wryed his Nose."

For all the hoopla and hype over the pun, H.W. Fowler's observation shows a great sensibility: "Puns are good, bad and indifferent, and only those who lack the wit to make them are unaware of the fact."[14] Redfern reminds us that puns do not have to be funny—but it doesn't hurt if they are! Some justification for the negative attitude towards the trope exists, just as there is often retribution against the one who (too) cleverly employ it. Those who can differentiate between the good, the bad, and the indifferent have their reward in the delight of language captured.

The task of this chapter is not to show that puns are good or bad, but to show why this subversion of logic, perceptions, and assumptions that wordplay creates is humorous. The previous chapters, on ambiguity and the formal structures of wordplay, provide the precondition for the humor. The inherent ambiguity of language allows sound to be played against sound, and meaning against meaning. In this balancing of sound and sense new possibilities are brought forth as ideas are compared and contrasted; we find contraction and expansion both phonetically and semantically. A reader may find "pleasure" in this balancing act and the contrast created by this particular collocation of linguistic features. Why is this so?

THEORIES OF HUMOR

The humorous element in a pun is not always obvious, partly because we have misconceptions about what "humor" is. What comes to mind most readily is "laughter," or worse, frivolity. The things we laugh at are sundry—quips and clever children; riddles, rhymes, and limericks; epigrams, aphorisms, and graffiti; slips of the tongue and on the bum; jokes, japes, and jests, and wheezes; Wellerisms and ... the pun. Some of these are witty, whimsical, absurd, droll, ludicrous—or just plain funny and pleasurable. The degree of laughter for these aspects of humor are similarly varied: we are amused, giggle, titter, guffaw, and even die laughing.

Even "simple" laughter remains basically opaque. We recognize laughter as a physiological reflex—facial contortions, expulsion of air from the lungs, and accompanying sounds. However, what biological purpose does it serve? This has led some to call laughter a "luxury reflex." Laughter is a complex mental state, like fear or jealousy, and a complex social interaction. We can neither agree on why we laugh, nor when it is appropriate to laugh.[15]

In recent years, theories of humor have been grouped into three categories.[16] The first theory stems from Plato and Aristotle. Aristotle says, "Comedy ... is an imitation of people who are worse than average."[17] We laugh because our situation compares favorably with the misfortunes of others. This theory is dubbed the *Superiority Theory* , since the one laughing is in some way "superior" to the one being laughed at. Hobbes argued similarly: "Sudden glory, is the passion which makes those grimaces called laughter; and is caused either by some sudden act of their own, that pleases them; or by the apprehension of some deformed thing in another, by comparison whereof they suddenly applaud themselves."[18]

The second theory, the *Relief Theory* , focuses on the physical aspects of laughter. Herbert Spencer was first to bring this aspect of humor to the forefront. For Spencer, built-up nervous energy required a muscular release; hence laughter comes about as a specialized release channel ("Only when there is what we may call a *descending* incongruity"—when "consciousness is unawares transferred from great things to small"[19]). Bergson and Freud fall into this category as well, but bring in the idea of subversion of structures (for Bergson, mechanism; for Freud, outwitting the censor).

The third theory is the *Incongruity Theory* . Kant argues that humor arises from the incongruity between what is expected to happen, and what actually happens. As Hazlitt says, "Man is the only animal that laughs and weeps; for he is the only animal that is struck with the difference between what things are, and what they ought to be."[20] There is a frustrated expectation and laughing arises from the accompanying emotional release.

The scholarly discussion of humor has continued and progressed in recent years, especially, but not exclusively, with insights drawn from psychology. The three theories discussed fall short of an adequate theory of humor, yet all three inform what is necessary for a comprehensive theory that accounts for laughter at humorous situations and laughter at non-humorous ones. Three recent attempts at a synthesis, one each from philosophy, psychology, and linguistics, will provide a working theory for our discussion of the humor of wordplay.

Philosophy . An enthusiastic spokesperson for the new attempts to articulate a comprehensive theory of humor is John Morreall, a philosopher when he is not trifling with humor.[21] Morreall suggests three features that can form the basis for a comprehensive theory of humor. First, there is the change in the psychological state of one involved in laughter situations. Second, this change must be sudden, we must be caught "off guard ... so that we cannot smoothly adjust to what we are experiencing." Finally, the sudden psychological shift must be viewed as "pleasant": "Enjoying self-glory, being amused by some incongruity, releasing pent-up nervous energy—all these feel good, and can cause us to laugh"; thus, "Laughter results from a pleasant psychological shift."[22] Important for our purposes, is the recognition that the shift may be either cognitive or affective and often both.

Psychology . In a similar fashion, C.P. Wilson, a psychologist, says that two associations are introduced in a single item, creating "cognitive imbalance"; the "associative strength" of one item will be greater that the other, thus producing a "surprising" perception of incongruity. The audience resolves the incongruity and balance is then restored; the resolution suggests a "pleasant" outcome.[23] The important part of Wilson's theory for our purposes is that one of the two items will have a greater associative strength than the other.

Linguistics . The linguist V. Raskin, arguing strictly for a semantic theory of humor (but recognizing that his theory is compatible with and resolves the difficulties of traditional theories), says that the "necessary and sufficient" conditions for a text to be funny are: (1) A text must must be "compatible" with two "scripts" (the semantic information surrounding or evoked by the word) which overlap "fully or in part." And (2) The two scripts must be "locally opposite" (antonymous or simply opposite in a particular discourse).[24] For our purposes, he informs us that jokes are non-*bona-fide* modes of communication because they ask us not to "cooperate" by disambiguating the discourse— "opposite" ideas are presented as one and the reader must entertain both ideas.

Humor, then, results from language used dissonantly, which, once recognized, results in a feeling of pleasure. Humor begins on a cognitive level since the reader (in our case) must recognize two locally opposite scripts in a single discourse. Since some rule or sense of (linguistic) propriety is violated, the reader will feel an imbalance (cognitive or affective). Once balance is restored, "pleasure" results (affective). Humor is enhanced to the degree that the imbalance is surprising and the restoration is sudden. Humor will not be found if the imbalance persists, nor if the imbalance is seen simply as uncertainty (either "this" or "that," but not both); no pleasure results since one feels frustration on the one hand or one imposes order without a sense of violation on the other.

The Language of Humor

For Peeters to connect both language and humor with wordplay is no accident. The connection is grounded in Bergson's and Freud's theory of humor; that is, that humor is the flouting of mechanism (Bergson), or outwitting the censor (Freud). Since wordplay goes against the "mechanism" of language, it is humorous. M. Douglas says of the Joker, "Safe within the permitted range of attack, he lightens for everyone the oppressiveness of social reality, demonstrates its arbitrariness by making light of formality in general, and expresses the creative possibilities of the situation."[25] The same could be said of the punster: He lightens the oppression of syntax, demonstrates the arbitrariness of sound, and expresses the creative possibility of words.

Peeters is in danger of erring when he presses the anomalous nature of the pun. A pun may subvert the conventions of language, but it does so, as Douglas says of the Joker, "Safe within the permitted range of attack." A pun is a skip in the sound, syntax, or sense, not a stumble or a fall. The boundaries of language are seldom breached, but are conquered by enlisting the enemy in the service of the text.

The relationship between language, humor and wordplay goes farther than the slightly skewed—or, in some eyes, the contrived—collocations we find in language use. In addition to "humorous language," there is, as W. Nash notes, a "language of comedy."

The language of comedy can be "quite unremarkable"; it "concerns a discursive relationship between all the parts of a text and its infrastructure."[26] Comedic language has to do with the overall plan—the use of embellishment that falls flat at the end, or personal control being undone by an non-personal element—and other such unifying strategies that depend less on lexical choice and "brilliance," and more on scheme.

Humorous language, on the other hand, deals with stylistic properties—words, phrases, or perhaps, sentences. Comic style and structure do not always produce witticisms or jokes. Wordplay falls into the category of humorous language, though some overlap is inevitable.

Humorous language is "funny" because of the collocation of letters, words, and phrases. Some words might be simply funny in themselves:

> Contusions are funny, not open wounds,
>   and automobiles that go
> Crash into trees by the highwayside
>   Industrial accidents, no.

The habit of drink is a hundred per cent,
  But drug addiction is nil.
A nervous breakdown will get no laughs;
  Insanity surely will.

Humour, aloof from the cigarette,
  Inhabits the droll cigar;
The middle-aged are not very funny;
  The young and the old, they are.

So the funniest thing in the world should be
  A grandsire, drunk, insane,
Maimed in a motor accident,
  And enduring moderate pain.[27]

However, more so than inherently funny words—if there is such a thing—
is simply the syntagmatic and paradigmatic choices an author makes, just as in
language generally. The syntagmatic features are "repetitions, parallels,
inversions" and the like; the paradigmatic selections come from a "zone of
choice"—a set of synonyms.[28]

Nash maps the humorous phrase or sentence as choices between
syntagmatic and paradigmatic relations. His example will help illustrate what he
means: *The lank sergeant sighed lugubriously* . If we begin with the phrase
"sergeant sighed" (which forms a syntagmatic, alliterative sequence), and want to
make a humorous statement, we might add an adjective describing the sergeant
and an adverb explicating his action. To do this requires paradigmatic choices—
synonyms of whatever feature of the sergeant we wish to describe. In Nash's
example, he wants a thin person, so the choices are "thin," but also "lank," "lean,"
"skinny," and "emaciated." The sergeant is going to have a "sad" *sigh* which
produces "sadly," "dolefully," "mournfully," and "lugubriously." To sigh "sadly"
effects a nice alliterative sequence, but "lugubriously" combines with "lank" to
produce a comic atmosphere ("lugubriously" also forces us to reconsider "lank"
at the beginning of the sentence).

Nash makes this important observation, "But examination will always show
that these apparently dynamic items are not self-charged. They are always
located in a context, or *allocated* to a position in a design."[29] In other words,
humorous language is a choice of words put into a particular context. As I
argued previously, wordplays come about less from true lexical ambiguity and
more from the omission of contextual clues that eliminate alternative readings.
Humorous language depends on a humorous context, one that allows for sound,
sense, and scheme to be played off each other.

Speaking specifically of the pun, Nash says, "The management of humorous
language is largely a matter of devising transfers ... until a happy confusion of a

double vision is achieved. At the heart of this process of continual and multiple transference, an important process aping the shiftiness of thought itself, is the apparent frivolous device of the pun; word-play is the lure, the spinning toy, that draws up the lurking and fishy meaning."[30] The author fishes for the right word that tugs the line from thought, to sentence, to humorous language. Nash, as also Peeters and others, thus connects language, thought, and humor in wordplay; the collocations of sound and sense that spin until consonants and meanings blend in confusion, then fusion as one, often unexpected, sense comes to dominate and delight.

CONCLUSIONS

The comic—that which we find humorous—is richly varied and covers the fatuous to the sublime. In its multiformity, humor is not unlike the pun; or perhaps better, the pun, because it is language used humorously, is richly evocative and diffuse. The variety is so vast that even by offering a general typology of the pun, one is forced, like Heller, Kelly, and Brown, to record the spins and deviations that both separate and coalesce in what we call wordplay. The locus and the power of wordplay are found in the interconnection between the play of language and humor. Thus when Peeters appeals to both language and humor to explicate wordplay, he gets to the heart of the trope; Peeters, however, appeals to language and humor to show the ability of puns to subvert language. The subversion of language occasionally does take place, but more often it is the use of language in such as way as to balance phonetics, semantics, and even syntax in compression and ultimately expansion in order to subvert our misconceptions and parochialism, not to subvert language *per se* . As Douglas says, the Joker passes "beyond the bounds of reason and society and gives glimpses of a truth which escapes through the mesh of structured concepts."[31] We find a similar thought in Morreall: "People with a well-developed sense of humor naturally look at things critically, because they are looking for incongruity."[32]

Rather than being simply frivolous, then, wordplay can be a strong heuristic device, "profoundly serious, or charged with pathos."[33] Wordplays lead us to look at the incongruities that surround us; they cause us to acknowledge that entropy encroaches on every thing we do. Parenetic punning.

Readers can delight—and wince—at the acerbic wit of Isaiah as he critiques his countrymen, or enjoy the extended play—and comic reactions— throughout the "Isaac" (יצחק, "laughter") narratives, but only if one first accepts the possibility of "play" in wordplay.

We come to this conclusion, then, that wordplay is a linguistic and literary undertaking that produces cognitive and affective relationships based on contiguities and differences of sounds, senses, and syntax.

My favorite cartoon is an old *New Yorker* one where a psychiatrist is talking to his patient. He says, "The good news is you have a happy self-image.

news is that it has no basis in reality." Does our sketch of wordplay have any basis in the reality of texts? Is wordplay multifaceted, fulfilling various functions within a pericope, and essentially humorous in the Bible? Part Two of this study will show that this conception of wordplay finds support not only in general theoretical considerations, but in the specificity of a text, the book of Micah in this case.

PART TWO
WORDPLAY IN THE BOOK OF MICAH

"[Wordplays] are a kind of code which the reader, spectator or hearer is invited to crack."

Redfern, *Puns*

INTRODUCTION
CRACKING THE CODE

The predominant mode of conceptualizing wordplay in biblical studies, precipitated in large part by Casanowicz, is as soundplay. Attention is paid to the phonological aspects of wordplay to the neglect of other aspects, especially semantic plays. In recent years, this preoccupation with phonetics has waned somewhat, and attention to ambiguity and to function has waxed (e.g., Peeters, Watson). Still, these transilient comments are, by-and-large, isolated, often embedded in commentaries, dissertations, or journal articles[1]; no systematic and sustained examination of the trope across the whole of the literature or in a particular book in the light of these more recent concerns is readily available. It remains to demonstrate that wordplay encompasses more than soundplay in the book of Micah and that it fulfils various cognitive and affective functions.

FROM THERE TO HERE

Part One, "The Universe of Wordplay," provides a vocabulary for talking about the various types of wordplay that we find in texts. Since wordplay is diverse not monolithic, we cannot expect to find every type represented in Micah. We can, however, isolate those kinds that are employed and establish a general range from which Micah[2] works.

Since the present approach to wordplay in the Bible differs markedly with most other approaches, and since the subject itself is inherently fluid— "ambiguity" entails movement—there will be a degree of interdeterminacy and opportunity for honest debate over the findings presented in Part Two. However, in order to crack the code of wordplay, we must be alert[3] to the possibilities of the enterprise as presented in Part One.

A danger exists of imposing categories upon the material. To guard against that, insofar as it is possible, we must examine of the sorts of wordplay found in the texts that are generally agreed upon to contain wordplay (e.g., Mic 1: 10-15). The study proceeds from what has already been mapped out and then extends the borders to include the less familiar—what we find in the text and what we know about the trope generally.

To locate the familiar, we must look at the history of interpretation. If we are to advance the study of wordplay, we must have a base from which to go forth. The history of interpretation provides a base. However, extending the work of our predecessors rather than simply recreating it, is both more interesting and more helpful; we must enlarge the circle, not wander around in it. The data from the history of interpretation is but a tool or a guide and not the main concern of the present study.

To show the ambiguity of wordplay, we must establish the semantic field of the word(s) in question. For a word to be ambiguous, a single sentence-form should convey two (or more) separate propositions; for example, the sentence, *Everyone knew Mary was smart* , can mean: a. Mary was intelligent; b. Mary was stylish; c. Mary was alert; or d. Mary was impudent. All four are possible, given the sentence-form above and an indeterminate context.

If a word occurs only in a particular context, then ambiguity is unlikely since the semantic field will be restricted. A single context seldom exists, however. In normal communication, a native speaker will work to disambiguate sentences that could, by form, express two distinct propositions. The native speaker will perform this task usually through the clues of the immediate context.[4] However, some sentences, like the example above, may require extra-lexical information: if the "audience" knows that Mary was an honor student, worked at a fashion store, or had a quick tongue, then any one of the other three possible readings would be eliminated, at least provisionally, excluding any further contextual clues. The extra-lexical information obscures the distinction between "world-knowledge" (historical-cultural information) and linguistic-knowledge (word associations); Raskin calls "extra-lexical" information "those semantic properties evoked by the words which are not usually accommodated in lexicons of any kind," information which is, nevertheless, essential for comprehending even some of the simplest sentences (monetary systems, superstitions, etiquette, and so forth).

To demonstrate that wordplay encompasses more than soundplay, then, requires showing semantic ambiguity by delimiting the lexical field and contextual clues, and using whatever lexical and extra-lexical information is still recoverable by non-native, non-contemporary speakers of Hebrew. The non-native speaker may sometimes have an advantage in recognizing wordplay since such a person would not "naturally" disambiguate sentences.

The data from the history of interpretation may also assist the exegete in exposing ambiguous sentences: if one scholar posits a single semantic possibility in a given context, and another scholar argues equally as forcefully for a second semantic possibility, then the term in question could be ambiguous in this context and would require further investigation to determine the source of the ambiguity.

The first task, then, is to show the varieties of wordplay found in Micah, varieties not only of sound, but semantics and syntax as well.

Naming, however, is not explaining, so we must push beyond "godfathering" to examine the literary and social functions of the trope. Sound, sense, and structure work to persuade the audience, or evoke from them a response. The reader recognizes or creates patterns of relationships; these relationships may be cognitive or affective. Chapter 7 focuses on the cognitive effects, and chapter 8 on the affective.

On a literary level, wordplays can provide unity, development or disruption, contrast or comparison, and foreshadowing or retrospection. Wordplays do these activities since sound and sense can clash or coalesce. These architectural—architextual?—designs are a reflection of the thought and purpose behind the words (whether by design or default), which appeal to both intellect and emotion; for example, Vickers maintains that oxymorons show "a strange harmony *which must be* expressed in such discords."[5]

The social function stems largely from the humorous element in wordplay, an element usually overlooked by biblical critics. One problem many have in seeing the ludic element in wordplay, especially in biblical studies, is the tendency to contrast play with seriousness. Play (or more narrowly humor) is not opposed to seriousness; indeed, players are often very serious when play begins. We can say that play is "non-serious" in the sense that it is a voluntary activity lying outside the realm of "normal" activity. However, play is orderly; it follows rules and has a beginning and ending; play is neither anarchical, nor infinite. Finally, play both includes and excludes; a "community" engages in play and thereby sets up barriers, either by accident or choice, for those who are not part of the "game." Play represents a celebration of freedom within its own parameters, one that unites a "community" with its implicit critique (exclusion) of another.[6]

Play, as an activity freely entered into that creates distinctions between groups and lies outside "normal" activity, is a subversive activity for it undermines the status quo. Redfern calls wordplay "underground literature." Wordplay is, then, both literary and social, and as such is a particularly apt trope for the prophet as he or she rolls out a persuasive argument, only to pull it out from under the audience—"you are the man!"[7]

A serious question arises: If wordplay works largely through indirection, then how can we recognize this recondite trope? Addison makes this observation: "The only way therefore to try a piece of Wit, is to translate it into a different language. If it bears the Test you may pronounce it true; but if it vanishes in the Experiment you may conclude it to have been a Punn."[8]

Addison does not hold puns in high esteem, yet beyond this unbecoming attitude lies a misguided premise. If "wit" vanishes in translation, it probably is humor since humor is context dependent; if the context vanishes, then the humor vanishes, or if the context is untranslatable (because if the peculiarities of a given language situation, lexical and extra-lexical), then the humor often will be as well. What marks wit is not its ability to transcend linguistic peculiarities, but "economy," as Freud informs us.[9]

Several items may alert a reader to the presence of wordplay, especially those that display "wit": an unusual collocation of words (condensation, displacement, opposition, repetition, etc.); words working together through the lines (image-linking, especially faulty reasoning or representation); or an indeterminate context (indirection, perhaps revealed through the history of interpretation of a passage).

The task is not an easy one since we are dealing with a subject that is elusive and defiant, one that works with what is not heard and seen as much as with what is. As such, it is necessary to work from the more certain to the less within each section. The initial observations within each section, I feel, will be more easily recognized by scholars than the latter observations. Similarly, the move from section to section is a move from the more certain to the less: it is easier to show the varieties of wordplay than to show the functions, and identifying the humor in a wordplay is more difficult to show than the function. No comment or section is determinative; the success of the enterprise is cumulative.

The approach outlined above is inclusive methodologically, yet flexible. The task is to make a consistent analysis of wordplay in the book of Micah in the light of the concerns outlined in Part One. These concerns correspond to the three subdivisions of Part II: *The Varieties of Wordplay* ; *The Persuasive Angle of the Text* ; and *The Ludic Angle of the Text* . Each section necessarily anticipates the following one, or adds something to the previous section—the sections are fluid even as the trope itself is.

SIX
THE VARIETIES OF WORDPLAY

Addison's worst fears have been realized; we have 'degenerated into a race of punsters.'

Mahood, *Shakespeare's Wordplay*

Micah employs both puns and paronomasia. Paronomasia is the more frequent and obvious device wherein wordplay is played out, at least according to commentators' observations. However, even in the most obvious text, Mic 1: 10-15, plainly not all the wordplays are paronomasia, especially the type based on the etymological associations of the placenames, real or imagined; rather, the wordplays are based on some extra-phonological, indeed, sometimes even extra-lexical information. Whatever a commentator makes of מספד בית האצל יקח מכם עמדתו (literally, "The mourning of Beth-Ezel he will take away his standing place"), it clearly is not paronomasia.

This chapter, then, will show that a variety of wordplays are found in Micah by examining 1: 10-15; 1: 6-7; 4: 14; 2: 12; and 3: 5-7.

MICAH 1: 10-15: WHAT ARE THEY SAYING ABOUT MIC 1: 10-15?

Who can add to what has already been said of Mic 1: 10-15? This pericope has been pushed and probed, twisted, turned, and scrutinized from every conceivable angle. Some commentators do little more than repeat the text; for example, A. Cohen says of "Beth-le-aphrah": "lit. 'house of dust.' The name otherwise unknown," and glosses "roll thyself" as "in grief and despair."[1] Other commentators find meaning in the unlikeliest places; for example, W. Rudolph finds in the words "the glory of Israel" a reference to the three mighty men who came to David while he was at Adullam (cf. 2 Sam 23: 13, 19).[2] Finally, some commentators emend the text beyond recognition in order to make some sense of it; for example, T.K. Cheyne reads "Jarmuth" for "Maroth" (v 12; cf. Josh 15: 35) and "Eshkol" for "Lachish" (v 13) even though he has already inserted "Eshkol" at v 10 for אל בכו ("Eshkol" at v 10 was used "only" to produce a wordplay, whereas at v 13 it has a "much more serious purpose"—Israelite pilgrims had a "fascination" with this sanctuary).[3]   To say something new about this pericope would seem to require a new universe of discourse.

Nevertheless, this passage stands as the supreme example of the paronomastic style we find in the text of Micah and, therefore, we must make some comments regarding the passage even if no new insights are forthcoming.

The task is to uncover the varieties of wordplay. Since the text is arguably the most difficult text in Micah, attention to textual difficulties is necessary; but these difficulties are not determinative for the direction of the inquiry since we are dealing with the text of the *book* of Micah, not with an author or some supposed "original" text. In other words, given the MT of Micah, what can we make of it with respect to wordplays that we find? Textual options are addressed as they influence how others have understood the wordplays in the pericope; our argument is on the character of the wordplay, however, not the character of the text.[4]

One way of addressing the nature of the wordplays in Micah is to ask two questions—questions which have become axiomatic in the American political arena during the 1970s and 1980s: What did he know? and, When did he know it? The "he" here, however, is not Micah, but subsequent commentators. What constitutes recognizable wordplay in the pericope as discussed and (dis)agreed upon by the commentators? At what point in the history of interpretation were these observations made explicit?

The history of interpretation is a separate inquiry, much as textual criticism can be; but no inquiry is completely unto itself and, at least the data from the history of interpretation impinge upon exegesis at important though perhaps not determinative points. An exegete does not come to a text *de novo* ; by identifying and accounting for the traditions that have shaped our understanding of the text we can show whether the traditional interpretations suffice or whether new questions are necessary for understanding the text.

As a strictly historical study, the history of interpretation, or the data that inform such a study, may yield fortuitous discoveries. An idea or tradition can become lost in the course of events, whether through negligence, misunderstanding or simply rejection because it counters the prevailing interpretation of the period. For example, תתגדדי in Mic 4: 14 is understood by medieval Jewish interpreters as "gather together" (based on the Tg); Eliezer of Beaugency, a pupil of Rashbam (Rashi's grandson), departs from this tradition and renders it, "cut yourself." Eliezer is largely overlooked by subsequent commentators, but his understanding of the verb is the one that is generally

accepted by modern commentators (independent of his study, of course).
Moreover, the same interpretation is found in Jerome; is Eliezer preserving an
alternative tradition to Rashi, one found also in Jerome? Or, has Eliezer arrived
at this understanding independently of a particular tradition? Either way, in
Eliezer we find an alternative understanding of a difficult text, one that countered
the prevailing tradition but has now become the accepted view.

The present study is less concerned with answering such questions about
descent and influence since that inquiry properly belongs to the history of
interpretation; however, sorting through the data to find what was recognized as
wordplay and when these observations were made is more germane to the task at
hand. Do the particular observations of commentators coincide with the general
studies of Casanowicz and others regarding wordplay? That is, is wordplay seen
solely or primarily as paronomasia? What constitutes wordplay as recognized
throughout the commentaries?

The data from the history of interpretation may further facilitate the
discovery of wordplay by exposing the ambiguities of a word or text, as noted
above. When two reasonably competent scholars say, "The text clearly means
X," and "The text clearly means Y," then a *possible* explanation is that the text is
ambiguous. (The text may also simply be uncertain or some other problem and
not ambiguous.) If the text is ambiguous, then exploration of the nature of the
ambiguity is called for.

By bringing in data from the history of interpretation, then, fortuitous
discoveries may emerge and a more particularly historical study is brought to
bear on the exegesis. This approach provides some historical controls, or at least
a historical context, for any departures that are made from the "consensus." I
want to set a context to show that in breaking with traditional understandings of
the text I do not do so willy-nilly or out of a sense that the previous work on
wordplay is irrelevant or entirely deficient. What I will offer as new comes out
of respect and learning from previous work.

The examination of the history of interpretation need not be exhaustive.
For our purposes, those commentators not working with Hebrew or having
recourse to the Hebrew text may be set aside. Although insightful comments are
possible even with commentators not working with the Hebrew text, diminishing
returns are more likely. Accessibility is another problem for someone exploring
the history of interpretation. Some very fine or interesting commentaries are
long out of print or are part of special collections of libraries. Nevertheless, a
representative study of periods and points of view is possible and provides the
necessary data for answering our questions, though not exhaustively.

The works of several commentators are examined: Jerome in the Patristic
period; Rashi, Ibn Ezra, Kimchi, and Eliezer of Beaugency of the Medieval
Jewish commentators, and Nicholas de Lyra, also of the Medieval period; Luther
and Calvin in the Reformation period; Edward Pococke and Ernst Rosenmüller in
the Post-Reformation period; and then the more recent critical commentaries,

especially those of J.M.P. Smith, W. Rudolph, L.C. Allen, J.L. Mays, R. Vuilleumier, H.W. Wolff, and D.R. Hillers.

<hr>

Excursus: Is Knowledge of Hebrew Necessary?

Is knowledge of Hebrew a necessary precondition for recognition or appreciation of wordplay? Certainly the "recognition" of most wordplays in the Hebrew text requires some knowledge, at least, of Hebrew, but knowledge of Hebrew is not a necessary condition for the appreciation of the trope. A translator may capture the "idea" of the wordplay, though perhaps not the particular play, and a subsequent reader could make what he or she wills of the result. For example, one can render בבית לעפרה עפר התפלשתי as, "In dustville, I will roll myself in the dust," or some such translation. A commentator or reader may then make observations on the literary and theological function of the wordplay in the oracle. Another strategy, taken by H.W. Wolff in his *Mit Micha Reden: Prophetie einst und jetzt* , is to create contemporary wordplays that give the reader a sense of what Micah created for his audience. One of Wolff's witticisms is "Schellenbeck muss zerschellen." The same strategy is carried out by the translator of Wolff's work, R.D. Gehrke: "Tacoma will give off a terrible aroma," and "Fort Worth will be called Power Dearth." A reader of Wolff/Gehrke can catch the tone, if not the specifics, of the wordplays, and in some cases catching the tone alone would not materially affect the exegesis.

Recognition of wordplay—or at least explicit comments upon it—is, thus, not tied to linguistic knowledge if the translation itself can convey the play in some form. Is, then, the recognition of wordplay—or perhaps simply appreciation for it—dependent upon a certain socio-historical milieu or linguistic approach? Would a commentator who considers "form" as important as content "find" wordplays more easily than someone who regards perspicuity in language and composition as pre-eminent? Casanowicz contends that wordplay (paronomasia) is more prevalent in Latin and French than in Greek or German. Granted this position is questionable, at best, but certain individuals or periods may have a greater interest in certain types of figures of speech; appreciation for wordplay may wax and wane, as in the case of eigthteenth-century England where Dr Johnson did not take kindly to Shakespeare's wordplay.

In the commentators examined, even those commentators such as Eliezer and the present generation who freely acknowledge the extensive presence of wordplay, precious little is said except that it exists. This omission is also true in their comments on the formal matters of composition—linking, contrasting, etc.

Allowance for ambiguity and persuasive strategy is lacking in most commentators' analysis of the text.

The two guiding questions—when and where wordplay was recognized—however, lead us back into the text, not necessarily for new insights but that interpretive options are clarified for us.

Wellhausen calls the dirge a "Kapuzinade" (a severe, but perhaps popular, sermon);[5] J.M.P. Smith says that it is the "most remarkable," as well as the most difficult and obscure, oracle in the book;[6] Rudolph does not limit his comments to the book but carries Smith's sentiment further to include "des ganzen AT."[7]

The text is so difficult that K. Elliger opts for radical emendation.[8] His hypothesis is an influential one, even reaching the halls of recent, moderately conservative scholarship (e.g., J.L. Mays[9]). Elliger suggests that the textual problems arose from purely mechanical damage to the right hand column of the "original" text, and thus the middle and end of a line require no reconstruction. Furthermore, he argues that each bicolon contains a place name, and all the towns lie within Micah's "field of vision"—the Shephelah. The latter part of Elliger theory is widely accepted, but his supposition that the text was damaged on the right column receives only sporadic support (most notably, S.J. Schwantes[10] and Mays).

An important critique of Elliger's theory comes from A.S. van der Woude, who questions the damaged-text theory saying that there is no evidence to support a "stichic," rather than a continuously written, line that Elliger's thesis requires.[11] He further questions whether the text is so damaged that it defies understanding; recognizing the metrical pattern (2+2 alternating with 3+2, and not just the 3+2 *qinah* -meter) suggests that there are two speakers in this pericope, not one, as is commonly supposed. "Wordplay" falls on the 2+2 lines, not the 3+2 lines, which, once recognized, yields a smoother sense for the text, so van der Woude argues. Finally, not all of the place names can be identified as lying in Micah's field of vision. Van der Woude, however, is followed more for his critique of Elliger than he is for his solution to the problems of the text (i.e., that two speakers alternate and that place names are not necessarily in the Shephelah).

The problems with the text , however, are not simply modern, critical problems. Pococke, in the midst of trying to explain 1: 11, stops and says, "How much more difficult will it be to reconcile so many translations as have *since* come forth?"[12] "Since" refers to Jerome, who already lamented of the situation and appealed to the assistance of the Holy Spirit to explain the great diversity: *Ut si quando indiguimus spiritu Dei ... nunc vel maxime eum adesse cupiamus* .

The object of the present inquiry is much more modest than solving the myriad of problems surrounding the pericope, though one cannot escape them entirely and some attention must be paid to the textual problems. The primary task in this chapter, however, is simply to uncover the varieties of wordplay, as evidenced in the history of interpretation of the passage and in the light of the concerns regarding wordplay outlined in Part One of this study.

1:10: בגת אל־תגידו: "In Gath, do not announce [it]." The same words occur in 2 Sam 1: 20, but in reverse order; אל־תגידו בגת. The MT of Micah is laconic, but comprehensible. Those in Gath are not to call attention to the disaster, which is portrayed in the following verses; or perhaps those in Gath are not to call attention to their grief, which follows immediately from the initial words, "neither weep." Presumably, the point is that the neighboring enemies would come against them to "finish the job" or scorn them if they vented their grief, as is clear in the Samuel passage: " … lest the daughters of the Philistines rejoice … " (RSV).

In spite of the relative clarity of the text, variance from the MT is found in both LXX and P; this variance is germane to the recognition and nature of the wordplay in the text. Schwantes argues that תגידלו, as evidenced by the translation of LXX (μεγαλύνεσθε) is a conflation of תגידו, as in the MT (cf. Tg, תחוון, and V, *annuntiare*) and תגילו, as in P (*thḏwn*, "rejoice").[13] Wolff and Hillers favour the reading of LXX, a reading perhaps also reflected in 1QpMic.[14] Hillers is cautious in adopting this reading but does so on the basis of Gath's being, at the time of this oracle, a Judaean territory lost to the enemy. The wordplay, he avers, works with either verb.

The easiest way to explain LXX is to suppose that its *Vorlage* read תגידלו. However, the translator may also simply be trying to make sense of the bicolon: If the translator associates Gath with the Philistines, as found in, for example, Amos 6: 2 ("… then go to Gath of the Philistines …"), then the injunction not to magnify themselves is appropriate. This understanding of LXX is supported by the following words in the LXX: "You in Akim, do not build out of the house according to laughter, [but] sprinkle dust according to your laughter." In other words, do not magnify yourselves because your time is coming.

The reading of P, *thḏwn* (Heb: תגילו; "rejoice"), serves as partial justification for a different wordplay from the paronomasia found in MT. For example, Mays favours the reading of P, and, on the basis of Elliger's proposal (cf. Schwantes), reconstructs "In the gardens of Giloh (בגנות גלה), do not rejoice (אל תגילו)." The reading of P and the reconstruction of the initial words, then, form a "popular" etymological play, a type of play that is found throughout the pericope.

Elliger's proposal is creative and enticing—but he may be acting as much as an author as he is critic. The only textual support is for the verb as found in P. What justification is there for supposing an "etymological" play in this bicolon? Indeed, since wordplay is not unequivocal in the initial colon, a reader cannot be certain that wordplay, especially etymological wordplay, is a major structuring device. Only as the text is further processed does wordplay become obvious (לעפרה עפר), and only as the entire pericope is examined can the type of wordplay involved be discerned. It is true that paronymic plays dominate, but I will argue that the wordplays are not of one type, and therefore one cannot always predict what type of wordplay will be found in a given place.

One may reject Elliger's proposal and still follow P, though little warrant exists for this emendation either. Allen says that P may be influenced by 2 Sam 1: 20. However, the verb in Samuel is תגידו, as in Micah; תשמחנה, "be glad," and תעלזנה, "exult," are also found in the verse. More simply, P arose as a suitable contrast to the following injunction, "do not weep."[15]

LXX and P obscure the paronomasia and the allusion to 2 Sam 1: 20 in an effort to make sense out of the prohibition, especially as this injunction relates to the following words not to weep. LXX provides the motivation (derision), while P creates a contrast (rejoice/weep). However, nothing necessitates adopting either reading as the original; both can be explained on the basis of תגידו and the desire to make sense of the whole colon.

The wordplay is formed by the alliteration and assonance between תגידו and גת. The paronomasia is present but does not demand that the reader notice it. (Indeed, in my perusal of the history of exegesis, I found no explicit mention of wordplay before Eliezer and then again in Rosenmüller.) Hence D.R. Hillers can say, "Paronomasia, if present at all ... ,"[16] while Mays does not quibble over the paronomasia, but reconstructs an unequivocal pun, בגנות גלה אל תגילו. The transformation of the consonants ג and ת in בגת and תגידו shows that what Ahl calls "anagrammatical" plays are employed.[17]

The repetition of the palatal and dental letters forms the paronomasia and suggests a connection between the town and what the inhabitants are instructed to do, or not to do in this case (אל). More important, however, than the relationship between "Gath" (גת) and "tell" (תגידו) is the relationship between this passage and David's lament in 2 Sam 1: 20. Mic 1: 10 is not a citation, as if it drew upon an existing text,[18] but it is an allusion in both form (wordplay) and content (lament). What follows in this instance is not the fall of a national hero, but a disaster that befalls the nation. The allusion, like the paronomasia, does not demand to be seen and, therefore, may be passed over or assigned to a later redactor.

LXX and P are incorrect to tie too closely the *sense* of the initial words with the following ones, but are correct to take into account the entire colon, hence:

בכו אל־תבכו: "Weeping, do not weep" or "Do not even wail." If translated woodenly (i.e., the first translation), these words are more problematic than the previous ones.

Rather than a placename and verb separated by a negative, as in the previous part of the colon, the MT has an infinitive and finite form of the same verb separated by a negative. The lines are coordinated structurally (noun/inf. +

neg. + pl. verb), and partially coordinated syntactically (pl. verbs preceded by negative) and phonologically (dental, palatal, and velar phonemes repeat); בגת and בכו correspond paradigmatically and alliteratively, but not semantically.

The dissonance created by these partial overlaps gives rise to conjectures regarding the text. Prior to Elliger's proposals, many translators and commentators read בכו as a placename: "In Akim" (LXX) or "In Baca" (J.M.P. Smith). Smith argues that several considerations favour reading "Baca" for בכו: a paronomasia is restored and the city lies in the region of Micah's concern; the loss of the MT is "easily" accounted for; and the LXX has a variant reading ἐν Βακειμ.

However, if בכו is a placename, then this is the only place in the oracle where two placenames occupy the same colon and not successive cola. Also, caution should be exercised since the placename is preserved only in the LXX, which is suspect because of misreadings or mistranslations throughout the pericope.[19]

Accepting the MT does not resolve the difficulties. Schwantes says, "All agree that אל as a negative is out of place here."[20] J.M.P. Smith omits the negative particle on the basis of dittography from the preceding occurrence of אל; Wolff reads the emphatic particle אף (following Elliger); Mays, following Schwantes, reads the emphatic particle ל; Allen ("Do not weep and sob"—a free rendering of the phrase) comments, "The structure of ordinary life will be so shattered that the customary and comforting ritual [of mourning] will go unobserved."[21]

The positioning of אל, however, is not without parallels in biblical Hebrew (GKC §113v, usually with לא) and is required by the "imitation" of syntax/structure with the preceding words. The construction, inf. abs. + neg. + verb, functions as an emphatic statement, as asseveration (prohibition, however, not a command as, e.g., Hillers argues).

The wordplay is paronomasia once again, specifically, a paronymic play on the verbal root. Moreover, alliteration with the first part of the colon is present (repetition of dental, palatal, and velar phonemes) and consonance between תגידו and תבכו. Finally, hyperbaton is also present with אל. As with the previous words, the wordplay is not obvious in the sense that it calls attention to itself. Comments on the wordplay are found only in those commentators (e.g., J.M.P. Smith) who posit reading בכו as a placename.

The colon can be rendered, "In Gath, do not announce [your grief]; don't even weep." The phonological and syntactical correspondences establish a link and the second part of the colon specifies what it is those in Gath are not to proclaim.

בבית לעפרה עפר התפלשתי: "In Beth-Leaphrah I will wallow in the dust." The problems with this colon center on identifying the placename and accounting for the 1st sg. verb in the context of the oracle.

The *qere* ("what is read") התפלשׁי , "roll yourself," is usually read in place of the *kethib* ("what is written") התפלשׁתי, "I will roll." Rashi says that this word is part of the language of *qinah* ("lament") and likens it to גלל (התגלגלי), "to wallow" (citing 2 Sam 20: 12 and Job 30: 14); his understanding is born out by the other occurrences of התפלשׁ, Jer 6: 26; 25: 34 and Ezek 27: 30, where the context is one of mourning.

Wolff, and most other contemporary commentators, read the pl. impv.; Allen says that the textual corruption went from ו to י to תי. However, what good reason can be adduced to argue against a corruption from any of those readings to any other one? All are possible corruptions from the others, and all have both merits and difficulties as *the* reading. The 1 sg. reading is the most difficult syntactically (and therefore the "original" on the principle *lectio dificilior*) but can be explained on the basis of the influence from v 8; the fem. sg. is syntactically acceptable but may have arisen because of the following verb (עברי); the pl. fits the context best (as a parallel to בכו), but smacks of being a harmonistic compromise. The text cannot be unequivocally decided[22] and does not affect the wordplay.

The identification of the placename does not affect one's understanding of the wordplay either, but a comment is in order since some proposals for the placename are tied to understanding the wordplay involved. Many commentators cite Josh. 18: 23, where the placename "Ophrah" occurs. Keil says that the *pathach* in the Mican text is for the sake of "paronomasia" with עפר, by which I take it he means assonance. But "Ophrah" is out of place if Elliger is correct in saying that all the towns lie in the Judaean Shephelah.[23] Some commentators omit the *lamedh* before "Aphrah" (J.M.P. Smith), but this emendation is resisted by Allen, Vuilleumier, Hillers, and Wolff of recent commentators. Hillers acknowledges that the form is unique; he is content simply to transliterate the difficult phrase as *Beth-leaphra* , a move that we can concur with since identification of the locations cited in this passage is less than certain in most cases.

Unlike the previous colon, the wordplay in this colon has long been recognized. Rashi comments that this colon and the next two cola, with the placenames "Inhabitant of Shapir" and "inhabitant of Zaanan," contain wordplay as well, and are part of the dirge. Calvin calls attention to the "alliteration," as does Rosenmüller. Luther says that "Bethleaphrah" is a "Hebraism" that means "in a house of dust."

The widespread recognition of wordplay in the colon has not met with a corresponding acceptance of the MT; in spite of its clarity, emendations are still proposed. Elliger suggests בכרמי בת-עפרה, "in the vineyards of ... ." Schwantes improves upon this by reading בחוצות in place of Elliger's בכרמי: "Since it goes better [than "vineyards"] with the עפר of the second stichos."[24] Schwantes proposal is worth noting in its entirety as a curiosity in the history of interpretation. התפלשתי, he argues, is a noun with a *tau* preformative to which a later redactor added the definite article, and the *yodh* is a *hireq compaginis* , which, he avers, is "rather common in poetry," thus, "In the streets of Bethaphrah—the dust of wallowing."[25]

Another curiosity worth noting in the history of interpretation, but one which has more merit than Schwantes' proposal as a general approach to this difficult text, comes from Pococke. Pococke, who, of course, does not work within a framework that allows for emendation, nevertheless discusses various proposals for understanding the colon. He notes that some take עפרה as a placename, while others, "because some of those names are not elsewhere found in Scripture, think, that they were not the usual proper names of the cities of the land, but names put upon them by the prophet, by which, and by descanting on them, he might declare, what he had to say of, or to the people, for making them sensible of what should befal them."[26] Thus the wordplays themselves are more important than an accurate citation of the places—than the ostensive reference— since the wordplays serve the message of the prophet while the placenames themselves serve the wordplays.

The wordplay of the colon is a rather straightforward paronymic pun on the place עפרה ל(בבית), a *nomen-omen* type of pun.

1:11. עברי לכם ישבת שפיר עריה־בשת: "Pass by, O inhabitant of Shaphir, [in] naked shame." With this verse we come to the heart of the problem of recognizing wordplay in Micah. Schwantes says, "There is nothing in the first stichos to constitute a word-play with שפיר of the second."[27] This supposition is true if wordplay constitutes only paronomasia (alliteration, assonance, and the like). Others, for example, Hillers, who say that the point of the saying may have meant something to Micah's contemporaries but is lost on us today, at least keep open the possibility that wordplay may entail linguistic features other than sound. My contention, of course, is that wordplay is more than paronomasia; this verse becomes a prime example to support that contention. My point becomes clearer if we first, however, address the intelligibility of the colon, which has occasioned some disagreement.

The problems arise with the first and last words of the colon. Duhm suggests inserting שופר at the beginning of the line, and reading עברי as a *hiphil* and לכם as a sg. fem. The result is: "Let the trumpet resound for you."[28]

Duhm's reconstruction is only convincing if the text is damaged or if paronomasia forms the basis of the wordplays throughout the pericope; no textual support from the versions is evident. The suggestion that לך should be read for לכם is picked up by some who do not favour the entire reconstruction (e.g., Hillers and Wolff). The syntax of the colon is anomalous (fem. sg. impv. followed by masc. pl.) but not without parallels of sorts in the book; indeed, a certain latitude in the agreement between subject and verb, and even between successive verbs is evident throughout the Hebrew Scriptures.[29] In commenting upon the anomalous grammar of the line, Rashi says that עברי is used for "they" (the inhabitants) are all as one, i.e., a collective, whereas לכם is used as he speaks to the many (individuals).   Neither emendation to לך nor the linguistic gymnastics of Rashi affect the wordplay of the colon; one need not press the grammatical logic too far in translation.

A more difficult syntactical problem involves עריה־בשת. The LXX tacks these words to the following colon; in doing so, however, the LXX omits בשת and the translator renders עריה as "her cities": "From her cities, she will not come out."   Schwantes, Rudolph, and Mays all follow this reading after a fashion; for example, Mays renders cities as sg. rather than pl. J.M.P. Smith omits בשת as a gloss; however, he treats עריה as "nakedness" and connects it with the preceding, not the following: "Pass ye over from Shapir in nakedness." If one does connect the word(s) with the following, then "cities" or some such reading, must follow, and no paronomasia is evident unless one inserts שופר at the beginning of the colon.

The relationship of עריה־בשת, as preserved in MT, is one of apposition where the person or thing is further defined by its attribute. Hillers cites Isa 20: 4 to support that naked exposure is an OT concept of punishment, especially associated with going into captivity: "Thus will the king of Assyria guide the captives of Egypt and the exiles of "Cush" [RSV: "Ethiopians"], young and old, naked and barefoot, bared buttocks, [to] the shame of Egypt."

We can hear echoes of עברי in עריה, and יושבת (the first use of this word in the pericope) in בשת , but these phonemic correspondences are subordinate to the pun on שפיר.[30]   The central play seems to reside in the juxtaposition of the placename שפיר, with its semantic sphere of "beauty," and the following terms, especially the rare term עריה. Wolff comments that the wordplay is "Sinnspiel": "Die Schöne wird geschändet"—the beautiful one is defamed. As far back as Jerome, we find a similar recognition of this juxtaposition, although Jerome does not specify the word(s) as a wordplay. The wordplay is a pun, though not a paronymic one, as with "Beth-leaphrah."   Rather, a contrastive relationship between the placename (beauty) and the following nouns (shame/defamation) is found.

לא יצאה יושבת צאנן: "The inhabitant of Zenaan does not flee." The words themselves pose little difficulty, but two minor problems are evident in the literature.   First, what are the limits of the colon?   Second, where is the placename or to what does it refer?

The brevity or starkness of the colon has caused some either to connect words from the preceding colon with these words or to bring in מספד from the following colon. Many commentators follow the LXX in the former, as noted in the previous discussion, while J.M.P Smith does the latter, emending מספד to מספרה in the process: " The inhabitant of Zaonan comes not forth *from her fortress* ." Neither move is necessary and both seem to obscure the wordplay as found in the MT.

Some commentators take צאנן as if related to צאן, "flocks";[31] more often, Josh 15: 37 is cited for the placename where the form appears as צנן (e.g., Mays, Wolff, Hillers). If צאנן is the placename—and we do not know this with certainty—then the insertion of the *'aleph* brings out the assonance between the placename and the verb (Mays).

Beyond the obvious paronomasia (alliteration and assonance) lies a possible pun. The name in its present form—the strange orthography (if the town is identified with צנן) and its collocation with יצא—suggests less the sense "flocks (צאן)" but more "going out (יצא)"; thus Allen remarks, "Its ironic destiny is to betray its name."[32] Hillers suggests, "Have not dared to come out to fight"; either that, or he admits that "the allusion escapes us."[33] If any connection with "flocks" is intended, it requires extra-lexical information that is lost to us. The play between יצא and צאנן still stands.[34] With wordplay a bit of indirection, where one thing is shown while another is adjusted, can often be detected; but if such an occurrence is present in this colon, we lack the vision to see clearly one or the other at our temporal distance.

מספד בית האצל יקח מכם עמדתו: "The Mourning of Beth-Ezel—'He takes his support'— from you!" Wordplay is not at all evident in the final colon of the verse: Hillers says that if the MT is taken literally, it is nonsense; Rashi and Calvin are quiet with regards to the presence of wordplay, and Rosenmüller seems to be straining when he links האצל with צל, "shade." The sense of the colon is also not self-evident; the problem(s) center on what to make of עמדתו.

Elliger reconstructs two lines from this "fragment" on the supposition that these were brought together after the text was damaged. Schwantes and Mays resist this radical emendation, though they, and Wolff, add עשה to the beginning of the colon: "*Erhebe* Wehklage ... " (Wolff). J.M.P. Smith, as noted above, reconstructs "The inhabitant of Zaanan comes not forth from her fortress (מספרה for מספד); Beth-ezel is taken from its site (ממעמדו for מכם עמדתו)." Other minor emendations include reading מספד as an absolute; ממך for מכם; and עמדתו for the 3 sg. suf. Hillers further emends עמדתו to חמדתך, "He takes away your treasures."

The difficult term עמדתו is variously explained. Pococke says that "its standing" is the "measure" or the "conjecture" that they will learn from what "you" suffered (לקח can have the sense of "teaching," as in Deut 32: 2). Pococke also records that "some Christians" (Arias Montanus, Junius, and Tremellius) translate צאנן as "flocks" and explain עמדתו as "sustenance," and that "a learned Jew" (Abravanel) renders it as "tranquillity" or "stability" (the enemy would take this away from the "daughter of Judah"). Calvin claims that the prophet is speaking "of the standing or station of the enemy." Allen says that Beth-ezel "withdraws its support from you"—it is a "further non-ally" (with Zaanan) of

Shaphir and is "too engrossed in mourning" to come to the aid of her neighboring town. Mays explains עמדתו as a place for standing "against attack."

Though our knowledge of Hebrew and the text of the Hebrew Bible has increased, Pococke's remarks have lost none of their relevance over the intervening years: "In such variety of exposition (and more may be found) the reader may have liberty of choosing: he will be hardly able to reconcile them."[35] There is no proposed explanation or alternative to עדמתו that suffices as a clear— and witty—wordplay, although the rendering "sustenance" picks up on צאן as "flocks" (a common understanding of צאן throughout the history of interpretation). Nothing in the text requires that we accept—or reject—the proposal.

Rather than positing an error in transmission, suggesting an emendation, or straining for an explanation, I want to suggest a another possibility: we lack the proper context for understanding the pun. Humor is context-dependent, and this passage requires a specific knowledge of places and events that we know only generally, if at all. עמדתו may truly be a pun, albeit the echo that signals the duplicity of the wordplay is muted by our historical and cultural distance. The problem seems less textual or linguistic and more anecdotal, something associated with the town, the extra-lexical information. That the dig is connected with "aiding and abetting"—or the inability to do so—is a good guess, but it remains a guess.

No discernible paronomasia is evident. The possibility of a pun between בת־האצל and לקח (Mays, Wolff) is more easily argued for than its presence in עמדתו. אצל ("take away") and לקח ("take; seize") share the same semantic sphere; אצל, however, also means "beside; near," and could have a link with the proximity of the locations; "neighboring" (האצל) towns "support" (עמדתו) one another.

1: 12. כי חלה לטוב יושבת מרות: "The inhabitant of Maroth aches for good." חלה is difficult, but the crux centers on לטוב. R. Gordis argues that לטוב is best translated "greatly" in this verse, thus making emendation unnecessary.[36] Schwantes objects that this rendering mars the essence of the verse, namely, "good" playing off both "evil" (רע) and "bitterness" (מרות). But note that rather than "bitterness," Rashi links מרות with "rebellion." In either case, Schwantes' objection remains since לטוב, "(moral) good," could contrast with "rebellion," or with "bitterness" if taken as "good (savory)"; however, if taken as "greatly," then the wordplay is destroyed.

Hillers makes a strong case for rendering לטוב as "sweetness." He cites Cant 1: 2-3, "For your love is sweeter (טובים; RSV: "better") than wine; than the scent of your precious (טובים, "sweet"?) oils."[37] Hillers further cites Ugaritic ṭb, and Akk. ṭabu , "sweet." "Sweet" has a certain poignancy when contrasted with "bitterness." Understanding לטוב as "sweet" also fits with J.M.P. Smith's emendation of the problematic חלה to יחלה, as if from יחל, "wait," and not חול/חלה, "become weak, ill." Allen, however, retains the MT, citing BDB for חלה in the sense of "anxious longing" in this passage and not "be(come) ill."[38]

Onc should not move too quickly to resolve the tensions in the text, especially since the wordplay is built upon a pun, not paronomasia. רע in the following colon (כי־ירד רע מאת יהוה) supports "rebellion" for Maroth—if rebellion is viewed as a "(moral) evil." "Good," then, for לטוב (rather than "sweet") implicitly plays off רע. "Good" for לטוב could further allow the MT to stand with חלה in the sense of "become ill": The inhabitants of Maroth were taken "ill" when the calamity (רע) that came to the gates of Jerusalem affected their welfare (טוב), perhaps even that their "goods" (טובים) were lost (Rosenmüller).[39]

Thus, sounds, words, and images trigger other sounds, words, and images; and we need not rule out the possibility of multiple plays on מרות and חול/חלה, especially with רע and ישלם in the following colon: one "becomes ill" when "evil" comes, one does not "wait anxiously" for it, and "good" corresponds with "peace." We find, then, a (con)fusion of possibilities and a tangle of associations: bitterness (מר) hopes (יחל) for sweetness (טב); bitterness (מר) produces illness (חלה); rebellion (מרה) corresponds with evil (רע) ; evil implicitly plays off good (טבה), which corresponds with peace (ירושלם), and further circles around to change hope (יחל) into illness (חלה).

The wordplay is in the form of a pun, *nomen-omen* , noted as early as Ibn Ezra (לאות). The play(s) move the thought forward:

כי ירד רע מאת יהוה לשער ירושלם: "When evil comes down to the gate of Jerusalem from the Lord." לשער presents a minor textual problem. Many earlier commentators follow the versions (LXX, Tg, P, but not V) in reading "gate" as pl.; of recent commentators, Rudolph alone follows this emendation of the MT (so also J.M.P. Smith of an earlier generation of commentators). Hillers says that the sg. is "acceptable" and Wolff explains the versions as a case of dittography. Nothing materially is gained by emending the MT, and the sg. recalls שער־עמי in v 9, thus linking parts of the oracle.

Mays argues that this colon is dependent upon the previous one, and that such dependence would break the pattern of independent poetic lines. Moreover, since the colon picks up on the language and themes of 1: 8 and other verses in Micah (notably 1: 3, the theophanic vision), Mays assigns it to a redactor. However, it is not altogether clear that the cola are entirely independent; contrasts and continuations are found throughout the pericope: 1: 10a is an injunction not to call attention to the situation ("announce"), while 1: 10b is a reversal of sorts ("weep/mourn") or a continuation of the thought (אל; "[Also] do not ...); in 1: 11 the "inhabitants" are starting and stopping (לא יצאה ...עברי); 1: 13a and b are connected (היא refers to לכיש or המרכבה); and Davidic motifs link beginning, middle, and end of the pericope (גה, ציון, and עדלם) These connections and others are loose, perhaps, but present nevertheless, and should not be overlooked.

The antonymous wordplay between "good" in the previous colon and "evil" in this one has long been recognized,[40] but few commentators note the implicit play—"if a wordplay is present"[41]—between Jerusalem ("welfare") and "evil." Rashi, Pococke, Keil, and J.M.P. Smith are silent on the matter. Hillers states that the "assonance" between ירד and ירושלם is "probably not significant."[42]

The wordplay is paronomasia, with the repetition of *yodh* , *resh* , and *'ayin*, and a pun on רע. The pun works within the line (ירושלם) and between the lines (לטוב). These are a contrastive relationships in both cases, each playing off different associations of the terms, as observed in the previous comments.

1: 13.   רתם המרכבה לרכש יושבת לכיש: "Harness the chariot to the horse, O inhabitant of Lachish." The difficulty with this line lies in the *hapax legomenon* רתם. Mays follows Schwantes by restoring אסרת (fem. impv.) since this is the technical term for harnessing; see also Rashi, who explicates רתם by saying אסרו המרכבה, "they harness the chariot." Most recent commentators simply vocalize the masc. impv. of the MT as an inf. abs. so that the verb and the subject of the colon agree. The inf. abs. still conveys an imperatival force (cf. GKC. §113 *aa* and *bb*).

If we opt for emendation, we run the risk of swallowing up a good, if rare, term. The context clearly determines meaning of רתם as "harness." Moreover, the use of little known terms (loan words, anachronistic meanings, and the like) is not foreign to wordplays. However, רתם does not appear to serve any special purpose within the colon or between cola (at least not as paronomasia). This observation, however, is true of אסרו as well (i.e., it does not form a paronomasia, nor a clear pun). The special significance of רתם, any extra-lexical associations—if indeed present at all— is now lost, but we gain nothing by emending the text.

The paronomasia between לרכש and לכיש is universally recognized by modern commentators; Wolff says that the colon as a whole displays a "schönsten Alliterationen."[43] The play is recognized as early Kimchi and Eliezer, but no explicit mention is made of it in Rashi or Calvin; Rosenmüller also calls attention to the paronomasia. Mays argues for the presence of irony in the statement: Lachish, being a fortress city, is commanded to make ready for flight, not fight. This interpretation, although not necessarily with the ironic overtones, goes back at least to Kimchi, who says that they hasten to go into exile (מהרו לגלות).

ראשית חטאת היא לבת־ציון כי־בך נמצאו פשעי ישראל: "It is the beginning of sin to the daughter of Zion for in you were found the transgressions of Israel." Just as universal agreement exists for the presence of paronomasia in the previous colon, so universal agreement exists for its absence in this colon. Allen says that Micah turns from "cameo to commentary," thus supplying his own paronomasia—and adding to Addison's fears that punning is infectious and not funny.

Schwantes, while recognizing that this is one of the few clear lines in the poem, engages his creative skills and comes up with באר־שבע for ראשית. This emendation stems from the fact that Lachish is not singled out by the prophets for having greater guilt than other cities with respect to the sins of Zion, but Beer-Sheba, along with Gilgal and Bethel, does receive special notice; he cites Amos 5: 5; 8: 14 for support.[44]   Furthermore, Beer-Sheba lies "close enough" to the vicinity of the Shephelah to be part of Micah's dirge, and "three of the original letters are still preserved"[45]—convenient, but unconvincing and resting upon the twin assumptions that the text is damaged and that all the wordplays are paronomastic plays.

We may not like the colon or we may assign it to a redactor, but it is one of the few clear lines in the pericope. Perhaps the colon works in much the same manner as a transitional paragraph in a narrative where drama is downplayed for didactic reasons; theology replaces tropes.

No obvious paronomasia or pun is evident. The colon is not, however, devoid of phonemic echoes. There is a repetition of *'ayin / 'aleph* and sibilants: ראשית חטאת היא לבת־ציון כי־בך נמצאו פשעי ישראל nevertheless, the line is more noticeable for its absence of explicit wordplay and presence of theological bent.

1:14. לכן תתני שלוחים על מורשת גת: "Therefore, give the dowry to Moresheth-Gath." The two textual difficulties do not affect the wordplay in this colon.[46] לכן does not seem to follow logically, so לך (Mays) or כן (Rudolph) is suggested, and emending תתני to either the pl. (Mays) or the passive (Wolff) is often done. Pushing the logic of this colon, as indeed pushing the logic of the entire pericope, too far is probably misguided exegesis. The addressee could be "Zion" of the previous colon (Hillers).

The German commentators of the nineteenth-century found what they considered an intentional play on מורשת / מארשת, "fiancé" (e.g., Wellhausen citing Hitzig; see also J.M.P. Smith), and שלוחים in the sense of "dowry" (or "gift" as in I Kgs 9: 16; cf., with Wolff, Ugaritic *šlḥ*, "ein geschank"). Earlier commentators, taking the lead from LXX and V, explain מורשת in terms of ירש, "Inheritance of Gath" (see Pococke). In this line of interpretation, שלוחים is either taken as "messengers," as in LXX and V, or as "gifts" (Pococke). Rudolph observes that the author reserves ירש for מרשה in v 15, which, if correct, pushes the association with ירש to the background.

Hillers, while at least tacitly accepting the argument that מורשה is related to מארשת, registers the objection that the two terms have only one root consonant in common. However, the author of 1: 10-15 is probably not a linguist, so this cannot be an objection to its use, only to the linguistic validity of its use—false etymologies abound in wordplays and often make the best puns. Etymologists are archaeologists, while punsters are sociologists.

The wordplay of the colon is formed by the pun between מארשת / מורשת and
שלוחים, as noted by the German commentators. The ideas originate from the
same semantic sphere—"marriage"—but show no etymological link. In addition
to "dowry," however, שלוחים can mean "divorce" as in Exod 18: 2, "Now Jethro,
Moses' father-in-law, had taken Zipporah, Moses' wife, after he had *sent her
away*" (RSV); "Divorce" would fit the context of judgment (and following
especially after לכן), but "dowry" fits with מורשה, "fiance." Perhaps the image of
a short-lived marriage is in view: from dowry to annulment.

בתי אכזיב לאכזב למלכי ישראל: "The houses of Aczib turn out to be false
to the kings of Israel." For the pl. "houses," which seems awkward, we find
emendation to the sg., "house" (Rudolph; J.M.P. Smith); to "daughter" (Budde,
Nowack); and to "inhabitants" (Mays, following Elliger, "restores" יושבת). Mays
further reads the sg. for "kings," though Rudolph and other contemporary
commentators resist this emendation. Allen, Wolff, and Hillers retain the pl.
"houses"; Hillers adds, "though the point of the line escapes us." Again, these
proposals do not affect the wordplay in any material way.

Beyond the paronomasia (assonance) between אכזיב and אכזב lies a
paronymic pun: *nomen-omen*. Ibn Ezra calls Achzib a "sign" (אות, as with
Maroth above) and cites two passages with obvious paronomasia מדמן תדמי (Jer
48: 2) and ערער תתערער (Jer 51: 58) "and thus many [other places]." Similarly,
Pococke says that Achzib finds an "allusion" in Achzab. אכזיב sounds like אכזב,
which is used elsewhere of a failing brook (e.g., Jer 15: 18), and thus Mays
comments: "The city of Achzib has failed the King of Israel; he relied on it for
defence, but the city disappointed him as a dry brook betrays the thirsty man who
comes expecting to find water."[47]

1:15. עד הירש אבי לך יושבת מרשה: "I will bring the heir/conqueror
unto you, O inhabitant of Mareshah." The 1 sg. verb אבי poses the biggest
problem textually. Most modern commentators (Rudolph, Allen, Mays, Hillers,
and Wolff) read the 3 sg. for the 1 sg.—"he will bring" (or take it as indefinite,
"one brings ..." or a passive, "A conqueror is brought ..."). J.M.P. Smith retains
the MT, understanding it as a word of judgment. The 1 sg. is easily explained on
the basis of metathesis (Allen),[48] and the 3 sg. fits the context; however,
throughout the pericope the "actors" slip in and slide out of position without
rhyme or reason and thus, again, the "logic" of the syntax should not be pressed.

The logic of the syntax should not be pressed, but in this instance the
wordplay may be affected by one's textual orientation: the choice is between
syntax (יבוא, 3 sg.) or theology (אבי, God as agent of the action), neither of which
is infallible in this pericope. The choice is also tied to one's understanding of ירש
to some extent. ירש could mean "heir" and the colon could be seen as a promise,
especially in the light of the following colon ("The glory of Israel will come to
Adullam"): "The heir will again come... ." In the context of the lament,
however, reading the colon as a threat and taking ירש as "dispossessor" rather

than "heir"[49] seems reasonable. The 1 sg. also fits with God as the one who brings "calamity (רע)" in v 12 and plays off the 3 sg in the following colon (even as עד / ע(ו)ד play off each other).

The paronymic play between הירש and מרשה has been widely recognized from Rashi onwards, although the wordplay was seen more often in terms of the alliteration rather than the pun ("dispossessor" of "heir-town"). Rudolph and Hillers make the point that this is a false etymological connection since "Mareshah" is elsewhere מראשה as if from ראש (cf. Josh 15: 44). Again, this objection only pertains to the linguistic validity, not to the wordplay itself—authors push and even violate "rules" in the interest of false or supposed wordplays.

עד־עדלם יבוא כבוד ישראל: "Unto Adullam the glory of Israel will come." The difficulty with this colon comes in the recognition of wordplay. The early commentators make no mention of wordplay and the more recent commentators are divided. Mays finds "assonance," but this reading depends to a great extent on his reconstruction, לא עד עד־עדלם.

The crux hinges on כבוד, "glory." Many commentators recognize the probable connection with David when he fled to the cave at Adullam (cf. 1 Sam 22: 1). Rudolph makes the ingenious, though unlikely—Hillers calls it "fantastic" (not, I take it, in the colloquial sense of "good")—suggestion that כבוד refers to the three mighty men who came to David while he was at Adullam (cf. 2 Sam 23: 13,19); Rudolph says: "Macht und Ruhm und Glanz." Pococke—not unlike Hillers' comments at various points in the pericope!—says, "There might be the reason either from its situation, or its strength, of beauty, why it is so called, tho' now unknown."[50]

We noted the syntactic plays between this colon and the previous one; if wordplay is present within the colon itself, it must lie as a pun, probably centering on עדלם and כבוד; the ties to Davidic traditions are obvious in the light of the whole lament (e.g., גת, etc.). Paronomasia does not predominate the colon (*pace* Mays, though assonance is present in עד־עדלם) and the extra-lexical evidence is illusive—"allusive" and therefore illusive?

GENERAL COMMENTS

This discussion of Mic 1: 10-15 is lengthy and convoluted because of the myriad of problems the commentator encounters, each problem impinging upon another in most cases. The resolution of the many textual, syntactical, and redactional difficulties[51] is not, however, necessary for uncovering the wordplays. Nevertheless, if we reject the damaged text theory, then errors of transmission are few (e.g., perhaps the vocalization of מספד in v 11c and יבא / אבי in v 15a). The syntactical problems, which cannot be resolved without extensive emendation of the pericope, are, perhaps, connected to questions of redaction.[52] Moreover, the redaction(s) need not be excised to understand the wordplays, and indeed, the redactional activity is sparse (perhaps v 13b): if the text has been extensively redacted, then the direction of redaction is from clarity to obscurity or from obscurity to even further obscurity, for the redactor left us with a difficult text. However, v 13 would suggest that this line of redaction is not the case since v 13b is among the clearest cola in the whole lament, and the most obviously out of place in the light of the remainder of the poem (no obvious paronomasia, but obvious theological bent).

The passage is difficult, but this difficulty is what we should expect from a text replete with wordplays and growing out of a situation that is not altogether recoverable for us today (textually or archaeologically). Presently, we do not possess an ideal text, only texts, especially if one rejects, in principle, extensive ambiguity.[53]

Much of the present discussion centers on who commented upon the wordplays in the passage; the data from the history of interpretation give some sense of where wordplay was located and what the wordplay entailed in the eyes of commentators. This investigation also turns out to be as checkered as a textual or syntactical investigations. Wordplay, as we defined it with respect to ambiguity and humor, is dependent upon linguistic slight of hand and cultural undertones for its effect; therefore, the reader must often work like a color-blind person trying to find the right pair of socks. The shades of meaning are easily overlooked or indistinguishable, and thus the history of interpretation cannot settle the issue of wordplay's presence, only suggest where a match may exist.

Most of the wordplays noted by commentators are what we term paronomasia. Rashi, Kimchi, Eliezer, Calvin, Rosenmüller, and the recent generation of commentators point these out, usually with little further comment—they exist. We also find that puns are recognized, but usually the *nomen-omen* type, as, for example, when Ibn Ezra says that certain cities are "signs." We could also include here the comments of those like Jerome and Luther who, while not specifying the words as wordplay, nevertheless recognize that "Shaphir" belies its name when it occurs in collocation with "naked-shame." Since naming is not explaining, these comments of Jerome (and others) where the "significance" of the name is expressed are in some ways more insightful than simply saying that the word in question forms a wordplay with no further comment or explanation.

Even though wordplay in Mic 1: 1-15 has been long recognized, the extent and variety of the wordplays are largely overlooked or deemed insignificant. With the exception of 1: 13b, "You are the beginning of Sin ... ," no universal agreement on wordplay exists, and certainly not on what constitutes the play. With 1: 13b universal agreement is that no wordplay is found in the colon. Beyond 1: 13b, the only other colon that approximates consensus, and again from the negative side that wordplay is not apparent, is 1: 11c, "Mourn, Beth-Ezel... ." Mays gives a resounding "perhaps" there is wordplay, while Hillers more simply calls the wordplay "nonsense." On the positive side, a number of commentators find wordplays with Beth-le-aphrah, Zaanan, Maroth, Lachish, Achzib, and Mareshah.

CONCLUSIONS

I began my comments by saying that so much has been said about this passage that no new insights may emerge. What did we find? The present study indicates that while paronomasia does predominate, we find a wide variety of wordplays in this lament. Paronomasia begins the pericope with alliteration and assonance in בגת ... תגידו, and continues in the paronymic play between בכו ... תבכו, which also alliterates with the previous paronomasia. Moreover, we noted the metathesis in גת / תג, or what we term "anagrammatical" plays (cf. also בשת / ישבת in v 11). We find further instances of paronomasia in 1: 13 with לכש ... המרכבה לרכש (Wolff, recall, calls this paronomasia a "most beautiful" alliteration). The entire colon beginning with כי ירד רע (v 12b) forms an extensive alliterative play. Finally, in spite of comments to the contrary, 1: 13b does have phonemic echoes, although it is certainly not an unequivocal instance of paronomasia.

Four wordplays involve a placename as well as another term linked phonetically and sharing a semantic field, real or supposed: לעפרה / עפר ;יצאה / צאנן ;אכיב / אכזב; and הירש / מרשה. Those in "dustville" roll in the dust; those in the "city of departure" do not go out; those in "Falsetown" live up to their name to the kings of Israel; and those in "Heirdom/Victorville" receive a new heir/victor.

Thus, paronomasia predominates. However, the play between מרשה and הירש may not be a "synonymous" play if ירש is understood as "dispossessor" (it would be an antonymous play between words with similar phonemes). And we do find contrasting plays that have differing "phonologies" (e.g., 1: 11c, which may be corrupt, but given the MT, no paronomasia is evident). In addition to 1: 11c, we find puns on the placenames and another term(s) not phonetically linked in 1: 11a , 1: 12b and c, and 1: 14a. These we term "antonymous" plays: שפיר / עריה־בשת ;לטוב / מרות / ירושלם / רע; and שלוחים / מורשת גת. The "City of Beauty" is shamed in nakedness; "Bitter-town" hopes (in vain) for sweetness; evil comes to the "city of Peace," and "Marriageville" receives a divorce (or a dowry, thus making it a synonymous play, but with contrasting phonemes).

אצל (v 11), as well as צאנן and מרות, raises the possibility of antanaclasis. אצל may mean "take away" or "beside." However, the nature of the pericope—obscurity and etymological plays (real or supposed)—makes it difficult to *show* the presence of antanaclasis. We need not press the point here since we can show antanaclasis elsewhere in the book.

Some questions are raised by the forms לעפרה, צאנן, and מורשת, which may be morphological plays of sorts; or, more simply, they may be evidence of non-standardized script/vocalization. The non-standardized vocalizations, however, serve the plays very well (e.g., צאן alliterates with יצא). We also find the homographs עד / עד(ו) being used in successive cola, an example of anaphora, which recalls the structural play at the beginning of the lament in 1:10a: בגת אל...בכו אל.

Finally, the plays on Gath, Jerusalem, and Adullam suggest another aspect of wordplay not often noted in discussions of the trope—allusion. Gath and Adullam are the first and last placenames, an inclusion of sorts, and Jerusalem is the middle placename (six on each side, if one counts "Zion" in 1: 13 as a placename). Alliteration between גת and תגידו is often noted, but assonance on עד עדלם is only infrequently mentioned. The implicit play on Jerusalem is not mentioned in medieval exegesis, but occurs rather frequently in modern critical commentaries. Gath, Adullam, and, obviously, Jerusalem all have connections with Davidic traditions, and the whole lament is set up by the "citation" of David's lament over Saul and Jonathan.

In saying that the pericope has a variety of wordplays, I think we have found a "new" insight, even if that insight seems rather obvious. We have seen a number of commentators "predicting" (reconstructing) a particular wordplay in a given colon (Schwantes and Mays are notable here). However, these reconstructions depend largely upon paronomastically based wordplays. As such, they are unconvincing since, if the present analysis has any merit, the text contains more than just paronomasia. Reconstructing wordplays in this complex passage should be an exercise in restraint, not creativity.

MICAH 1: 6-7 : OF EFFIGIES, SNAKES, AND GARMENTS

In the light of 1: 10-15, 1: 6-7 seems simple, perhaps deceptively simple. We certainly do not find the extreme textual difficulties, and as a consequence neither do we find the, sometimes, wholesale emendations by scholars. Nevertheless, problems are present and various solutions are offered to overcome the problems.

As with 1: 10-15, the predominant, though not exclusive, mode of wordplay is paronomasia; no paronymic or etymological plays on placenames are present, however. What we do find is the curious occurrence of אתנן being used three times within four cola. This play off a single lexical form poses the biggest problem for commentators and raises the possibility of a further variety of wordplay, one based on pun more than paronomasia.

The crux comes in v 7, but v 6 presents an interesting paronomasia that is often overlooked. 1: 6 is a fine example of a carefully balanced line of Hebrew poetry.[54] Both cola begin with 1st. sg. verbs: "I will make .../I will pour ..."[55] The verb of colon a is followed by "Samaria," which shows up in colon b as a pron. suf., "*her* stones." The "field" is preceded by לעי in colon a, while לני precedes "her stones" in colon b. Each colon closes with a phrase that balances the colon, but shows no paronomasia.

The presence of לעי before השדה is difficult. Some commentators (e.g., V. Fritz,[56] Rudolph) omit לעי; Hillers says that the word here "is scarcely right." Mays stays with the MT and cites Mic 3: 12 (עיין), Jer 26: 18 (which is a citation of Mic 3: 12), and Ps 79: 1 (a lament): שמו את-ירושלם לעים, "They make Jerusalem ruins," as evidence for its use. A closer examination of the paronomastic parallels in the verse will help us to determine the suitability of the term to the context.

The phonemic correspondences are worth noting. Casanowicz cites v 6b, והגרתי לני אבניה (repetition of *gimel*), as an instance of paronomasia. A similar correspondence between letters, however, is found in שמתי שמרון in colon 6a with the sibilants and *mem* (not cited by Casanowicz). Thus in each colon we find paronomasia, but might there also be a correspondence between the cola in לעי and לני? Carreira thinks so,[57] and it seems likely since the terms occupy similar syntactic positions in successive cola, and '*ayin* and *gimel* approach phonological similarity.[58] If this is the case, then לעי, though difficult, need not be emended; לעי is a phonemic parallel to לני.

In addition to being a phonemic parallel, לעי is also a foreshadowing of עיין in the oracle against Jerusalem in Mic 3: 12, especially with the presence of שדה in both passages. Moreover, parallelism and phonological correspondences are found in 3: 11 as well. Rather than alliteration, however, we find "rhyme" (consonance) between the terms: ראשיה...כהניה...נביאיה and ישפטו...יורו...יקסמו. Note also the anagrammatical (chiasm) alliteration between בשחד and בכסף. 3: 12, in addition to picking up on עי and שדה from 1: 6, picks up on במות from 1: 5. Samaria and Jerusalem share a same fate; the theophanic acts are interrelated. Thus we find paronomasia within and between the cola, and between 1: 6-7 and 3: 11-12 (anticipation/retrospection). The most interesting paronomasia, however, lies in the difficult לעי and its counterpart לני, since these may indicate a phonological correspondence not commonly noted or accepted between ע and נ.[59]

The repetition of אתנן in v 7 is obvious, and, though not so noted in the commentaries, is a wordplay.[60] Is there more to the repetition than paronomasia?

Before answering the preceding question, a minor exegetical issue calls for our attention. קבצה causes consternation because an object is not expressed. The versions (Tg, P, and V) translate it with a pl. pass., "They were gathered"; others supply a suitable object, "She gathered *them*" (cf. Hillers; RSV). Another possibility is that קבצה is an indefinite sg. used as a passive. We find such a use with שם עלינו מצור in Mic 4: 14: "One has laid siege against us" is equivalent to "A siege is laid against us" (see also GKC §121*a*). Thus 1: 7 should read, "For from the hire of a harlot one gathered [them]; and unto the hire of a harlot they will return." קבצה follows from עצביה, a phonological play (alliteration and anagrammatical; note also the alliteration in אשׁים שׁממה), and contrasts with the pl. verbs in the rest of the verse (even as "hire" in v 7 contrasts with "images" in v 6). The text most often appealed to for illumination of the colon is Gen 3: 19: "... till you return (שׁובך) to the ground, for from it you were taken (לקחת)... ."

The crux of this brief oracle is with the first occurrence of אתנן in the initial colon, which stand paradigmatically to פסיליה, "her idols," and עצביה, "her images." The link between the "hire/gift of a harlot" and idols is not obvious. Three options are available to a commentator. First, omit the words; Rudolph says that these words are palpably a later addition and should be excised. A second option is to emend the text. Mays is representative here (drawing upon Wellhausen). He avers that אתנן was drawn from the following words to "repair" a damaged text, which read "Asherah" (אשׁרה). However, if that is so, the repair job seems poorly done since the text is still problematic.

The third option is to stay with the MT. In this case, two further possibilities are open to the commentator. First, one may choose to adapt the traditional, or usual, meaning of אתנן; that is, "gift," "fee" or "hire." Hillers adopts this approach saying that a "whores' fee" is appropriate in the context of statues and idols.[61] He further cites the evidence of Tg, מעותהא, and P, dhlth who translate אתנן as "her idols." This line of interpretation is taken in a similar fashion by Rashi, who says "all this wealth" (כל ההון הזה) was gathered by the prostitute, and Ibn Ezra, who says that אתנניה are that which they gave to the pagan prostitutes. Thus the אתנן stands metaphorically for the idol or the payment (the coins themselves).

The second possibility is to retain the MT, but translate אתנן differently from the standard translation. Hence, J.M.P. Smith appeals to Arabic tanna , "be measured, made comparison," and suggests the root תנן, "resemble, be equal." Smith further suggests תנן is related to שׁנה ("repeat") and concludes: "From this point of view the use of אתנן here is seen to be paronomasia, very characteristic of Micah."[62]

G.R. Driver also appeals to comparative Semitics for illumination. He says that the traditional translation is "nonsense" and Wellhausen's emendation ("Asherah") is "needless." Like Smith, Driver suggests the root tnn , possibly an Aramaic loan-word (תנה for Aramaic שׁנה) and Arabic tinnun ("equal, like, companion"). Driver, however, suggests "effigy" for a translation: "All her graven images shall be beaten to pieces and all her effigies (אתנניה) shall be burned with fire... ."[63]

More recently, Watson suggests an Ugaritic background, tnn (which is spelled with prothetic 'aleph in Micah), meaning "sea-serpent, dragon": "The poet is alluding to the tradition recorded in the Ugaritic 'Snake' tablet and at the same time playing on twin meanings of 'tnn . It is a measure of his skill that he could provide an alternative pronunciation of *tannin* to achieve the desired effect, which, with its obligatory element of irony, belongs fully to a long tradition of idol-polemic."[64]

We should note that these attempts to find a translation for אתנן somewhat different from "hire" is not a modern quest. Kimchi, without any textual citation, glosses אתנן as "pretty garments" (הבגדים היפים) which, he says, were in the "houses of the idols." He says that they honored the idols with "silver, gold, and comely garments (בגדים נאים)."

CONCLUSIONS

Neither the traditional rendering nor the proposed alternatives offer air-tight solutions. The emendation of Wellhausen has lured only a few scholars (e.g., Mays), and the suggestions by Kimchi, J.M.P. Smith, and Driver have met with even less success. The suggestions do, however, open the possibility of polysemantic plays—puns. If אתנן is used in two different senses, we have an example of antanaclasis. This contention, however, requires closer inspection; Watson's proposal will serve as a test case.

Watson's proposal is interesting and appealing in a number of respects, not the least of which is because he is sensitive to the workings of wordplay with its ambiguity and allusions. The obstacle to Watson's proposal is *showing* the dependence he suggests. The Ugaritic text deals with a "bride-price," not a prostitute's fee, and the "serpents" are not cult objects.[65] Watson is certainly right that if his proposal is correct, it is a "measure of [the prophet's] skill" to use the allusion and words in such a creative manner.

The price for the more traditional reading does not, however, need to sacrifice the skill and wit of the prophet. Sandwiched between the two concrete images is an abstract image—the money solicited by the prostitute. Equating the idols with the money is out of place, but only if the audience is overly literal. אתנן is literal to the syntax, but metaphoric to the sense; that is, syntactically, אתנניה is appropriate in relation to the pl. nouns with fem. sg. pron. suf. The syntagmatic relationship with "idols" and ישרפו באש ("shall be burned with fire") however, cannot be taken literally. Thus, "hire" must stand for the broader context from which it came, either associated with the idol (Hillers), or the "coins" (Rashi), and not the abstract payment for services rendered.

The text, then, is either playing meanings off one another, as Watson or others propose, or playing metaphor off letter. The former is certainly an achievement by the "author." The latter is preferred here as a simpler explanation—and the achievement is no less since both the literal and metaphoric senses of אתנן survive in the single text. The oracle requires two readings: the first reading suggests striking out the literal rendering of אתנן in the first colon. However, in the light of v 7b, where the literal reading is entirely appropriate, one is forced to reconsider the previous encounter with אתנן. A balancing between the literal and the metaphoric takes place; in effect, the "idols" and the "hire" are one and the same.[66]

Thus in Mic 1: 6-7 we find paronomasia—alliterative plays (assonantic and anagrammatical), but also an example of consonance (עצביה / פסיליה / אתנניה). The alliteration between ע and ג is noteworthy and worth looking for in other texts. The central wordplay, however, is the pun on אתנן, perhaps an instance of antanaclasis, but more likely a literal/figural play, a more specialized form of antanaclasis.

The oracle raises two questions. Can a wordplay be "inadvertent"? Is the occurrence of שמרון שמתי and שממה and אשים, for example, simply due to a "poverty" of the Hebrew language or some similar, mundane, explanation? Secondly, if a metaphoric meaning of a word can be played off a literal meaning, or combined with its literal meaning in the same colon or oracle, can an image created by our words be played off other word-created images and be properly called wordplay or an extension of wordplay?

MICAH 4: 14 : DID I SAY THAT?

"Inadvertent" wordplays, it seems, are a natural part of our linguistic experience. Through analogous thinking, or simply by accident, we produce alliterations and even puns without consciously creating them.

To speak of inadvertent wordplays implies some notion of intentionality—a point we are avoiding in this study. I cannot say that we find what I would consider a clear and demonstrable example of an inadvertent wordplay in the book of Micah. There are, however, "throwaway" wordplays—wordplays that are present, but serving minor functions, adding little to the message or displaying marginal wit. Not every wordplay is funny or serves an important function in the discourse.

Mic 4: 14-5: 2 provides examples of "marginal" wordplays, but also, one of these soft-spoken puns becomes amplified in an influential subsequent interpretation of the passage, Matt 2: 6. First, the more obvious plays.

In 4: 14, Carreira finds alliteration between מצור and שׁט. More often noticed by commentators is the paronomasia between שׁבט and שׁפט, where only the middle consonants differ (yet both are labials). 5: 1 continues the alliterations. Carreira contends that the dominance of *mem* and the persistence of *'aleph* / *'ayin* in 5: 3 are part of Micah's *Kunstsprache* :

ואתה בית־לחם אפרתה
צעיר להיות באלפי יהודה
ממך לי יצא להיות מושל בישראל
ומוצאתיו מקדם מימי עולם

Is the presence of such combinations, however, any more noteworthy than the dominance of any letter *x* in any given language? What is achieved by the juxtaposition of מצור and שם? The same question is true of Carreira finding correspondence between אפרתה and באפלי, and צעיר and יצא. That there is alliteration of sorts is true, but we appeal to the two most devastating words in the English language, so what? The alliterations hold no structuring significance, display no wit, nor add anything to our understanding of the words or the message of the prophet.

More striking than the alliteration between מצור and יצא is the play between יצא and מוצאתיו in the following colon, especially given the unusual form of the second term. The paronymic play in 5: 2 between יולדה and ילדה is along the same line, though this latter play does not have the unusual construction of the previous play.

With the exception of שבט and שפט, and the possibility of יצא and מוצאתיו, these alliterations offer little by way of exploiting the ambiguities of language or creating a particularly memorable rhetorical effect. They fall under the category of "pretty paronomasia," and are subordinate to the dominant wordplay, בת־גדוד תתגדדו (see the discussion in Chapter Eight below).

Tucked away in these alliterations is an interesting pun that gets overlooked in our efforts to bring perspicuity to the text. באלפי is less a play on אפרתה, and more a play on מושל. אלף means "thousands" as in a military unit or subdivision of a tribe, and can even be used, by extension, of the clan itself; for example, I Sam 10: 19, "And now present yourselves before the Lord by your tribes (לשבטיכם) and your clans (ולאלפיכם)." It is also used of a district; for example, I Sam 23: 23, "I will search him out among all the districts of Judah (בכל אלפי יהודה)." Furthermore, אלף occurs in stylized phraseology, "the heads of the clans of Israel" (ראשי אלפי ישראל; cf. Josh 22: 21).

Mic 5: 1 personifies "Bethlehem Ephrathah," but "Ephrathah" is more properly the district in which Bethlehem is situated (e.g., Ruth 1: 2);[67] and since אלפי follows from this (and even has some sonic affinities), one would do well to translate אלף as "thousands" or "districts." However, the following colon, with its parallel phrases, should be considered:

להיות מושל ישראל	To be ruler of Israel
להיות באלפי יהודה[68]	To be among the thousands of Judah.

The מושל, "ruler," draws one back to reconsider the previous line, which suggests a metaphoric reading of באלפי, especially in light of the personification that begins the colon, "And you, Bethlehem... ."

Is there more to the play than a metaphoric reading or against a literal reading of אלפי? I want to suggest that rather than simply a metaphoric reading,

אלפי calls to mind the homonymic אלוף, "tribal chief"; cf. Gen 36: 15: אלה אלופי בני־עשׂו, "These are the chiefs of the sons of Esau." אלוף is not present graphically but certainly aurally.[69]

The drama does not end with this embedded pun, for in the history of interpretation a quite deliberate transformation of the oracle based on the aural reading takes place.[70] At Matt 2: 6 the scribes "quote" Mic 5: 1 and render באלפי as ἡγούμενος, "rulers." That this citation is deliberate seems likely in the light of the drastic departures that we find in the Matthean quotation of Mic 5: 1.[71] At every departure a christological point is made, a fact which is especially true of "rulers" for באלפי: in using this term here, Matthew is affirming "the superiority of Jesus over his predecessors in the Davidic dynasty" and later uses ἡγέμων to assert Jesus's superiority over Pilate as well.[72]

Commentators have long noted that the Mican passage appeals to Davidic traditions in citing "Bethlehem Ephrathah." However, "Bethlehem Ephrathah" has connections with the patriarchs as well as with David. I Chr 4: 4 cites "Ephrathah" (the father of "Bethlehem") as the son of "Hur," who is the son of Judah. It is Judah who receives the blessing that "the sceptre shall not depart from [him], nor the ruler's staff from between his feet" (Gen 49: 10, RSV). Gen 49: 10 is considered a "messianic" passage by some.[73]

The personification of "Bethlehem Ephrathah" then is a point not lost on Matthew not only in his rendering of "thousands," but also perhaps in a way similar to that of the LXX, that is, as a possible link with the patriarchs. The connection with the patriarchs underscores the messianic status of Jesus, especially in the light of Matthew's genealogy, which goes through Judah back to Abraham (in contradistinction to Luke's which goes back to Adam). A further link with the patriarchs and the royal line is found in Matthew's rendering "Ephrathah" of the MT of Mic 5: 1 as "land of Judah"; Gundry says of this rendering, "Matthew wants an allusion to Judah, the progenitor of the royal line … in order to heighten the stress on Jesus' kingship."[74]

The reading of Mic 5: 1 that suggests not only monarch (David) but patriarch (Judah) receives support from the enigmatic colon that closes the verse: "His 'origins' (ומוצאתיו) are from before, from the days of old (מימי עולם)." The medieval Jewish commentators Eliezer of Beaugency and Kimchi seem to be the first to suggest that these words refer to David and not to "eternity."[75] Many commentators have followed this interpretation.[76] However, the colon is indeterminate at best; Hillers says that there "is a strong flavor of myth here, for 'of old' has the suggestion 'primeval, from the beginning, as an order of creation.'"[77] Hence understanding "Bethlehem Ephrathah" as a subtle reference not only to David but patriarchal legends as well is suggestive.[78] The personification of the initial colon in the light of the indeterminate phrasing of the final colon pushes the reader to look beyond David to the days of yore, the patriarchs.

CONCLUSIONS

These observations support the suggestion that Matthew is not "misquoting" his Hebrew text; rather, he is picking up on the wordplay of his OT source, and bringing a second, latent conceptual association of the word to the forefront in order to heighten the status of Jesus as the greater ruler. "Thousands" (אלפי) is a subtle play with "ruler" (מושל / אלוף). The play is set up by both the personification of the initial colon and the further play between יצא and מוצאתיו. It is left to (the text of) Matthew to exploit this clever pun (in the text) of Micah.

Two general observations can be made. First, even if we speak of "inadvertent" or "marginal" wordplays, that does not preclude subsequent readers from forming their own wordplays or finding significance where, perhaps, none is obvious. This observation supports an understanding of reading as a partnership between text/author and reader; the text as artifact and whimsy. The reader, Matthew, exerts his freedom with respect to the text, but the reader does not have complete autonomy in this case since the text and the reading display recognizable affinities. In the case of the LXX rendering ("And you, O Bethlehem, of the house of Ephrathah ... "), the reader has wrested more control from the text: the sum of Matthew's reading is an extension of the text, whereas the sum of the LXX is a different text, especially as it continues, "... are few in number to be among the thousands of Judah." A demarcation line exists between freedom and autonomy, but we must resist drawing this line in the abstract. The drawn line requires the constraints of a particular context, from philology to ideology.

Second, perhaps "innocent" wordplays are not entirely innocent. This second point I want to underscore by looking at one further example of a wordplay that does not serve "lofty transformations" of meaning.

MICAH 2: 12: EMPHASIZING EMPHASIS

Mic 2: 12 displays an undistinguished wordplay between אסף and אאסף and between קבץ and אקבץ. These "wordplays" follow the norms of Hebrew syntax— the infinitive in connection with its finite verb is frequently employed "*to define more accurately* or *to strengthen the idea of the verb* " (GKC §113 *l*); in other words, for emphasis.

To say that these wordplays follow grammatical norms and are used for emphasis is not devoid of significance when one is examining stylistic devices. In this particular text, we find this particular stylistic device and not some other (as, e.g., in Mic 1: 10 with בכו אל תבכ, another way of showing emphasis). We may not gain exegetical insights, but we gain in our understanding of the text in relation to other texts and the stylistic potentials.

MICAH 3: 5-7 : BEYOND HOMONYMY

A second question was raised from the study of 1: 6-7. Clear instances of paronomasia—plays on the sounds of words—are evident, but also evident are plays with the multiple meanings of words—puns proper. Do we also find plays in texts that go beyond the phonological and lexical correspondence(s) to the connotative associations—symbol or image—of words?

The plays in 3: 5-7 are less obvious because phonological similarities are not exploited—indeed, they are hardly used at all. Neither are meanings played off one another. We find rather an additional variety of play—a play with images, rather than sound and sense. The plays in these verses unify the passage and contribute to the message much as the wordplays in 2: 6-11 (see the discussion in Chapter Seven below). Not only do these plays have a similar rhetorical function, but they also form a thematic correspondence: this oracle "resumes the indictment of crowd-pleasing prophets of 2: 11" and displays several verbal affinities with that passage as well.[79]

There is at least one phonological and semantic correspondence that is obvious in this oracle that is otherwise noteworthy by the absence of paronomasia and pun. The significance of the play rhetorically, linguistically, or literarily is questionable in much the same way as the "pretty paronomasias" of 4: 14-5: 2 are—the play is more an "accident" of the language, as Driver derogatorily says of such uses. In these three verses, על occurs six times with various meanings, forms, and grammatical functions. In v 5, על־נבאים is translated, "*Concerning* the prophets"; אשר לא־יתן על־פיהם, "He who does not put [anything] *into* their mouths"; and קדשו עליו, "Proclaim Holy [War] *against* him"; in v 6, באה השמש על־הנבאים, "The sun will set *upon* the prophets"; and קדר עליהם היום, "The day will grow dark *over* them"; and in v 7, עטו על־שפם, "[All of them] will cover their moustaches" (על used in a idiomatic expression and untranslated).

These uses of על are noticeable and interesting, but little is made of them in the text; neither proximity, form, nor meaning is "exploited." That is not to say that these are insignificant, of course, since that word is found and not some other; however, they form the background of the passage, not the foreground—linguistic Musak.

There is also a degree of "near rhyme," or what we refer to as consonance within these verses because of the frequent pl. noun/ptc. and pl. pron. suf. endings: for example, הנביאים / המתעים and בשניהם / פיהם. Note also the occurrence of שלום, מקסם(ו), and היום. Again, the instances of consonance do not play a significant structural role, nor is attention drawn to them by unusual word order or form. However, the mention of מקסם is noteworthy because of the use of מהחזון in the previous colon. The text as we now have it, with its vocalization of מקסם as an infinitive, the recurrence of preformative מן and following guttural (ק/ח), and both words occupying the final position in the cola, suggests the possibilities of a more deliberate "rhyme," at least in the mind of the Masoretes. This consonance reinforces the parallelism of the cola.

The more significant—and perhaps obvious—plays for our purposes, at least structurally, are the two sets of images employed with respect to mouth and speech, and with darkness and sight. In v 5, the prophets who "lead astray my people" (cf. 2:10) "cry" (קראו) "peace" for those who give them something to bite (הנשכים בשניהם), but "declare" (קדשו) "(*holy*) war" for those who do not give them anything to put in their mouths (לא־יתן על־פיהם). The "mouth-speech" imagery pervades the verse.[80]

In v 6 the images change to *darkness-sight* . The result of prophesying for gain is that there will be "night" (לילה) for them "without a vision" (ההזון), and it will "become dark" (חשכה) "without divination" (מקסם); the "sun will set" (באה השמש) and the day will "be black" (קדר).[81] As Hillers observes, the images of night, dark, and sunset "exploit" the associations both of vision and the more threatening, ominous link with darkness generally. "Dark" plays with "vision" and implies "threat."

The *darkness-sight* and *mouth-speech* images are combined in v 7, thus bringing a unity to the passage. The consequence of the "prophets" being without an oracle (vision) is the obvious shame they will experience (בשו and הפרו). Because of their shame, they will cover (עטו) their upper lips (שפם) for there is not a word from the Lord (כי אין מענה אלהים).

Hillers again makes an interesting observation: covering the moustache is associated with mourning and a sign of a leper; thus, "It is symbolically congruent ... with another association of "night," namely, death and exclusion from society."[82] Hillers connects the final image with the *darkness-sight* imagery of v. 6, but one should not overlook the connection with the *mouth-speech* imagery at the beginning of the oracle. Indeed, though the darkness imagery is present, following as it does from the previous verse, it is, nonetheless, in the background, subliminal. The mouth imagery and not the sight imagery is visibly brought back into play by employing both שפם and ענה.

CONCLUSIONS

In these verses we do not have phonological and lexical plays structuring and contributing to the message of the oracle, but more broadly semantic or logical plays—imagery and root metaphors. The use of these images suggests that wordplays move in the direction of metaphor or even allegory.

The distinguishing feature between wordplay and devices beyond, I think, is that connotation becomes the constitutive element and denotation shifts to the background. The correspondence is not sound, etymology, or a meaning of one word played off another meaning of the word, but the meaning of separate lexical items that share similar semantic spheres being played off meanings of other terms sharing a different, but overlapping semantic sphere. That is, extra-lexical associations come into play more so than the phonological or specifically lexical (i.e., lexicon) items. Thus, in Mic 3: 5-7, "they" shall "cover their lips," hence they shall not speak; however, the covering also coveys darkness—speech-sight coalesce. The reader (audience) does not need to re-read the passage, as is often required of the pun, but they do have a fusion of images not unlike the lexical fusion that can take place with puns.

CONCLUSIONS

Although the preceding analysis could be challenged on minor points, it is clear that wordplay not only involves soundplay but morphology, semantics, and syntax as well.

Paronomasia predominates throughout the passages examined. Alliteration and assonance are common; for example, עפר / לעפרה (1: 10). We have instances of consonance; for example, in Mic 3: 5-7 we find several forms with the masc. pl. ending, the masc. pl. pron. suf., and then also the words מחזון / מקסום / היום / שלום. We also find anagrammatical plays; for example, בשחד / בכסף (3: 11). A paronomasia worth noting occurs in 1: 6, לני / לעי; the correspondence between *gimel* and *'ayin* is not a commonly accepted one.

We also discover puns that work in similarly diverse ways as the paronomasia. In addition to the puns in 1: 10-15 involving placenames, we have an instance of אתנן being used in both literal and figurative senses, or in different senses (Watson)—antanaclasis. Furthermore, we have the interesting play in 5: 1 between מושל and באלפי, with its "hidden" play on אלוף—Mahood's "unspoken" pun.

Finally, we find the possibility of syntactical play and broader semantic considerations. In Mic 1: 10-15 we detect an example of anaphora (עד / ד(ו)(ע). Mic 7: 11-12 displays a more impressive instance of anaphora and hyperbaton (also paronym, repetition, alliteration, homonyn, and other wordplays):

יום לבנות גדריך
יום ההוא ירחק־חק
יום הוא ועדיך יבוא
למני אשור וערי מצור
ולמני מצור ועד־נהר
וים מים והר ההר

The wordplays are diverse and extensive; but the anaphora with יום and למני, and the hyperbaton in the final colon are noticeable,[83] and illustrate more clearly the use and effect of such devices.

The preceding discussion was lengthy and detailed, but was necessary to show that the constraints in seeing the varieties of wordplay in Micah (and the Bible generally) are largely conceptual, not factual. The wordplays, and the fluid boundaries between them and between wordplay and other rhetorical devices, are present; the requirement to recognize their presence in a text is patience rather than moving head-long towards finding perspicuity.

Some of these plays examined are crucial for understanding the passage (e.g., אזן in Mic 1: 6-7), while others work quietly to unify, support, or move the cola along (e.g., the etymological plays in Mic 1: 10-15 and the imagery in 3: 5-7). It is this aspect of wordplay—the function of wordplay in a pericope—that also requires close examination since biblical scholars seldom comment on this role of the trope.

SEVEN
THE PERSUASIVE ANGLE OF THE TEXT

The 'message' of nature, of 'moral evil and of good' is never free from ambiguity ... it is an ambiguity that is rooted deep in the perceptual process itself, below the threshold of consciousness.

S. Prickett, *Words and the Word*

Biblical scholars often treat rhetoric as mere dress, something added to the self-evident message of the author. In the past, these self-evident truths were delivered by God—the human authors were "inspired." More recently, we have shelved God and introduced a community—scholarly consensus. If this appeal to self-evidence is left to stand, whether the self-evidence stems from a divine source or an authoritative community, then rhetorical devices are superfluous; argumentation is reduced to mathematics.

The prophets deliver their message through argumentation, dialectic, analogies, metaphors, and even wordplays, among other strategies and devices. The truths may be self-evident to the prophet, but in the communication of the superiority of his (or God's) position, the truth is not simply announced, but shown, often through the use of rhetorical features. It is, in the final analysis, persuasive discourse, not logical discourse that suffices—the distinction between the two is aptly illustrated by the poor philosopher's dilemma: "Sex is better than logic, but I can't prove it." Wordplay is evocative, not explanatory.[1] Perelman puts it this way:

> In identifying this rhetoric with the general theory of persuasive discourse, which seeks to gain both the intellectual and the emotional adherence of any sort of audience, we affirm that every discourse which does not claim an impersonal validity belongs to rhetoric.[2]

The formal aspects of composition do not simply contain the message, but contribute to the message itself. We cannot, of course, equate the form with the message either; the semantic content is necessary for the text to "mean" something.

In the course of showing the rhetorical features of wordplay, the varieties of wordplay will continue to be addressed. The major concern of this chapter, however, turns to the cognitive effects of the trope, the role or function that wordplay serves in structuring the message of the text. The question is, What role does wordplay play in the text? The final chapter will continue to explore the rhetorical role of wordplay by examining its affective result, the humor of wordplay.

MICAH 2: 1-4: WHAT GOES AROUND COMES AROUND

Watson argues that a function of wordplay is to denote reversal. In Mic 2: 1-4 figure is combined with sense and structure to show that human intention is reversed by divine action; man proposes, God disposes. Specifically, an image is created to convey the idea that justice undergirds reality: those who act unjustly will receive their due.

The pericope begins with a warning against those who "devise" (חשבי) "evil" (רע) upon their beds (על־משכבותם) and then carry out the deed because it is in their capacity to do so (כי יש־לאל ידם).[3] Specifically they seize fields (שדות), take away (נשאו) houses, and oppress a man and his inheritance (נחלתו). The initial verse is a tightly constructed poem against those whose plans were carefully laid and carried out.

The reversal comes in v 3 with the Lord speaking: "I will devise (חשב) evil (רעה) against this family (על־המשפחה הזאת)[4]." Here we clearly see reversal or antithesis, but more specifically, we find wordplay used to depict poetic justice— "tit-for-tat," מדה כנגד מדה. The words are hurled back at the attackers like a snowball that narrowly misses and lies at the foot of the quarry; they receive measure-for-measure. The theme of the passage is poetic justice and the form reinforces the message, word-for-word, action-for-action.

Understanding the passage as an instance of poetic justice is noted by many commentators: Allen ("retribution"), Wolff ("Maß und Art der Strafe sind genau von Maß und Art der Schuld bestimmt"), and Mays ("Their punishment will be directly correlated with their guilt"), among recent commentators. Thus this observation is not unduly noteworthy in itself; however, once we recognize this reversal, the more subtle reversals can emerge. But to find these, we need to tarry and see just how cleverly the words—the permutations of sound,

morphology, semantics, and syntax—play off one another in these four verses to
underscore the reversal.

The wordplays are extensive and subtle. First, we have a wordplay
involving simple repetition with חשׁב being employed in the same sense in vv 1
and 3; both the "wicked" and Yahweh "plan" their action. We also have a "pretty
paronomasia" (alliteration with labials, sibilants, and gutturals combining to
create their sonic effect), not often noted,[5] in משׁפחה and משׁכבותם. More subtly,
we have an instance of a pun (specifically, antanaclasis) between רע in v 1 and
רעה in v 3. In v 1, רע suggests "moral evil" or a misdeed (cf. און, the parallel
term in v 1), but in v 3 the idea is probably closer to "calamity."

"Evil" (רעה) creeps into the text again with the phrase כי עת רעה היא (v 3).
The phrase occasions no major problem of translation; but in the light of the
author's using (ה)רע in two different senses, one must enquire as to its sense here.
Is the time "evil" because of the "evil-doers"? Or, is it "calamitous" because of
the work that Yahweh will perform (the "yoke" laid upon their necks)?

Early on in the history of interpretation, commentators have taken the
עת רעה, perhaps too quickly, in the sense of calamity. Wordplays do not only
separate senses, as we see in vv 1 and 3, but also fuse. J.M.P. Smith says: "It
[רעה] states the accomplishment of Yahweh's purpose as indicated in the first line
of the str. ["I will devise evil ..."], and thus brings the str. to a well-rounded
close."[6] The "well-rounded close" is even more impressive by covering not just
the "strophe," but the whole oracle, if we do not rule out the undertones of moral
evil—the time is "evil" because of the actions of people who perform evil deeds
(v 1) and is "disastrous" because Yahweh will execute retribution for these deeds
(v 3).

Wordplays invite a reader to look over one's shoulder to identify the vague
sounds and senses that echo throughout the text, not just the line. Most of the
occurrences of עת with רעה have the sense of a calamitous time; for example, Jer
2: 27-28, "In the time of their trouble they say, 'Arise and save us!' But where
are your gods that you made for yourself? Let them arise, if they can save you,
in your time of trouble" (RSV). However, these occurrences are not entirely
unambiguous: in Jer 11: 12-14 we find a situation similar to that of Jer 2: 27-28,
where the people are crying out to God in the "time of their trouble." Their
trouble is caused by their moral lapses—the stubbornness of their "evil heart (הרע
לבם)" and turning back to the "iniquities" (עונת) of their fathers and whoring after
other gods (vv 8 and 10). Also, at Amos 5: 13 we find an injunction to be
"prudent" (המשׁכיל) for the time is evil (כי עת רעה היא), an assertion that is
followed by, "Seek good (טוב) and not evil (רע) that you may live (RSV)." In a
passage such as Mic 2: 1-4 where words are reversed, where they carry their own
consequences, the echo of "moral evil" that precipitates "calamity" is certainly not
excluded by the context; indeed, it seems entirely justified.[7]

Beside these initial wordplays that highlight the reversal between the evil-doers and Yahweh, other semantic and phonemic correspondences occur. In v 3 the *qal* and the *niphal* of שׁדד are employed side-by side, and the noun and verb of the root חלק show up in successive cola (v 4). Moreover, in v 3 we have the *hiphil* of מוש and the *qal* in v 4. These are paronymic wordplays in our terminology. We also have in v 4 the preposition ל employed with two different uses in successive words: "He takes it away *from* me (לי), and *to* the 'faithless' (לשׁובב) he divides our fields." And, a point to which Allen has called attention, we should not overlook the paronomasia of מֹשׁ תּוֹמִישׁוּ in v 3, משׁל and ימִישׁ in v 4, and משׁליך in v 5.

We also detect paronomasia between שׁדוד נשׁדנו and שׂדינו in v 4. The occurrence of שׂדינו in v 4 recalls שׂדות in v 2, another instance of sounds echoing throughout the text. The "fields" of v 4 that are handed over to others belong to the lamenters, those who "confiscated" the fields of v 2—hence, poetic justice.

The correspondence between ימִישׁ and תּמִישׁוּ was noted, but we find a correspondence (assonance) also between ימִישׁ and ימיר (v 4). In this context and as parallel terms, we might also suggest a (partial) semantic correspondence between the terms: to "exchange" (ימיר) the חלק is akin to "removing" (ימִישׁ) it. The idea of "withdrawal" or "separation" overlaps even as the phonemes and morphology overlap. Moreover, if we are driven back to the previous verses by the correspondence between שׂדינו / נשׁדנו, then we also look back because of חלק and the paronomastic נחלתו in v 2. Both terms have connotations of "property" (whether "land" or more general "goods"). The "portion" (חלק) is taken away in the same way as the "inheritance" (נחל) of the lamenters' victim was apportioned—a situation not unlike that with the fields exchanging hands. Poetic justice rounds out the lament.

A final example of reversal leads us to a difficult portion of text. In v 4 a משׁל will be "lifted" (ישׂא) against those who "lift" (נשׂאו) houses (v 2). The verb נשׂא is used in the sense of "take away" in v 2, and "sing" in v 4 (antanaclasis).

The words following משׁל in v 4, which have long puzzled commentators, require investigation. Pococke, nearly alone of the commentators, mentions the obvious paronomasia: "There are here three words [נהה נהי נהיה] in the Hebrew eloquently joined of *much like sound* , or agreement between themselves... ."[8]

J.M.P. Smith, together with a host of others,[9] omits נהיה as a dittography. However, the versions all support *something* being read in the text, though not necessarily a verb, as the MT has it. The LXX, ἐν μέλει, and V, *cum suavite,* hang together by taking the word almost adverbially ("metrically"?; "melodiously"?). Tg renders the three words by employing the synonyms "lamentation" and "dirge," ואיליא ובעיניתיה; and P employs '*wlyt* ', "lamentation," for נהיה.

We cannot rule out the possibility of dittography here; however, we have also made the point that wordplay tends to be preserved *simply because it is memorable*. So once again we should pause and ponder the text before we emend a possible wordplay. What options are available?

Rashi seems to take נהיה as a *niphal* of היה, citing Zech 8:10 for support. Furthermore, he mentions "others" who make reference to נהייתי. in Dan 8: 27. Keil also cites Dan 8: 27, and offers this: *actum est!* —"it is all over!" (an exclamation of despair). Earlier commentators often took נהיה as a feminine form of נהי, hence Rosenmüller, *lamentum lamenti,* "a mournfully mournful song." That the phrase should be taken as a superlative is similarly argued by E. Pusey[10] and Rudolph.[11]

It is not easy to decide what to make of נהיה. It may be that we should treat the phrase as a משל, a "proverbial" statement of sorts,[12] since it follows immediately from this statement;[13] the content of the "taunt-song" (RSV). If so, taking the three words as cognates has something to commend it. Allen produces an intriguing and appealing translation: "Groaning, moaning, and bemoaning." At the least, we have consonance, or perhaps "feminine rhyme." Indeed, the effect of this "crisscrossing of sounds" in the משל is almost onomatopoeic, a mournful sound-link—"moanin' 'n' groanin'."

Caution must be exercised here. Watson makes a distinction between onomatopoeia and mimicry. The latter is simply the imitation of a sound by a human, whereas the former is a *language-dependent* word that resembles the sound it denotes. Onomatopoeia become part of the lexical stock.

The words employed in our text are language-dependent—they are part of the lexical stock. The effect of the phrase, however, does not lie in the word itself, but in the unusual combination of the words: three apparently cognate words; a verb followed by two nouns (or verb-noun-verb, if נהיה is a *niphal* form of היה), and אמר following without any marked coordination. It is not quite the same as, say, *moo* or *buzz* — an animal or implement (e.g., a drill, hammer, and so forth) sound in which the word imitates the sound it denotes, although the nasal quality of the words may imitate the sound of lament. However, in onomatopoeia, the sound is recognized as a convention within the culture.[14]

Sasson suggests "farrago" as a designation of such tropes as *helter-skelter* . These, he says, are confused, often ungrammatical collocations of terms. Farrago does suggest a mixture, but it is not a common literary or linguistic designation of such occurrences; words like *helter-skelter* have little reason, perhaps, but certainly "rhyme" and thus some coherence. A better term might be "iteration,"[15] which suggests a repetition, even a rhythm.

What are we then to make of נהה נהי נהיה? There is iteration, but not in the same way as *helter-skelter* . The Hebrew words are separate lexical items with a "confused" (unusual) grammatical construction, whereas *helter-skelter* , and the like, is only a lexical item as a unit. The crucial question becomes, is this phrase a *conventionally* understood sound-imitative phrase? The words involve sound mimicry (perhaps), but also sense. Since we have no other occurrence of this phrase in the extant literature, we cannot say with much certainty whether it is a convention or not. However, if מֹשֶׁל is a designation for the phrase (the phrase being a particular *kind* of מֹשֶׁל), then seeing it as a *literary convention* , if not a linguistic one (as would be the case if the phrase were onomatopoeia) is more probable.

CONCLUSIONS

In the final colon of the pericope, we find sound-coherence (paronomasia, iteration), but also grammatical coherence, if we are prepared to understand נהיה as a fem. form meaning "lament."[16] The phrase is not nonsensical in the same way that *helter-skelter* is nonsensical—that is, afforded sense not by sense and syntax, but by its particular use in a stylized construction. If it does have the effect of iteration (or even onomatopoeia), then looking for a transparent translation may be futile (like trying to find out the meaning of *helter* and *skelter* as separate lexical items in a dictionary).

The form of the "parable," whose content is to taunt (עליכם not in the sense of "about" or "over" you, but "against" you), is iterative (alliteration; feminine rhyme). The proverbial statement emphasizes the plight of the evil-doers and perhaps amuses by mimicking or suggesting a plaintive quality of the lament— lachrymal lament.

Through contrasting the intentions of the evil-doers and the determinations of Yahweh, a unity in the oracle is achieved; sound and sense echo throughout the pericope where nothing is left hanging; each point has a counterpoint. The point and counterpoint, exhibited in trope, structure, and content, invite the reader to accept that justice will prevail—ביום ההוא.[17]

MICAH 2: 6-11: ENTRAPPED IN WORDS

In Mic 2: 1-4 words are played against one another even as the oracle of God is played against the plans of men. A specific kind of reversal, poetic justice, comes in both form and content. In the following oracle, 2: 6-11, we find another reversal; the "evil-doers" words are not so much hurled against them as they become trapped by their own words. The reversal is not poetic justice in this pericope, but is of a different, specialized form—what Watson designates as "appearances can be deceptive." Beyond the reversal we again find wordplay functioning as a structuring device linking parts of an extended oracle together.

No other passage in Micah, save 1: 10-15, exhibits as many exegetical problems as 2: 6-11. Hillers says, "This passage is corrupt or doubtful at so many points that even the general progression of thought is uncertain."[18] Again, however, we do not have to settle all the textual problems to discuss the wordplays in the pericope as we now have it.

The varieties of wordplay in the passage are not as rich as those in other passages. We find a paronymic play in v 10, תחבל וחבל, much as we found in Mic 2: 12, and alliteration in v 11, שקר and לשכר.

תחבל וחבל is often emended to the passive, usually citing LXX διεφθάρητε. Others (e.g., Wolff) argue that the *waw* rightly belongs to the verb and only later attaches itself to the following noun because of their proximity. The wordplay, however, is not affected materially by either the MT, LXX, or the conjectural emendations. Neither is the wordplay particularly interesting for our purposes—it lacks surprising linguistic usage or functional importance (though it does have philological interest since the noun only occurs here and in Job 21: 17).

The following paronomasia is similarly undistinguished. שקר and שכר alliterate, but no apparent contrast or fusion, concealment or revelation between the words or ideas is made. Perhaps strong drink and deception are being equated; Mays says, "His preaching would intoxicate them in drunkenness that freed them from facing reality."[19] However, this collocation of the words seems more convenient than surprising (no unusual positioning or form highlights the play).

Allen suggests a possible wordplay with the phrase לו־איש הלך רוח in v 11. רוח means both "wind" and "spirit" and the איש הרוח is a synonym for "prophet" (e.g., Hos 9: 7). Allen says: "What should have been inspiration was nothing more than wind."[20] As such, רוח forms an implicit polysemantic pun—syllepsis.

The more difficult and interesting wordplay occurs in vv 6 and 11 involving various forms of נטף. V 6 begins: אל תטפו יטיפון לא־יטפו לאלה. Two relevant questions arise: Is the prophet using נטף in the same sense in all three occurrences of the word? Who is doing the speaking?

נטף is used in the sense of "drip" in such passages as Judg 5: 4, "The heavens dropped (נטפו), yea, the clouds dropped (נטפו) water" (RSV). By extension, we find a metaphorical use, especially in the *hiphil* , of letting words "drip"; "drivel." Holladay, *Lexicon* , associates this with prophetic ecstasy.[21] However, the passages do not require ecstasy as a precondition for the prophetic utterance; for example, at Ezek 21: 2, Ezekiel is simply told by Yahweh to "set your face toward Jerusalem and preach (הטף) against the sanctuaries; prophesy (הנבא) against the land of Israel" (RSV).

In the history of interpretation we find a varied approach to the meaning of the three words. The LXX and P do not treat the various forms of נטף in their figurative sense of "speaking" (especially of prophesying). The LXX reads: μὴ κλαίετε δάκρυσιν, μηδὲ δακρυέτωσαν ἐπὶ τούτοις—"do not weep with tears, neither (should) they weep concerning these (things)." On the other hand, V and Tg take נטף in its figurative sense. V is interesting because he possibly reverts to a non-figurative sense for the third occurrence (and translates the pl. as a sg.): "Speak ye not, saying, 'It [perhaps "he"] shall not drop [perhaps "speak'[22] (*stillabit*)] upon these'" (Douay Version).

Throughout the history of interpretation, the figurative sense has prevailed, although those dependent upon the LXX, of course, find alternative explanations. Theodore of Mopuestia, for example, interprets the "tears" as a rueful act—οὐ μεταμελείας: "Do not regret [but suffer greatly over the consequences of your bad deeds]." The medieval Jewish scholars treat נטף as a verb of speaking (and not "dripping"): "The prophet narrates what the "evil family" [cf. 2: 3] were saying (היו אומר) to the prophets of God" (Ibn Ezra). Similarly, Luther and Calvin, though noting the literal sense and difficulties of נטף, take the words figuratively.

While we cannot assume that the term is used in the same sense in all three instances, there is nothing in the history of interpretation to commend a different sense, nor is there anything within the text to necessitate or suggest a non-figurative reading: translating נטף as "drop" in any of its three positions presents more difficulties than it could possibly resolve.

Attempts at emendation are made to overcome the difficult text. The last use of יטיפו in v 6 is variously treated as a sg. (V), or a 2nd pers. (P). J.M.P. Smith simply omits לא יטיפו. יטיפון is translated with a noun by LXX (and P), and a ptc. by V; J.M.P. Smith emends it to נטיף.

Neither lexical considerations nor proposed emendations commend a resolution that has gained widespread acceptance. Indeed, the solution cannot be divorced from the question regarding the identity of the speakers in the oracle. The more usual way to make sense of the pericope is to suggest that words belong to different speakers.

The exercise of sorting out the speakers very quickly resembles the classic "Who's on first?" comic routine. Most agree on the first speaker(s); for example, Hillers says: "One may reasonably suppose that it begins with quotations of pious phrases from the religiously secure who oppose the prophets."[23] In a similar fashion, Eliezer of Beaugency ascribes the saying to the false prophets (נביאי השקר), and Calvin says that the Jews speak the first words.

The pl. impv. at the beginning, as Hillers says, "if the text is correct," indicates that the speaker(s) is rejecting not only Micah, but any prophet of his persuasion ("doom and gloom" prophets?). The same idea with the sg. of נטף occurs at Amos 7: 16; Amaziah is speaking specifically to Amos (as quoted by Amos): "You say, "Do not prophesy against Israel, and do not preach (תטיף) against the house of Isaac ... '" (RSV). The injunction not to prophesy (pl.) is found also at Amos 2: 12, where Yahweh says, "You command the prophets, 'Do not prophesy' (לא תנבאו); Behold, I will... ." Opposition to the prophets is part of the prophetic tradition.

Calvin reports the interpretation that God speaks the second word: "'Distel ye not,' —'[Nay] they shall distel!'"; the idea is that it is not in the power of the Jews to oppose the prophets of God since it is God who sent them. J.M.P Smith reports the interpretation that Micah is taking up the conversation of his audience: (Speaker 1): "You must not speak." (Speaker 2): "O, let them speak." (Speaker 3): "They must not speak such things as these."

The more common solution is to see the second bicolon as reportage by Micah: "'Do not preach,' thus they preach" (J.M.P Smith, Allen, Mays). Hillers says that the retort, especially if pejorative, is ironic: You say, 'Do not prophesy such things,' but what of this since you are little better than soothsayers yourselves. In English we lose the wit of the remark because we lack a single term that suggests both aspects: "flowing words" (prophecy) and "flooding words" (drivel). The wit is also served in the compactness of the statements—this!-that! What rhetoricians call "epitrochasmus," a swift movement from one thing to another.

The third occurrence of נטף in v 6 is no less problematic than the first two. The negative particle אל contrasts with the initial negative לא. Does this imply another reversal? Calvin suggests that God is speaking to those who would try to limit the work of those he has sent: They shall indeed 'not prophesy' that they will no longer be reproached by you, and you will have nothing to stand in the way as you rush headlong to your evils, and hence your doom, for I will take away my prophets from you. Eliezer of Beaugency suggests a similar understanding: "Surely it is fitting that my prophets should not preach to those who are nothing but scorners of their words."

This understanding eliminates a problem with the *lamedh* following the verb. Usually translators resort to "*concerning* these things" (cf. RSV: "One should not preach *of* such things"; or NIV: "Do not prophesy *about* these things"). However, if Calvin is correct, then we could translate the phrase as, "You will not prophesy to those [who speak thus to you]." In v 11 *lamedh* is used first as "to" (לך) and then as "concerning" (לי), following נטף. Moreover, the understanding that God is the third speaker eliminates the problem of the 3rd pl. verb following from the pl. imperative in the opening words (usually both terms are ascribed to the same speaker).

Alternatively, the phrase לא יטפו could be the words of the opponents, the initial speaker(s). This is the most common understanding (Mays, Hillers). Allen, however, argues that the subject of the third verb is the same as the immediately preceding one, and introduces the content of the prophecy, "Humiliation won't overwhelm us." In a similar fashion, Keil understands the final hemistich as a conditional, "If they (the true prophets) do not prophesy to these (the unrighteous rich in vers. 1, 2) ... shameful destruction will burst upon them."[24]

The switch from 2nd pers. to 3rd pers., and the like, is awkward, but not unusual throughout the Bible and even in the book of Micah (e.g., 7: 19). Moreover, as noted, the *lamedh* here could function in much the same way as it does in v 11, אטף ... ליין, "I will speak ... *concerning* wine ..." where it introduces the content of the speech.

The crux of v 6 lies in the final colon, לא יסג כלמות, where textual and exegetical difficulties again abound and little consensus emerges. The textual problem is with יסג, and the exegetical concern lies chiefly with the subject of the sg. verb since no subject is expressed and "reproaches," the logical choice syntactically, is pl. (and fem.).

Modern solutions to the problems take the form of suggesting that the *samekh* and the *sin* are not distinguished, and thus יסג is not from סוג / נסג, but from נשג, "overtake." Thus Mays: "Disgrace shall not overtake us" ("us" being supplied as a suitable object). We find this tactic in various forms in Allen, Wolff, J.M.P. Smith, among modern commentators. Hillers, though slightly different, is still part of this troop: "Such reproaches will not come to pass."[25]

The modern solution has its roots in medieval exegesis and even earlier. Ibn Ezra says the the *samekh* is like a *sin*. Similarly, V translates יסג by "comprehendet," which is used elsewhere for ישיג (cf. Zech 1: 6). Ibn Ezra further supplies the object "us" in his comments and treats כלמות as a sg. All the versions seem to treat כלמות as a sg.: LXX, ὄνειδη; V, *confusio* ; Tg, אתכנעו; and P, ḥsdʾ. Similarly, they all take it to mean a "disgrace" of some sort. Schwantes suggests that the versions are taking כלמות as an abstract sg.[26]

The notion that the homophones ס and שׂ are interchangeable (or confused) has a long tradition and makes the best sense in the present passage.[27] The subject of the verb, however, is less certain. Rashi and Eliezer find a warning in the final clause to the prophet(s) of God; Rashi cites Prov 9: 8: "Do not reprove a scoffer [or he will hate you]." Most modern commentators attribute the phrase to the "scoffers."

Does the recognition of wordplay help us settle the issues in v 6? The wordplay is simple repetition (or antanaclasis if one can find the sense "drop" suitable in any of the three positions). Morphological play may exist between the words in the three different forms that are employed: the imperative (with a negative); the 3rd pl. (with *nun paragogicum*); and 3rd pl. (*sans* final *nun* , but with a negative particle, although different from the initial negative).

The form with *nun paragogicum* calls attention to itself and may be employed for emphasis (GKC §47*m*)—thus distinguishing itself from both the former and the latter? According to this understanding, we have three different forms corresponding to three different speakers, all with reversals of sorts occurring. The reply, set off by form, comes as a reversal of the initial command, which is supported if this second occurrence carries a pejorative association (Hillers). The third occurrence may accept the meaning of the first—that the true prophet should not speak—but implies that this will not turn out like they (the opponents of the prophet) envision; rather than being for your benefit, it will be for you detriment (because לא יסג כלמות). If this is the case, then beyond the paronomasia created by the repetition lies a more subtle pun where the second term carries pejorative connotations that are not evident in the first: "'Do not prophesy!' thus they prattle; [prophets] should not prophesy to these [who prattle thus] for [their] reproach will come to naught [whereas our reproach is certain, though they heed it not]."

However, nothing about the wordplay itself necessitates finding significance in the forms—just as there is nothing either linguistically or exegetically that settles the issue. The different forms are suggestive (and introduce morphology play along with sound and sense) but not determinative. Wordplays are illusive, after all.

The understanding that the second occurrence of נטף is used pejoratively (and involves a morphological play), however, finds support in the uses of נטף in v 11. נטף occurs two times in v 11. Again, two different forms are used and two different speakers are often suggested, indicated by quotation marks in modern translations: "Wenn einer mit Wind daherkäme und Trug lügen würde: 'Ich predige dir von Wein und Bier!'—das wäre ein Prediger für dieses Volk da" (Wolff).

The oracle that intervenes between the opening words and these closing words details the contemptuous treatment that the "people" receive at the hands of those who call into question the prophetic message of reproach (following as it does from 2: 1-5, the same who plan evil upon their beds). The closing cola then, as Wolff says, come as "galligem Humor"—only a spokesperson who lies and offers the promise of sensual pleasure is a "prophet" for "these folks" (contrasted with "my people" in v 8).

The implied sarcasm at the beginning of the oracle between the words of the opponents and those of the prophet becomes overt and comes full circle at the end with the image of a prophet after their own hearts: Mays says, "Micah flings at his audience a job-description of the preacher they prefer,"[28] and Hillers puts it this ways, "This preacher you prefer is surely the sermonizer you deserve."[29] The wordplay provides a caricature of the opponents and brings unity to the oracle by employing the same terms at the beginning as as the end.[30] Indeed, the reoccurrence of the words here forces the reader back to the beginning, and thus, perhaps, makes the implied contrast in v 6 sharper.[31] Thus what may simply be heard as paronomasia in the beginning is seen as a pun by the end.

CONCLUSIONS

The text suggests that appearances can be deceptive; those who scoff warrant our scoffing. Perhaps there is a critique of language here, certainly a critique of those who misuse it—the sarcasm is harsh. The text pushes the words (of the opponents) to carry all the weight that the prophet can give them, but not more than they are able. Those who speak can not escape through their words, but become enmeshed by them. The become the butt of their own diatribe and object of our scorn: humor as superiority.

CONCLUSIONS

Further examples of paronomasia, puns, and syntactical plays are found in these two passages from Mic 2. We can, however, add onomatopoeia, or something very similar to it, to our list: the presence of נהה נהי נהיה in 2: 4 is suggestive of onomatopoeia, at least.

We also see wordplay used to bring coherence to the pericope. Each evil deed (רע) is met with calamity (רעה) until both evil and calamity mesh, baneful, cankerous or miasmal (כי עת רעה היא), and all that the evil-doers can do is whine (נהה נהי נהיה). If evil deed receives its own recompense in Mic 2: 1-4, then injudicious words are given their significance in 2: 6-11: be careful what you utter for it may be more appropriate than you realize. Those who oppose the people of God become trapped by their deeds and words. Mimesis: form imitates message, language mirrors nature.

If wordplays bring coherence to individual pericopes, they also bring coherence to larger structures. In the previous chapter, I argued that Mic 1: 6-7 and 3: 11-12 each contain wordplays but also correspondences between the passages: עיין in 3: 12 recalls לעי in 1: 6 (שדה and במה find echoes as well). This relationship of coherence or anticipation/retrospection not only works within a book but between books, as I suggested with the lament of David over Saul and Jonathan (2 Sam 1: 18-27 and Mic 1: 10-15), as well as the allusion to patriarchs in Mic 5: 2. Between books this relationship is better termed "allusion," but only if understood in a broad sense of verbal correspondences and not necessarily textually based (texts seen as documents or sources).

I think we can also speak of the dramatic effect of wordplay in the "characters" in these passages. In the first oracle, "evil-doers" plan "evil" (רע), but Yahweh plans "calamity" (רעה); they will seize "fields" (שדות), but will end up being "destroyed" (שדוד נשדנו); they will take a person's inheritance (נחלתו), but their fields will be divided (יחלק) among others. In the second oracle, the "scoffers" are not witty, but unwittingly fall into Yahweh's hand (אל־תטפו ... יטיפון). The reader is led to accept that justice will prevail and that

Yahweh is the one who ensures that justice. Puns, as Mahood says, reveal character, and in these passages we find that Yahweh is the true punster throughout the pericope.

In speaking of Yahweh as the punster, we must not overlook another instance of wordplay used to denote a reversal. However, the reversal in this pericope is less an act of justice and more a gracious act. In the famous passage of Mic 6: 1-8, Yahweh asks, "How have I wearied you (הלאתיך)? ... For I brought you up (העלתיך) from the land of Egypt ... " (vv 3-4). By simple metathesis[32]—or an anagrammatical play in our terminology—"weary" (לאה) is turned into "redemption (עלה)."

Moreover, these reversals reveal something about wordplay and not simply character. As a reader, I can find "pleasure" in the mirror effect of the use of words in both passages: every act of the evil-doers in Mic 2: 1-4 is thwarted by a counter plan by Yahweh, and the sarcastic comments found in Mic 2: 6-11, though pointed (Wolff calls them *galligem* —"spiteful") are "clever."

I think we can move beyond simple pleasure and speak of the humor in these passages. Humor, we argued in Chapter Five, is built upon dissonance or incongruity—two opposite scripts being brought together in a surprising way. In Mic 2: 1-4 the "evil-doers" plan an action expecting a particular result—seizure of "fields." The text is built around the premise of their faulty thinking: rather than "reward," they will receive "recompense." The faulty thinking is also seen when their plans go awry—when "caught" they expect no consequence, they whine over their lamentable situation (נהה נהי נהיה). The opposing scripts is: "they" think their action will result in reward, but in fact it receives recompense.

In Mic 2: 6-11 the reversal is less dependent upon faulty thinking and more dependent upon indirection. Mic 2: 6-11 also shows the more "phthonic" (φθόνος: "ill-will; malice") side of humor—humor as superiority. The sarcastic remarks of the "prophet of God" belies a position that, under "normal" circumstances, borders on arrogance: the prophet of God portrays his rival as a drunk who is not laughable, but risible.

Wordplays, thus, work affectively as well as cognitively, and the following chapter will bring to the forefront a particular affective function, that of the "play" of wordplay.

EIGHT
THE LUDIC ANGLE OF THE TEXT

[Sometimes he relied on mere similarity of sound.] But more often there is a kind of accompanying twist in the situation itself, playful or grotesque, which raises the humour above the exasperation of sheer verbicide.

P.E. More, "Thomas Hood"

As a reader, I appreciated the "poetic justice" I found in Mic 2: 1-4. Appreciating poetic justice seems universal—provided the poetry is against another person and not personal. The sarcasm of Mic 2: 6-11, though "spiteful," was similarly affective—I was "relieved" that my words did not entrap me this time, but others got caught in their words. Moreover, I delighted in Matthew's handling of אלפי from Mic 5: 1, and enjoyed the fusion of speech-sight imagery in Mic 3: 5-7. To say that wordplay may be humorous or playful is only to acknowledge what experience—and the dictionary definitions—already tells us.

The play or humor of the passages from Mic 2 can be seen in the content (faulty thinking; sarcasm) or the structure (reversal; "poetic justice"); however, it is not simply the content or the structure but the linguistic fixtures of the text that produce the humor. Or, rather, the content and structure is humorous because this particular juxtaposition of sounds, words, or syntax have triggered something in me as a reader. As a reader, I was "pleasantly surprised" by this collocation of words and the resulting incongruous situation or image portrayed.

The humor of wordplay, then, is not simply dependent upon the "content" of the passage—the broader context, as, for example, is the case with irony and, usually, sarcasm—but is dependent especially upon the linguistic collocations present. This distinction is only one of convenience, however, because it is the combinations of sound, sense, and syntax together with extra-lexical information that shows the faulty reasoning, indirection, and other strategies that we find incongruous, and, therefore, humorous. This distinction between the content and the linguistic collocations helps when considering non-humorous wordplays. Not all wordplays are "funny." The affective aspects of wordplay come to the forefront the more the wordplay works as a trigger in the overall discourse; one may still feel "pleasure" with a "pretty paronomasia," but the intensity of the response depends upon the dissonance triggered by the linguistic feature and the reader's ability to recognize the role that imbalance plays in the passage.

Excursus: "Gallows Humor."

Mic 1: 10-15 poses a problem if we are arguing that wordplay is playful: Few people would find a recent—or impending—invasion "funny." Perhaps, in utilizing wordplay in this dire situation, a forceful literary device is used that further has a mnemonic role (wordplays are memorable, as biblical critics often remind us). But if memory were simply the case, then a well-constructed poem with vivid metaphors would serve equally as well. And the poem in 1: 10-15 is anything but artfully constructed in the sense of forms, words, and images balancing one another—it has jumbled syntax, contrived paronomasia, slippery puns, and obscure allusions. Wherefore humor?

By form, the poem is a lament, a common form not necessitating the *qinah*, or 3+2, meter. Embedded within the literary genre is wordplay, a stylistic device, again, not foreign to the form of the genre.[1] The wordplays come as a volley of invectives ridiculing the towns that proved ineffectual against the unnamed invader. Through either "etymological" exploitation or simple associations, a cause and effect relationship between the town in question and its name or the character of its inhabitants is created: their names contained their fate, by comparison or contrast, in form or content.

The poem displays the "iconoclastic power of wit" (Redfern). The complacent optimism, which is later described in the book as "they lean upon the Lord saying, 'Is not the Lord in our midst? Evil cannot come upon us'" (3: 12), is shattered first by the event which prompted the lament, and second by the words of the author who sees this event as an inevitable outcome of the practices of the inhabitants, even foreordained by the very names of the cities.

Beyond the ridicule is the social control of humor; it is not humor-for-humor's sake, but humor-for-a-purpose.[2] By wit and imagery, the audience/reader is forced to contemplate the unthinkable, that this event was purposed by the Lord (v 12) because of the trust the inhabitants put in military might, which proved fruitless (v 13 especially).

The way through this judgment is mourning (v 16), as evidenced by the action of the prophet himself (vv 8-9). And this is perhaps where form and content come together in social control: humor opens the door to hope, a sense that there is something beyond the immediate, desperate moment,[3] while the lament form itself often moves from "mourning to dancing" (Ps 30: 11). In prophetic laments, the prophet's concern is "with rebellion against God rather than external catastrophe" that the prophet must "bewail ... as a mortal fate"[4]—or moral fate. In Micah, the two, rebellion and catastrophe, are combined; the catastrophe is an outgrowth of the rebellion. The lament and wordplay work together to push for repentance in the face of moral lapse and mortal danger.

The prophet makes light in this dire situation to shatter the complacency of his countrymen and point to a course of action: you are not to lament over a fallen hero, but a fate that befell you. To say that something is "playful" or humorous does not preclude its being serious as well.

JOKES, POEMS, AND PROPHETS

Jokes and poems work with disparate ideas and condensation of thought. Nowottny captures this principle when she says, "In poems, as in jokes, the point of using such a locution in such a context may well lie not so much in the separate interest of each set of relationships, but in the very fact that two spheres of interest are brought together or superimposed."[5] Disparate ideas are superimposed or condensed in a single expression.

From the side of humor, Freud argues similarly when he makes condensation the mark of nearly every joke technique; it is, however, an economy of a special sort, an economy of great trouble that "must often first transform one of the thoughts into an unusual form which will provide a basis for its *combination* with the second thought."[6]

Not all jokes are poems, any more than all poems are funny. With humor, it is not simply disparate ideas, but more specifically opposing scripts that are brought together, and the condensation is not simply economy, but a single item that signals the opposing scripts.[7]

Jokes and poems do, however, condense word and thought to bring alternative ways of looking at a situation. In many respects, then, poems and jokes are fitting vehicles for prophetic oracles. R.R. Wilson argues that prophets fulfil two social roles in a society; some prophets work on the fringes of society, while others are centrists. In either case, values are questioned; the one group pushes for radical social change, while the other opts for a more orderly transition.[8] The prophet resembles Douglas' jokester: "Safe within the permitted range of attack ... [the jokester] expresses the creative possibilities of the situation."[9] Prophets present, through their words, images, and actions, creative alternatives to the immediate situation or prevailing attitude.

Douglas argues that all jokes are subversive. Redfern, limiting his comments to puns, says it this way: "Yet, at their best, pointed puns are a way of countering insolently ideological double-talk, an improper gander which, like the Roman ones, can act as watch-dogs."[10] Jokes challenge the balance of power (Douglas), and puns are practised as underground literature (Redfern). The words of the prophets are not comforting but confronting.

In this chapter, my concern will focus on the affective aspects of wordplay, its ludic effect, especially as it confronts the ideology of complacency.

MICAH 4: 14: HOMOGRAPHS, NOT HOMONYMS

The initial words of Mic 4: 14, תתגדדי בת־גדוד are usually seen as homonyms by both translators and commentators. The reason given for taking the words as homonyms, however, is misguided. Rather than homonyms, the words are homographs. Moreover, seen as homographs, the spirited wit of the wordplay becomes evident.

תתגדדי בת־גדוד forms a recognizable wordplay based on alliteration with the consonants ת/ג/ד—apparently a paronymic play, a device we have seen throughout the oracles. The form, however, is not as important as the play itself for understanding the phrase. The play on בת־גדוד moves in two directions. First, paradigmatically with בת־ציון, "Daughter of Zion," in the previous verses, and then syntagmatically with the paronomastic תתגדדי. Several considerations—text, philology, structure, and the role of humor—need balancing to follow the lines of the play. To get from homonym to homograph requires some explanation.

Recognition of the wordplay goes back at least to medieval Jewish exegesis; Eliezer of Beaugency remarks גדוד לשון נופל, "[The word(s)] גדוד [and תתגדדי form] a wordplay." More recently, Mays says that the play is based on the "assonance" between the vocative and the imperative (and "not on the sense of the words"). Wolff concedes that the "alliterative" play makes the interpretation of גדוד uncertain. Although we find disparity about the nature of the wordplay, there is no disagreement that it does, in fact, exist.

Hillers, while accepting that there is a play, nevertheless argues for emending the text. He objects to the attempts at translating the phrase as an epithet of a city: "But בת גדוד "daughter of gashing," if not impossible, seems without good parallel as an epithet of a city... ."[11] We should note that of course "gashing" does not make a good epithet, but "marauder" or a similar designation, though without exact parallel, is possible. Although Hillers objects to Mays' citation of ישבתי במצור at Jer 10: 17 as a parallel, it is an *analogous* form (the *qere* reads the sg., ישבת). Moreover, the words are not syntactically anomalous; the use of the construct state with an appellative noun is common enough (GKC §128 *s-v*).

Throughout our study of Micah, settling the textual issues was not always necessary for understanding the wordplays; wordplays may be created in the transmission of the text, although as a general principle that seems less likely than "authorial" creations.[12] By settling the text and lexicography of Mic 4: 14, however, the wordplay comes to the forefront.

I would argue that the MT is the earliest *recoverable* text—the text by which the other textual witnesses can be explained.[13] The Tg is representative of supporting the *textus receptus* , though it departs more radically from the MT than the LXX. The three texts are:

MT: תתגדדי בת־גדוד

Tg: כען תסתיעין במשרין קרתא

LXX: νῦν ἐμφραχθήσεται θυγάτηρ Εφραιμ

The textual transmission of the LXX shows a degree of uncertainty regarding תתגדדי בת־גדוד, both in terms of the words themselves (ostensively the translator is confusing *daleth* and *resh*) and to what they refer (epithet or common noun): the translation and transmission is confused, but at some point a translator supplied a "suitable" epithet—"ephraim."[14] Similarly, Tg has problems with what he finds in the text. The Targumist, however, errs by seeing 4: 13 and 14 as being (logically) connected and "adjusting" the translation to make sense of the context.[15]

Any exegete or translator is confronted with the variance between 4: 13 and 14. 4: 13 is a word of weal, whereas v 14 is, at least on the surface, a word of woe. Reconciling the variance is problematic and takes diverse forms. The Tg replaces בת־גדוד with קרתא, "(O) Town," and renders תתגדדי as תסתיעין, "join in troops." The word of woe is made explicitly a word of weal: "daughter" is omitted altogether, and the "troops" are exhorted to join together to lay siege "against *her*" (עלינו is replaced with עלה). The derogatory—or at least highly ambiguous—reference to "Zion" (what one might reasonably expect after "daughter" based on the preceding verses) is circumvented altogether. We need not suggest a different textual tradition, only an exegetical difficulty that the translator "resolves."

Presumably the addressee is Jerusalem/Zion in 4: 14, as it is throughout this section, especially after v 13. However, the appellation is derogatory, and seems anomalous, following as it does from the exhortation in v 13 to "arise and thresh." The problem, of course, only arises if v 14 is seen as ensuing from v 13.

Although not everyone in the history of interpretation of these verses perceives the verses as logically connected, a significant breakthrough in understanding them came with the rhetorical studies of B. Renaud and J.T. Willis.[16] These studies are supported and supplemented by the more recent study of D. Hagstrom.[17] These scholars argue that a pattern of present hopelessness contrasted with future victory forms the structural design of the pericopes within chapters 4 and 5. Disagreements persist over the particulars; however, by seeing that 4: 14 does not logically belong to v 13, as the Tg and others suppose, the problem of translation eases. 4: 14 begins a new, independent pericope.

Thus, בת־גדוד תתגדדי is the earliest recoverable text, the start of an independent oracle (although also part of a series of oracles sharing similar themes and structures), and גדוד stands in a paradigmatic relationship with "daughter of Zion." What, then, is the meaning of גדוד? And what is the semantic relationship between that and תתגדדי?

We find throughout the history of interpretation that commentators are frequently influenced by the meaning of גדוד, however it is construed, for their interpretation of תתגדדי (the exception to this rule is Hillers who wishes to translate גדוד as "gashing," evidently on the basis of תתגדדי.

Occurrences of גדוד are clustered around Kings, Chronicles, and Job. Throughout the literature גדוד carries the general association of a (para)military group, but in arguably "early" texts the context suggests malevolent activity on the part of the members of the group. In Kings, גדוד is translated "raiding party" as, for example, at 2 Kgs 6: 23, "And the Syrians came no more on raids into the land of Israel" (RSV; BDB, "marauding band"; Holladay, *Lexicon* , "raiding party").

In unequivocally late literature, it carries the more "institutional" designation, "troops; detachments." 2 Chr 25: 10 reads, "Then Amaziah discharged the army (להגדוד) that had come to him from Ephraim ... " (RSV; see also Job 29: 25).

In the prophetic literature, we find the connotations that we find in Kings; e.g., Hos 6: 9, the priests are גדודים ("banded together") like those who "lie in wait" (כחכי) for a man, and they "slay" (ירצחו) those on their way to Shechem and generally act in a "villainous" manner (זמה[18]). We also find the same connotations of גדוד at Jer 18: 22, which the RSV translates as, "May a cry be heard from their houses, when thou bringest the *marauder* suddenly upon them."

Thus the connotations of malevolence are suppressed, if not totally absent, only in the decidedly post-exilic literature.

We are still left with the Mican reference, and the relationship between גדוד and תתגדדי. At Deut 14: 1 and I Kgs 18: 28, the *hithpolel* of גדד means "inflect cuts on oneself" as in mourning or cultic practices. The *qal* occurs at Ps 94: 21 with על, evidently with the sense of "assemble together against"; however, the text is not without its difficulties, and the understanding of "assemble" derives from the Tg as much as it does from anything within the text itself.

The only other reference besides Mic 4: 14 cited for the *hithpolel* of גדד as meaning "band together" is Jer 5: 7 (So BDB; Holladay, *Lexicon*, simply lists "inflict cuts on oneself" as a meaning; KB opts for emendation). The Tg of Jer 5:

7 has מסחיעין, as in Mic 4: 14. However, Jer 5: 7 could refer to cultic practices, as it does throughout the rest of the book (e.g., Jer 16: 6, "And no one shall lament for them or *cut himself* or make himself bald for them"). Jer 5: 7 would then read, "How can I pardon you? Your children have forsaken me, and have sworn by those who are no gods. When I fed them to the full, *they gashed themselves* in the houses of harlotry."[19]

If the preceding observations on the text and lexicography are correct, we are left with, "Gash yourself, O Daughter of Marauder." We face phonetically similar lexical items in Mic 4: 14, words that appear to share a similar root, but which, in fact, differ in meaning. However, the phonetic similarity has caused interpreters to find a semantic similarity as well—homonymy has suggested synonymy. Through a process of "associative etymology" (Ullmann), the two terms came to be interpreted, erroneously, in the light of each other. Hillers is thus correct when he says that translating תתגדדי as a denominative of גדוד is wrong-headed, but he is wrong to base this judgment on syntactic grounds; rather, the terms belong to two different semantic spheres.

If we treat the terms as separate lexical items, another picture emerges. The prophet, through an accident of sound, brings two terms together for their poetic and witty effect. If we reduce the phrase to its more prosaic meaning, we lose the effect: "You leaders of Zion are no better than *goyim* who practise abominable rites." The effect comes in the "witty compression" of the (dis)similar terms. We get "concords of sound and discords of sense."[20]

Thus, because the terms are homographs and not homonyms, dissonance is created—גדוד as "marauder" and תתגדדי as "gash yourself" require the reader to work out a balance. Dissonance is further created by the problem of the negative designation "marauder" as an appellative of "Zion" to which it is related paradigmatically. Thus, both the syntagmatic and paradigmatic relations function dissonantly, not consonantly.

Looking at the words in the light of the form and function of humor helps "resolve" the dissonance. The expected appellation following "daughter" is "Zion" in chapter 4. However, it is precisely at this most crucial point that we do not get what we expect. Rather, Zion, as a personification of the leaders of Jerusalem, whose penchant for bloodshed is well-chronicled in the book (e.g., 3: 1-3; 9-11), is little more than a marauder or brigand. In Hosea the priests are likened to "robbers" (גדודים), so also in Micah the whole of the leadership of Judah (Zion) is addressed as בת־גדוד. The phrase frustrates the reader's expectations—not so much in its form (Hillers), but in its place in the pericope. At the same time, גדוד functions as a critique of those in power: Zion's exalted position does not lie in the quality of her leadership, but on the reputation of her God (cf. Mic 4: 2-4). Both the frustration and the critique are facets of humor's form and role.

The paradigmatic play between "Zion" and "marauder," however, is sublimated and emerges only after certain assumptions about the structure of the passage and the meaning of גדוד are accepted. The more overt play—the syntagmatic play—rests on the relationship between גדוד and תתגדדי (and the crux, the meaning of גדוד).

It is the accident of sound between גדוד and תתגדדי that creates the dissonance (and thereby the ludic effect), but it is this same accident of sound that causes the joke to become lost as a reader disambiguates the phonetically similar, but semantically dissimilar words.[21] The misapprehended etymological connection—תתגדדי coming to mean "assemble" based on its contextual proximity with גדוד, and גדוד having simple associations of "troop" rather than the more descriptive "marauder"—comes about not by the prophet, but by later interpreters who failed to catch the joke (helped, in part perhaps, by the preceding word of weal in 4: 13). A coincidental phonetic find becomes an inadvertent party to semantic gymnastics.

Thus, rather than being an anomaly requiring emendation (Hillers, *et al.*) or requiring exegetical gymnastics (the versions), the phrase functions as a clever play on a name and a behavior. The "pleasant surprise" comes in the recognition that גדוד plays off both תתגדדי and "Zion." Other epithets may have worked, but גדוד works both paradigmatically and syntagmatically, which, I feel, is doubly surprising and, therefore, increases its effect.

The understanding of the verse as a derogatory reference to the leadership of Jerusalem is further supported by the wordplay between שבט and שפט in the following colon. The "judge" (שפט, who may be the king), rather than "shepherding" the people with his "staff" (בשבטך; cf. Mic 7: 14), will be struck with a "rod" (בשבט).

CONCLUSIONS

In this passage, we find a juxtaposition of homographs not homonyms; disjunction rather than conjunction. A false unity is created by this juxtaposition, a misconstrual that corresponds to the false impression that the leaders of Jerusalem are בת־זיון, when in fact they are really בת־גדוד.

The wordplay is an example of a "denigration" joke, which is common in political humor. The "logic" of the joke, the opposing script, is that under "normal" circumstances, the political leadership of Jerusalem is referred to as בת זיון, but in the present circumstances, it is בת גדוד. גדוד "triggers" the opposing scripts, and works both paradigmatically and syntagmatically.

MICAH 1: 2-5: BACK TO THE BEGINNING

By and large the wordplays in Micah are not obvious ones; that is, the wordplays do not call attention to themselves. Indeed, even at Mic 1: 10-15, the obvious paronomastic plays are not the whole story, and what we find are more subtle plays involving sense and associations. Similarly, at Mic 4: 14, where one could argue that the wordplay is forced ("Troop together, O Troops"), our study suggests that the ostensive play is a mask for a deeper play.

Throughout this study I have suggested that since wordplays are easily overlooked, many of the passages require a re-reading—"retrospective redefinition" (Nowottny). Something in the text causes us to look back over something that was read too quickly or faintly heard at first, verbal sleights of hand where we say, "Let's see that one again."

In the light of these subtleties and the need for re-reading, I want to take a look at the opening passage of the book, Mic 1: 2-5, a passage not noted for its paronomasia or wit. In doing so, I want to suggest that Mic 1: 2-5 differs from Mic 4: 14 in that the humor is not compressed in the juxtaposition of paronomastic words, but in a chain of events that culminates with a morphological or syntactical play. The audience is set up through indirection in much the same way as Mic 4: 14 where "faulty logic" is exposed ("you think x , but, in fact, y"). The trigger is unusual syntax rather than an accident of sound and sense.

The opening oracle of Micah sets forth a number of important themes that are woven throughout the book. The passage presents few problems of translation, though historical-critical studies of the past one hundred years have found difficulty showing the compatibility of the oracle in vv 2-4 with the verses that follow.[22]

The problem of the pericope arises because v 2 appears to be against the nations, but v 5 specifies "Samaria" and "Jerusalem" as the object of the prophet's words (cf. Mic 1: 1; see also Isa 34 for a similar pattern). I would suggest that it is precisely this tension that creates the possibility of humor. In between the "set up" in v 2 and the "fall" in v 5, precious little is given to resolve the indeterminacy that produces the joke.

V 2 borrows language from a *Gerichtsrede* , a covenant lawsuit or legal dispute. "Hear" is frequent on the lips of the prophets, and in Micah we find it at the three major divisions of the book: 1: 2, 3: 1, and 6: 1.[23]

What follows the summons to hear gives rise to one of the few exegetical problems in the pericope. At 3: 1 (and 3: 9) the summons is followed by "heads of Jacob and leaders of the house of Israel." Here we have, "Hear you peoples all; Listen earth, and her fulness." To whom and to what do "peoples" and "earth" (or "land," אֶרֶץ) refer?

Some commentators argue that "peoples" refer to those living in the "land" (אֶרֶץ), that is, the "Israelites" (Kimchi). Others argue that "peoples" refer to all nations, and אֶרֶץ refers to the whole earth and not simply Palestine (Rosenmüller, Marti, J.M.P. Smith, Mays).

The latter option, the oracle being against all the nations, seems the simpler sense. For example, Ps 24: 1 reads: "The earth and her fulness belong to the

Lord; the world and all who dwell in her." This interpretation suggests that עמים should not be restricted to Israel, but refers to all the people of the earth. However, עמים can refer to the tribes of Israel, as in Hos 10: 14-15, "Therefore the tumult of war shall arise among your people (בעמך) ... Thus it shall be done to you, O house of Bethel" (RSV[24]). Moreover, "the earth and her fulness," refers to the land of Israel in Deut. 33: 16.

The indeterminacy, such as it is, comes about from the context more so than lexical considerations. Ostensibly the words עמים and ארץ efer to the nations and the whole earth, especially since "oracles against the nations" are suitable subjects for the prophets (cf. Amos 1-2). The immediate context however, does not preclude the possibility of a reference to "Israel," and the larger context supports the more restricted reference to Israel. Indeed, the indeterminacy of the initial words in this oracle is heightened by its present context, and its relation to the rest of the book and the parallel (allusion?) story of Micaiah ben Imlah (1 Kgs 22). First, Mic 1: 1, granted an editorial addition, states that Micah's vision concerns "Samaria and Jerusalem." Moreover, the parallel statements in 3: 1 and 3: 9 are addressed to the leaders of "Jacob" and "Israel," and 6:1 is an oracle against "his people." Finally, at 1: 5 we are told that "all of this"—presumably, vv 2-4—is because of the "transgression of Jacob and the sins of the house of Israel."

Ways exist to disambiguate the colon. The more precise "heads of Jacob and leaders of the house of Israel" serves that purpose well, or, conversely, "nations" (גוים) as in Isa. 34: 1, would equally identify the addressee more precisely. The oracle would then clearly be addressed to either the Israel or the people of the earth, and any uncertainty is resolved. However, the colon is ambiguous as it stands since either reference is *not excluded in the present context.* Disambiguation takes place with the reader, not by anything in the text itself.

The "ambiguity" of the initial verse continues with the subsequent verses. "The Lord will be a witness against *you* ." The antecedent to the sg. pron. suf. is "peoples," but "you" does not further specify the reference. Some commentators translate בכם as "among you" (G. A. Smith;[25] Keil), but the preposition can serve a number of semantic and syntactic functions; at Num 5: 13 ב- לעד means "against you," a meaning that accords well with this verse. Keil argues for "among you" on theological grounds: The Lord would not condemn a people to whom his word was not given. J.M.P. Smith turns the theological argument around: Micah would not conceive of Yahweh as a fellow witness with the nations against Israel; the wrath of Yahweh against Israel serves as a testimony against the nations "who are even more guilty." Thus, the phraseology of the colon, even in a broader "theological" context, does not eliminate the ambiguity of "peoples" or "land and its fulness" in the initial colon, and, indeed, may almost innocently perpetuate it.

A similar ambiguity occurs in the final colon of v 2 and the initial colon of v 3, both of which can be treated together. As with v 2, commentators fall into two camps. The easiest way to understand, "The Lord from his holy temple," is the temple in Jerusalem, as in Ps. 5: 7: "But I ... will enter thy house, I will worship toward thy holy temple" (RSV). However, the "holy temple" can refer to Yahweh's heavenly throne as well, as in Ps 11: 4: "The Lord is in his holy temple; the Lord's throne is in heaven" (RSV; perhaps also at Hab 2: 20 and Zech 2: 13).

In the following colon, where we might expect some clarification for the phrase "holy temple," we get, "The lord will go forth from his place." This second colon does little to resolve the uncertainty of the first. As with "peoples" and "earth" in v 2, the "b" colon appears less specific—or certainly not any more specific—than the "a" colon in the parallel statements.

We do find unambiguous terminology in other passages. For example, Amos 1: 2, a passage very similar to the present passage, reads; "The Lord roars from Zion and utters his voice from Jerusalem; the pastures of the shepherds mourn, and the top of Carmel withers" (RSV). And even at Mic 4: 1-2, we find a clear reference to the temple in Jerusalem; v 2 reads, "And many nations shall come, and say, 'Come, let us go up to the mountain of the Lord, to the house of the God of Jacob ...'" (RSV).

The uncertainty, as evidenced by the commentaries, regarding the addressee in the initial verse, continues through these subsequent lines regarding the abode of the Lord. If the addressee is Israel and Judah, then these lines have a provincial reference, the temple in Jerusalem (e.g., Pococke). If the addressee is the whole earth, it may be more reasonable to adopt a cosmological stance, the heavenly abode (e.g., Hillers, with qualifications). A careful balancing act is going on; the two possible readings are created in a context that moves back and forth between a nationalistic, earthly scene, to a universal, cosmic one.

At 1: 3 we find an unspectacular wordplay between ירד and דרך. This is not a usual word-pair, however, and difficulties arise. The LXX and 1QpMic omit the latter term (cf. also J.M.P. Smith and BHK). This emendation is resisted in more recent treatments (Allen, Mays, Wolff, and Hillers); the terms, so Hillers maintains, are appropriate in theophanic descriptions.[26] Moreover, the kind of wordplay, an anagrammatical alliteration, has parallels in Micah (e.g., 1: 10 גת / תג).[27]

The metaphoric language of v 4 is striking, almost catachretical—mountains melting and valleys being cleft. Indeed the language is unusual to the point that the LXX feels compelled to transpose the verbs "melt" and "shaken" (σαλευθήσεται for נמסו and τακήσονται for יתבקעו) so that the mountains will be shaken and the valleys melt like wax.[28] We are no longer confronted by ambiguity, but we are confronted by the imagery,[29] a reversal of the natural order before the presence of the Lord. There is little that we can call wordplay in this verse, unless one is inclined to extend wordplay to metaphor, but the words and images are artfully juxtaposed—balancing, reversing, and heightening the effect of the unusual imagery.[30]

The mountain imagery seems prompted by the phrase "Upon the *high places of* (במותי) the earth," which precedes it. Modern commentators take this interpretation as a literal reference to "heights" of the earth. Some earlier commentators understand "heights" metaphorically: "All that is highest, exalted in the land, or among the people ... towers, and strong places, their princes, and chief ones... ."[31]

Consideration of "high places" leads to the final verse of this study. 1: 5 is a connecting link between the theophanic vision (vv 2-4) and the laments over Samaria (vv 6-9) and Judah (vv 10-16). As a connecting link, this verse is very important, and, I would suggest, provides a "punch-line" for the "joke."

The Hebrew syntax is stark: בפשע יעקב כל־זאת, "For the transgression of Jacob all of this." This colon is paralleled by, "And for the sins of the house of Israel." No question remains whether the addressee is the "nations" or the "nation," nor is there any question why Israel is the addressee; she is addressed for her "transgression."

The final colon introduces another ambiguity, not an ambiguity of sense or referent, but of syntax. Most translators read מי as "what" rather than "who," the usual translation of the term. As early as Qumran there was an easing of the difficult syntax by substituting מה.[32] No exact parallel for this usage of מי exists, but Gen 33: 8 and Deut 4: 7 offer approximations; for example, Deut. 4: 7 כי מי גוי גדול would be translated into English as, "For what great nation... ." GKC §137 notes that "it [מי] is used of the neuter only when the idea of a person is implied." The words immediately following the interrogative pronoun, however, are "transgression" and "high place;" the "person" comes by way of personification, "Jacob/Samaria" and "Judah/Jerusalem."

Thus the total meaning of the sentence differs from the syntactical assertions: the syntax, although literal in its employment, becomes metaphoric in the context—"who" questions involve people, not things ("transgressions") or places ("Samaria").

Another unexpected feature occurs in the parallel colon. Parallel to "transgression of Jacob" is "high places of Judah." Both the pl. form (במות) and the term itself are problematical;[33] one "expects" a parallel term to the sg. פשע, perhaps one that forms a word-pair, חטא, as in the previous colon. Indeed, the LXX reads ἁμαρτία, supplying the expected word.

"High places" (במות), however, produces several effects. First, it is parallel to "sins" (ובחטאות) in the previous colon,[34] producing consonance. Moreover, as a parallel to both "sins" and "transgression," it defines the nature of the offence, the general and the particular, כלל ופרת.[35] Although condemnation of cultic high places is not uniformly carried out in the OT, cultic apostasy may well be the issue at stake (Mays). Furthermore, the term is retrospective, recalling the "heights" of 1: 3, where "heights" appears to refer to topographical heights.[36] Recall also that topographical and cultic connotations of במה are found at Mic 3: 12—a coupling of the literal and metaphorical.

"Coupling" also reminds us that wordplays not only fuse words, but link passages; this play sets the reader up for the play at 3: 12, or, once at 3: 12, the reader must retrace his or her steps to see the forest for the trees (the oracles may be part of a larger structure and are not isolated fragments). Similarly, חקשׁיבי in 1: 2 alliterates with וקציני in 3: 1, thus providing a link with another oracle.[37]

The effect of this play upon words (ambiguity, uncommon syntax, and "intertextuality"), I would argue, is cumulative. The oracles in Micah are against "Samaria and Jerusalem" as the superscription suggests. However, the indeterminate terminology introduces a counter-movement right at the beginning of his message that creates an extended context that is neither restrictive (Israel only), nor exclusive (the nations *sans* Israel).[38]

CONCLUSIONS

Micah begins by calling a "people" to witness against "you" and proclaiming a startling theophanic vision: the Lord is Sovereign over topography, even reversing the natural order ("mountains melting" and "valleys clefting") even as he is sovereign over the mundane as well ("water-troughs"[39] and "wax"). One possible reading of these initial words is to understand their function as phatic language; that is, the words are employed less to convey information and more to gain a hearing. Once the audience is lulled into listening (or set up through reading), a shift occurs. At the very beginning of the book lies a concealed trap; through the "web of words," the audience falls victim to the obvious: "As so often with deliberate ambiguity, there is a strong dose of pedagogical intent present here ... [the author] must resort to enigma, image, paradox, and even contradiction, to tease or shock the audience into giving thought to the obvious, and thus enable them to see what is staring them in the face."[40]

The ludic effect depends upon indirection, a certain chain of events that points in one direction while moving in another; the expectation is that the nations are being castigated (although that is never unequivocal—the audience may well "disambiguate" the words prior to the reverse being made obvious, of course). If the ambiguity is resolved before the "unmasking" of v 5, then the humor disappears. Who is the object of God's theophanic wrath sets up the opposing script, and the trigger is 1: 5, "Who?—You!"

CONCLUSIONS

The humor of wordplay results from the juxtaposition of linguistic items that trigger an incongruity or two opposing scripts. One script is ostensibly obvious ("more plausible" on a first reading), but the reader comes to recognize that a second script is present as well, and not only present, but "intended," nullifying the initial or more obvious reading. The surprise at this recognition produces "pleasure"; the reader delights at the economy of words that allows for two contrasting readings of the same material. The leaders in Mic 4: 14 are not בת־צִיּוֹן, but בת־גדוד; in Mic 1: 2-5, the Lord is not coming against the nations, but the Nation.

This way of looking at humor (and the text) also allows for us to explain why some readers miss the humor—indeed why most readers have failed to find any humor in the Bible. If a reader/critic does not accept the presence of two opposing scripts, then no possibility for humor exists. In the history of interpretation, we find that commentators go to great lengths to "disambiguate" the text—we, as readers and commentators of Scripture, explain away ambiguities and are often left with philological and archaeological notes, sometimes with a homily to satisfy the faithful. At best, a word or phrase is said to be "ironic," but no mention is made of "play" or "pleasure." Whitehead, though erroneous, has won the day by default: "The total absence of humor from the Bible ... is one of the most singular things in all of literature."[41]

CONCLUSION
WORDPLAY RE-BOUND

'I just want to say one word to you ... plastics."
                    Mr. McGuire to Benjamin, in "The Graduate"

Wordplay, like religion, is a particularly human devising: "If punning did not exist, man would have to invent it to save society from the rigour mortis of syntax."[1] Like Moses at the burning bush, theologians have sought to limit the phenomenon—wordplay is a mnemonic device; wordplay is a literary embellishment; wordplay is a figure of speech. But perhaps no fetter of the pun is as pervasive in biblical studies as the fixation on the phonological aspects of wordplay. Even the valuable studies of L. A. Schökel and Watson do not muffle these locutions since they subsume wordplay under the general rubric of "sound."[2] Outside the field of biblical studies, the fascination with phonetics is hardly voiced at all. In Exod 3: 12-14 God answers Moses with a pun, a mystery to explore,[3] but more so a direction, an activity;[4] follow the bouncing ball.[5]

Wordplay defies definition by its variability and indeterminacy. It is a slur, a stutter; a lisp or stammer—or a strikeover. A pun points in one direction and runs in another. Unless the reader recovers quickly enough, the pun vanishes around the bend. Puns are elusive.

Wordplay is not a precise "speech-act", it frustrates linguistic expectations or subverts logic. Hence wordplay is not only language, but play. Humor, that luxury reflex that separates us from our primogenitors, is an outgrowth of language used dissonantly. It spans mere play—no easy feat—to fecundity and pathos—expansive thought and intense emotion. Whether emphasis is on play or pathos, it seeks to alter the audience's state through compression of thought or expansion of vision, sometimes managing both. Wordplay is persuasive.

The present study, with its focus on Micah, was an attempt to point out the *elusiveness* of wordplay, but also to *point to* wordplay. Wordplays can be snatched. We found in Micah that the forms of wordplay are diverse, that "soundplay" is too limiting for what we find in the text. We also found that wordplay is more than "embellishment," that it functions variously in a pericope, functions of coherence and disjunction within and between pericopes. We also suggested that wordplay can be playful, often resulting in pointed, tendentious humour.

The study left much to do. First, I am sure that I have not exhausted the wordplays in Micah, either in form or function. More are to be discovered. Also, some of the observations will, no doubt, require some modification as we bring more precision to the recognition of the workings of wordplay. Second, the question of the "sound" of biblical Hebrew needs further examination— wordplay does involve soundplay and the subtleties of the soundplays are diverse and support various structural and affective function in a text. I still suspect, however, that the results of that enquiry will necessarily be tentative. Third, I consciously avoided reference to an "author" in this study, but obviously some author lies behind the text; therefore, the relationship between authorial style and text can be explored (see further in Appendix One). Finally, the relation of wordplay to the larger structure(s) of the book or the "allusions" to other books will benefit from further enquiry. These allusions, especially with their variations (a technique known as "hankadori"), are there, but what we can say about them is another question.

Some practical observations about how critics approach texts arise from this study as well. I want to suggest two. First, as critics we need to exercise caution in using wordplay to make or support conjectural emendations. Since wordplay does take a variety of forms, "predicting" what form a particular text "requires" seems hazardous. Second, and more important, as critics we need to realize that language (and thought) is not always transparent and univocal; perspicuity and a single meaning are not necessarily desirable features in a text. Tensions and ambiguities are occasions for breakthroughs in meaning.

In sum, wordplay involves the "infinite plasticity"[6] of sounds, words, images, and syntax. Like the cockroach and the shark, wordplay is pervasive and perdurable, lingering in dark corners or lurking in the deep, ready to serve, subvert, and work its power of persuasion.

APPENDIX ONE
CARREIRA, MICAH, AND STYLE

The foregoing study of wordplay in Micah needs some justification since J. Carreira has undertaken a detailed study of the trope in Micah already.[1] My critique of Carreira is twofold: (1). Carreira, while broadening the discussion and finding numerous wordplays that have gone unnoticed, still is working with a too narrowing defined view of wordplay. (2). More importantly, Carreira ties the trope too closely to a specific social situation (Wisdom). The following comments will help clarify both the present study and the critique of Carreira.

Most studies of wordplay by biblical critics are either quite general, selecting examples from different authors and genres, or highly specific, focusing on a particular instance of the trope (a word or pericope). A notable exception to that tendency is the study by J. Carreira on Micah. Carreira seeks to locate wordplay as an essential ingredient of the author's style and draws several important conclusions from this observation.

As a figure of speech, wordplay is part of an author's repertoire, the fonts he has to alter the image of his type. Writing of Chaucer's wordplays, Baum says, "These examples, moreover should not be taken as a collection of little jokes, but as a contribution to the study of Chaucer's style."[2] Wordplay is not extraneous to the message, but contributes to the overall effect of the author's program, both content and form, and reflects authorial choices.

"Wordplay," as a distinguishing feature of Micah's style, is one of the few things in Mican studies that is universally accepted. The famous lament over the destruction of the Judaean countryside in 1: 10-15 is the most notable example; however, Carreira contends that wordplay is not occasional, but frequent throughout the book. In addition to 1: 10-16, he finds instances of wordplay in 1: 6, 7, 8a, 9b; 2: 4-11; portions of chapter 3; 4: 8, 9, 12, 14; 5: 1, 3; and 6: 9-12. Thus wordplay runs throughout the whole book with the exception of chapter 7.[3]

Carreira draws two corollaries to the pervasiveness of wordplay in the book. Wordplay is very much a part of the author's style, indeed, not an isolated device, but a central part of how the author communicates his message. And, thus wordplay becomes an additional criterion for establishing authenticity: "Es ist an der Zeit, die Alliteration als zusätzliches Kriterium für die Ermittlung der Authentizität zu benutzen."[4]

For Carreira, then, the examination of wordplay has important implications for how we view the book and the prophet. The title of his article, "Kunstsprache und Weisheit bei Micha," indicates where he will eventually take his study, but before we address his ultimate destination, we need to examine what Carreira means by "Kunstsprache."

Carreira does not define *Kunstsprache* ; however, he does limit its scope by saying, "Micha ist ein Meister in Stilmittel des Wortspieles."[5] Through his comments on the text it becomes clear that "Wortspiel" is not defined strictly in terms of phonetics—assonance, alliteration, and the like—but encompasses semantics as well. An example will clarify what Carreira means by wordplay. At 1: 12 the play comes more with the sense than the tone. Two contrasting ideas play off the meaning of the two placenames, Maroth and Jerusalem. Maroth, *Verdruß* ("displeasure; vexation"), will not receive the *Glück* (לטוב) that she waits expectantly for, and Jerusalem,

Frieden ("peace"), is contrasted with *Unheil* (רע). After examining other texts, especially Mic 3: 12, Carreira comments, "Wortspiele mischen sich mit Sinnspielen."[6] It appears that *Wortspiel* is more than sound associations.

Sinnspiel , however, is a general term and does not carry the same sense that "pun" carries in our terminology or what Mahood and others usually mean when they say that wordplay may involve a play on the sense of a word. For Carreira, *Sinnspiel* is not polysemy or ambiguity; rather, it is a play based on paronomasia and a corresponding (often contrasting) connotation of the words that create an ironic effect. The play at 3:12 from which Carreira makes his remarks illustrates this distinction. There is assonance between בגללכם and לכן, and perhaps also between שדה and חחרש, and עיין and יער. The "sense-play" comes in the final colon. Since the Israelite temple (הבית) has turned into little more than a Canaanite shrine, a "high place" (לבמות), the punishment will fit the crime: the temple will be a במה, but not a cultic high place, as במה is often translated;[7] rather, it will be a (mountain) "height" (overgrowth)—as Carreira says, "ein wildes Gebüsch."

The emphasis for Carreira is not on the polyvalency of words (although that is not completely absent), but on the contrast between what the people are doing and expecting, and what Yahweh does contrary to their expectations. Carreira is correct in his ironic assessment of the words, but he makes no mention of the contrast between the literal meaning of the colon and the figurative undertones. The play is not only on הבית and לבמות, but on במה, "height/high place," and עיין, "rubble." The pun is set up by עיין, "plain," and then יער לבמות in the sense of uncultivated foliage, and carried through in the juxtaposition of הבית and לבמות with connotations of temple/shrines. The words are literal to the syntax but metaphoric in the overall sense of the passage.

Carreira, then, is still working within the rather well-established framework of phonetically based plays; indeed, the bulk of his examples are assonantic and alliterative plays, and the few instances of semantically based plays owe as much to irony as they do to the pun. Carreira comments not on ambiguity and disparate senses, nor "anguish" over the nature of language, but on consequences or opposing actions.

Many of Carreira's examples of assonance and alliteration are commonly recognized, as he himself acknowledges. These wordplays were recognized as early as the Middle Ages by such scholars as Ibn Ezra and Kimchi. For example, at 4: 14 the plays between תתגדדי and גדד, and between שבט and שפט, are usually recognized as paronomasia. Other plays, even within these generally recognized passages, have gone unnoticed. Carreira contends that at 4: 14 מצור plays off שם, especially with the sibilants, but also with the *mem*. Carreira finds further play in 5: 1 between אלפי and אפרתה, and between צעיר and יצא. In 4: 12 and 13, he points out paronomasia between קבצם and אשים, and between גרנה and קרנך.

Correspondences between certain letters in these words cannot be denied. Also, some of the plays may be "better" than others; Watson talks of "near-alliteration," which involves similar sounding consonants which are considered to be equivalent, and cites Casanowicz' list of consonants: א/ע; פ/ב; ג/כ/ק; ח/כ; ז/ס/ש/צ; ד/ט/ת.[8] However, do these correspondences mean that any corresponding terms with sibilants, gutturals, or perhaps laryngals form an alliterative wordplay? Carreira questions neither the consciousness of the author in these plays (may we assume that since Micah is a "master" of wordplay that these are consciously employed?); nor does he consider the "accidents" of language, especially a language that has a preponderance of sibilants, gutturals, and the like.[9]

Granted, alliteration need not have consonantal similarity in the initial syllables, and the alliterative words need not be adjacent, but, some consideration of position and proximity, as well as lexical choice available to the author, needs to be given. Two words in close proximity with similar sounding characters where one of the terms is a "rare" term that "replaces" a more common word would certainly increase the likelihood of deliberate paronomasia. (Is the phrase above— "Micah is a Master of wordplay"—a case of alliteration? Had it read, "Micah is a Master of monotonous mingling of words," we would recognize the deliberate alliteration, not the least because it is forced! Coarse wordplays such as that rub us the wrong way while subtle ones often slip by unnoticed.)

Casanowicz offers these criteria for establishing the existence of paronomastic plays: frequent occurrence (thus near formulaic, like word-pairs); unusual words; plays upon proper names; accumulation (which would indicate design); syntactically coordinated words (as opposed to subordinated); and a passage of "elevated" diction.[10] A.A. Hill offers criteria for what is *not* to be taken as a pun.[11] Among his suggestions we find: the "nonexistence" of the pun word (i.e., lexical evidence shows that the meaning required for the pun did not exist at the time of the writing); puns dependent upon foreign terms;[12] if the text is manipulated to produce the second meaning or the secondary meaning does not fit the "dramatic or emotional tone" of the passage; and if the pun relies on a narrow context that does violence to the larger context. These criteria are not exhaustive, but they suggest that distinguishing the presence of wordplay, whether paronomasia or pun, from "normal" composition is both necessary and possible.

Considerable freedom in creating paronomastic plays is likely. Nevertheless, some systematic and convincing examination of how and why it works is required. To find alliteration so prevalent, and so often entailing "partial alliteration," as Carreira does, requires a great deal of imagination—sinister steps on the stairway and not simply the creaking house of language as it cools in the night.

Recognizing the extent of alliteration is troublesome, especially with no hard and fast guide-lines to discriminate its presence from whatever occurs in language when it is not present. A potentially more serious problem with his analysis is the conclusion that Carreira draws from the observation that Micah uses wordplay extensively.

Carreira contends that wordplay is a central characteristic of Micah's style, and, therefore, that this style can have bearing on issues of authenticity. The correlation of style and authenticity is certainly permissible, but highly difficult to argue for; and Carreira has not produced the necessary evidence to correlate, unquestionably, wordplay, style, and authenticity in Micah.

Style is not a pointed subject, as Turner states: "Stylistics must therefore deal with a particularity it can never reach, ever indicating and lighting up what it cannot capture."[13] He suggests that choices are manifested in *parole* but described in reference to *langue* .[14] An element of choice is involved, and thus lexical examination is necessary; however, linguistic knowledge is insufficient since one must show how the word or phrase functions in the discourse. Thus H. G. Widdowson says: "In order to understand what it is that a writer is trying to express, we must know what means he is using in relation to the linguistic resources at his disposal.... . We must also know what ends are achieved in terms of the communicative effect of the language used."[15] Delineation of an author's style must make recourse to the function of the lexical and syntactical choices in the immediate context, and to the relationship between these choices and the extended context of the genre and larger linguistic setting.

Carreira has begun the study of Micah's style by identifying a linguistic trait in the text. However, much more needs to be done, especially in showing that wordplay is part of Micah's stylistic *choices*. Comparison with other literature of the period is necessary to show the element of choice,[16] yet the task is extremely difficult to achieve since the materials we possess are scant and since questions of historicity and authenticity easily turn to circular arguments.

Carreira carries this question of Micah's style one step further by asking the source of Micah's rhetorical style. Carreira locates the source in wisdom circles, as the title of his article indicates.

The rhetorical features Micah employs—alliteration, assonance, playing on words—stem, so Carreira argues, from a master teacher, a wisdom teacher. Carreira finds such a teacher in a "school": "Kunst und Kraft dieser Sprache setzen eine Auschildung, eine Schulung voraus."[17] Further support for his supposition that Micah's style come from a teacher is found in the "vetitive" and "prohibitive" statements that Micah's uses. These statements necessitate a school as well.

Carreira addresses the problem of where this school would be located and suggests that if it is not found in Moresheth-gath (Micah's supposed home-town), then in another city in the provinces: "Auch wenn Micha keine Schule in der Stadt Moreschet oder in den anderen Landstädten der Provinz Juda besuchen konnte, ist nich auszuschließen, da er eine Schule besucht hat."[18]

Carreira also reminds us of the wisdom influence on Amos and Isaiah, and gives examples of verbal affinities between Micah's words and wisdom terminology—false weights and measures and similar terms. Thus, the style, terminology, and wisdom influence on other prophets of the eighth-century B.C.E. place Micah in the general context of wisdom and schools.

The existence of schools, however, is not a foregone conclusion in pre-exilic Israel. J. Crenshaw argues that a considerable diversity existed in Israelite education, and preoccupation with schools "threatens to obscure this significant fact."[19] Once again, Carreira has identified an important feature of Micah's style, a particular linguistic trait, but moves beyond a formal element to construct a literary and sociological universe from that trait—wisdom schools. Moreover, in this case, Carreira does not account for alternative features—the presence, for example, of "prophetic" language and style (e.g., extensive use of direct address, especially with God as the one who addresses an "audience").

Even if we grant that wordplay is a stylistic trait of wisdom circles, alternative explanations are possible for how an author may have obtained his knowledge of the trope or how one might have put such a style to use. Kökeritz (on Chaucer) and Mahood (on Shakespeare) both show that these authors were aware of the rhetorical devices and schools of thought in their day, yet these scholars do not argue that either author was a rhetorician or formally trained in rhetoric. Rather, they locate the effective use of wordplay in common affairs, a colloquial background—what one would find in the "taverns": "Chaucer's play on words, then, as we have seen, is quite in accord with medieval rhetorical practices.... Yet, only a poet with a keen sense of humor like Chaucer could occasionally transform this formalized word-play into a display of wit, sometimes subtle, sometimes coarse.... [Some of Chaucer's puns reflect] the chit-chat of the office and the tavern, at streetcorners or in the marketplace."[20] A keen ear and wit, not a mentor, are necessary for creating wordplay.

In the absence of hard evidence, and the uncertainty of any biographical explanations when we know virtually nothing of the author and only little of his times, it is hazardous to depend upon the existence of schools to explain Micah's literary style. We are on safer ground to locate Micah's wit in the affairs of everyday life—at the "gates"—at least as a methodological starting point.

CONCLUSIONS

Carreira opens up the question of wordplay as a characteristic style of Micah, but has not adequately established a sufficient base for his argument and probably errs by locating the impetus for its use in wisdom schools. With so little concrete evidence to build upon, we must proceed with caution in arguing for the authenticity of the Mican texts on the basis of wordplay; nevertheless, linking style and authenticity is a legitimate enterprise.

My study of wordplay in Micah has focused on the phenomenon of wordplay rather than authorial style, not because authors have no importance, but because we can talk about the form and function of wordplay without adding the burden of introducing intentions or unrecoverable background information. Finding a historical Micah is the subject of another study.

APPENDIX TWO
WORDPLAY AND NOMINAL REALISM

The study of Mic 1: 10-15 raised a question that we did not anticipate: What is the relationship between wordplay, especially etymological wordplays such as we find in 1: 10-15, and nominal realism?

At the end of Allen's commentary, he makes this observation: "Micah is not playing clever word games for the amusement of his listeners. Words for him and his audience are a web of associations for good or ill, a prey of mystic spells, which in the adverse sense are akin to the irrational superstition that surrounds the number thirteen for many today."[1] Allen suggests that words are portents, an idea that is often carried further: words have power. Words as having power can be particularly evident or noticeable in texts where etymological connections—real or supposed—are made.

The supposed power of words in the OT has enjoyed a vigorous and influential life. Allen is only echoing what others have said more blatantly not only of the OT but of the ancient Near East (and "primitive" man or languages) generally.[2]

There is no doubt that names in biblical Hebrew often, if not always, have lexical significance: "The meaning of a Hebrew name is for the most part deliberate; it is religious in large measure, and the emotions it suggests are the solemnity and the joyfulness of the confidence in God."[3] The distinction between lexical significance and the efficacy of words is important for linguistics and theology: the one does not lead inevitably to the other in either case. Mic 1: 10-15 gives rise to such speculation, however, and lends itself to such analysis.

J. Fichtner's study is now over thirty years old. In recent years, a number of studies have challenged the facile relationship expressed between a word and the thing it signifies, or the word as having some inherent power. J. Barr, as we have come to expect, unmasks the false sentiments regarding this myth. Barr admits that some names may be regarded as powerful, and some usages, especially of God, come close to the sense of denoting the "essence" of someone or something—but "some" does not mean "all." A. Thiselton observes that convention and the "appropriateness" of the person are more important than the word itself. Words have power because they are employed "performitively" through certain conventions—e.g., blessings and curses. Or the appropriate power figure—God, the King, or a prophet—utters a word; thus, the word carries more weight than if a farmer from Tekoa utters it. The sociologist S. Tambiah writes: "Since words exist and are in a sense agents in themselves which establish connections and relation between both man and man, and man and the world, and are capable of 'acting' upon them, they are one of the most realistic representations we have of the concept of force which is either not directly observable or is a metaphysical notion which we find necessary to use."[4]

Barr, Thiselton, and Tambiah, who are suggesting that words often have significance, caution that one cannot translate that formal linguistic trait into a theory of language where words are efficacious and are part of a "primitive" mentality. Words are not neutral since they establish important relationships; but even "magical" thought or language has a referential and structural basis just as "scientific" language does.[5]

A recent field study by S. Scribner and M. Cole supports the more theoretical discussions of Tambiah, Barr, and Thiselton.[6] They examined the role of literacy on "metalinguistic" knowledge (explicit knowledge about language that one can articulate, not just knowledge about speech activity). In theory, one should expect literacy to increase metalinguistic knowledge, which, among other things, entails some understanding of the arbitrary relationship between a sign and the thing to which it refers. They found that metalinguistic knowledge was not unitary; that is, no significant correlation emerged between the various degrees of literacy or between one area of metalinguistic knowledge and another.[7]

Scribner and Cole give a detailed account of one man whose "test" indicated a high degree of nominal realism—the name and the thing, in this case "moon," were one and the same. Upon questioning him further, they found that he made distinctions between man-made and God-created objects; words and things were independent concepts. The correlation between a thing and the name given that thing was based on a theological understanding of the thing in question and did not reflect a linguistic phenomenon.

These studies by Thiselton, Barr, Tambiah, and Scribner and Cole suggest that correlations between a word and a thing are not necessarily tied to a theory of language and especially not to cognitive development, but reflect the complex interplay of any cultural belief system.

Concerning Mic 1: 10-15 we make the following observations. The plays on "Maroth" and "Achzib" give the strongest support for a theory akin to nominal realism. Ibn Ezra suggests that these names are "signs", and even Pocock hints at this notion as well. Moreover, the wordplays on "Zaanan" and "Mareshah" appear as etymological ones (even if falsely based, according to our understanding of Hebrew). Less obvious are "Beth-leaphrah" and "Moresheth-gath," though the lexical significance of the placenames "suggests" the counterpoint—wallowing in the dust of "Dust-town," and the fiancé of Gath will be given a dowry or divorce. "Shaphir" and "Beth-Ezel" are problematic since the intended pun—if there is one—is not obvious to us. Certainly the linguistic connection between the placename and the pun is lacking. Finally, the wordplay with "Lachish," which we do appear to understand, is based on phonological correspondences and irony, not on semantic equivalence or ambiguity.

Rather than words having an independent power, or some ontological connection with the thing signified, they appear to be evocative. The connotative associations evoke images that are either brought to the forefront—"in Staubenhausen (*Bet-le-afra*) walzt euch im Staube!" (Wolff)— or denied—צאנן יושבת יצאה לא, "Do not exit, O Inhabitant of Egress." Moreover, as with Lachish and perhaps Adullam, some association with the town itself, not the word, evokes an image.

At a minimum we can say that Micah is not working with a clearly defined or consistent practice of nominal realism. However, words do not appear as arbitrary signs either. Words are not so much portents as evocations—they have "connotative energy." We need to be wary of moving from a descriptive analysis of formal aspects of a language to a metalinguistic notion. In the absence of linguistic discourses about Hebrew in antiquity, such as we find in Greece or Rome (Varro), the metalinguistic observations must be tentative.

NOTES

PART I

Introduction

[1]I.M. Casanowicz, *Paronomasia in the Old Testament* (Boston: Norwood, 1894). This study is considered the classic treatment of the subject and continues to determine the tone of discussions about wordplay.

[2]By using "perdurable" I am, perhaps, giving too much corporeality to wordplay; however, writing is representational and we do speak of a "body of language."

[3]I am not using "trope" or "figure" in a technical sense in this study; I reserve these terms to cover "figures of speech" generally. B. Vickers, *Classical Rhetoric in English Poetry* (London: MacMillan, 1970), argues that "trope" works on the conceptual level and "figure" on the physical level, the "shape and structure of language," 86. Vickers' distinction has some merit, but I remain unconvinced that we can separate so facilely the conceptual framework from the structural. Indeed, Vickers himself, in discussing the functions of figures appeals to their "emotional" and "intellectual" power, and their "organic nature" with respect to literature, which implies work on some conceptual level, at least, of connotation if not denotation.

[4]E.S. McCartney, "Puns and Plays on Proper Names," *CJ* 14 (1919), 343-58.

[5]Cf. Casanowicz, *Paronomasia* : "It must, however, be borne in mind that in the older rhetoric these figures were not considered from the point of view of the similarity for its own sake, but rather as an element of the periodical structure, to mark the end, or help the recognition of its divisions," 1. This function is all but lost in Casanowicz' study of paronomasia in Hebrew Scripture.

[6]Cf. W. Redfern, *Puns* (Oxford: Blackwell, 1984), "While Aristotle valued highly the ability to recognize differences in apparently similar things and noted in his *Rhetoric* the effectiveness of jokes which depended on a shift in the meaning of a word, he also had reservations; he sensed danger" because of the lack of clarity that might result, 7.

[7]W.G.E. Watson, *Classical Hebrew Poetry* (Sheffield: JSOT, 1984), 222-250.

[8]L. Peeters, "Pour une interprétation du jeu de mots," *Semitics* 2 (1971/72), 134, 140, cf. also J. Friedrich, *Extinct Languages* (NY: 1957) who cites Egyptian hieroglyphs that symbolize by picture phonetically similar, but conceptually dissimilar items (cited in F. Ahl, *Metaformations* [Ithaca: Cornell University, 1985] , 19).

[9]R.H. Blyth, *Oriental Humor* (Tokyo: Hokusiedo, 1959), 1-15.

[10]J. Huizinga, *Homo Ludens* (Boston: Beacon, 1955 [reprint]), 122.

[11]Ibid., 136-37, but also more generally the whole of the chapter entitled, "Mythopoiesis," 136-45; see also Redfern, *Puns*, 33-37 and 163 for references to puns in African cosmologies.

[12]R. Frank, "Some Uses of Paronomasia in Old English Scriptural Verse," *Speculum* 47 (1972), 209-13.

[13]Casanowicz, *Paronomasia* , contends that the phrase in Gen 1:1 was "unavoidable" and therefore not an instance of paronomasia, 26; however, E. König, *Stilistik, Rhetorik, Poetik in Bezug auf*

die biblische Litteratur (Leipzig: 1900) makes a rejoinder to this omission on Casanowicz' part and cites Hos 1:2 (תחלת דבר־יהוה בהושע) as an alternative possibility, 287.

[14]Casanowicz, *Paronomasia* , 36.

[15]C.J. Ackerley, "'In the Beginning was the Pun': Samuel Beckett's *Murphy* , " *AUMLA* 55 (1981), 15-22; Ackerley says at one point, "Janus-like, the pun faces both creation and chaos," 19.

[16]C.K. Barrett, *The Gospel According to John* (2d ed.; Philadelphia: Westminster, 1978), 544.

[17]Cf. E. Richard, "Expressions of Double Meaning and Their Function in the Gospel of John," *NTS* 31 (1985), 96-112, for a discussion of the objections to Barrett's understanding and possible responses to them. See specifically, R. Schnackenburg, *The Gospel According to St. John* , vol. 3 (London: Burnes & Oates, 1982) who rejects Barrett's interpretation, and R. Brown, *The Gospel According to John: xiii-xxi* (Garden City: Doubleday & Co., 1970) who rejects a double meaning as well.

[18]W.L. Holladay, "Form and Word-play in David's Lament over Saul and Jonathan," *VT* 20 (1970), 153-189; see also M. Dahood, *Psalms II: 51-100* (Garden City: Doubleday, 1968).

[19]Line 344 as cited by Frank, "Scriptural Verse," 218-20.

[20]J. Swift, "The Dying Speech of Tom Ashe" cited by Redfern, *Puns* , 126.

[21]J. Crosbie, *Dictionary of Puns* cited by Redfern, *Puns* , 127.

[22]The present study will show that Casanowicz has defined wordplay too narrowly for the varied types of the trope throughout the OT; also, in spite of the immense value of Casanowicz' study, there will always be disputed areas; e.g., Gen 1:1.

[23]C.J. Fordyce, "Puns on Names in Greek," *CJ* 28 (1932-33), 44-46.

[24]J. Culler (ed.), *On Puns* (NY: Blackwell, 1988); but see the article by D. Fried ("Rhyme Puns") who cautions about assigning too much significance to puns.

[25]G.R. Driver, "Playing on Words," *Proceedings of the 4th World Congress of Jewish Studies* , vol. 1 (Jerusalem: World Union of Jewish Studies, 1967), 121, *passim*.

[26]One cannot neglect a theory of language when dealing with wordplay, but in the current debate over theories of language, I remain skeptical that we can find a satisfactory theory of language (cf. G.P. Baker and P.M.S. Hacker, *Language, Sense and Nonsense* [Oxford: Blackwell, 1984]) and that endeavor is better suited for a philosopher of language rather than a biblical theologian with a proclivity for working with peripheral issues. Moreover, and in a more positive light, the humorous side of wordplay is often neglected, and never more so than in biblical studies, so focus on the play element is justified.

[27]A. Guillaume, "Paronomasia in the Old Testament," *JSS* 8-9 (1963-64), 282-90.

[28]J.M. Sasson, "Wordplay in the OT," IDBSup, 968; cf. also, B. Beitzel, "Exodus 3:14 and the Divine Name: A Case of Biblical Paronomasia," *TrinJ* (n.s.) 1 (1980), 5.

[29]J.J. Glück, "Paronomasia in Biblical Studies," *Semitics* 1 (1970), 50.

[30]J.H. Charlesworth, "Paronomasia and Assonance in the Syriac Text of the Odes of Solomon," *Semitics* 1 (1970), 13

[31]M. Black, *An Aramaic Approach to the Gospels and Acts* , 3d ed. (Oxford: Oxford University, 1967), 160.

[32]H. Kökeritz, "Rhetorical Word-Play in Chaucer," *PMLA* 69 (1954), finds plenty of examples of "confusion" and "lack of precision" in defining terms in post-classical textbooks on rhetoric, 943.

[33]In order to disentangle the confusion regarding the distinction between paronomasia, pun, and wordplay, I, somewhat hopefully, looked at the *Dictionary of Confusing Words and Meaning* (ed. by A. Room, London: RKP, 1985), which, under the entry "pun/riddle/conundrum," helpfully offered, "a 'pun' is a play upon words."

[34]L. Spitzer, "Pun," *Journal of English and Germanic Philology* 49 (1950), 354.

[35]Redfern, *Puns* , 16.

[36]Casanowicz, *Paronomasia* , adopts paronomasia as the comprehensive term, based, he avers, on

ancient rhetoric and traditional use, 4, note 4. Since his study is restricted to "figures of sound," he is correct. Our argument, however, is that his whole enterprise is too narrowly based to do justice to these diverse figures of speech and writing, so we are justified in seeking a different term, one more comprehensive.

Chapter 1

[1]Redfern, *Puns* , is quoting Jennings (ed.), *Pun Fun* (Feltham: Hamlyn, 1980) but not with approval, 28.

[2]Casanowicz, *Paronomasia* , 4.

[3]Ibid., 12.

[4]M. Mahood, *Shakespeare's Wordplay* (London: Methuen, 1957), 7.

[5]See, e.g., Kökeritz, "Chaucer,"; Frank, "Scriptural Verse." Frank sets out to examine the deliberate "playing with the sound of key words," but in his discussion of these words he comments on the "ironic and startling collocation of sound and sense," 210.

[6]H. Wildberger, *Jesaja* (Neukirchen-Vluyn: Neukirchener, 1982).

[7]R.E. Clements, *Isaiah 1-39* (Grand Rapids: Eerdmans, 1980).

[8]O. Kaiser, *Isaiah 13-39* (Philadelphia: Westminster, 1974).

[9]In a noteworthy comment, Casanowicz, *Paronomasia* , contends that Isa 28:10 does not contain paronomasia for its effect; rather, the effect is created by the sense, 26.

[10]Holladay, "David's Lament," 157.

[11]To Casanowicz' credit, he recognizes the dangers of studying paronomasia by foreign readers or in a dead language; "It must be borne in mind ... that since paronomasia exists for the ear, not for the eye, harmonies of sound may be overlooked by the reader of a foreign, and especially of a dead, language," 27.

[12]Professor David Gunn has pointed out that "wind" in connection with "spring of action" (as in a clock) does suggest the verb (and hence a pronunciation that would rhyme); however, as it stands grammatically in the sentence, the pronunciation as the noun is required. This example illustrates some of the many possibilities of sound and sense, as well as syntax, combining with the playfulness of language, but within the constraints of the particular language system. A similar "rhyme" was used with great fun in the musical, *Babes in Arms* , 1938 version (lyrics by Lorenz Hart): "Folks go to London and leave me *behind* /I'll miss the crowning, Queen Mary won't *mind* /I won't play Scarlett in "Gone With the *Wind* "/that's why the lady is a tramp."

[13]E.A. Havelock, *The Muse Learns to Write* (New Haven: Yale University, 1986) argues that simply the creation of an alphabet by the Phoenicians produced ambiguity: "Drastic economy [i.e., an alphabetic sign for the previous phonetic signs] ... was purchased at the price of drastic ambiguity," 60.

[14]Frank, "Scriptural Verse," 215.

[15]Watson, *Poetry*, 222, quoting J. Culler, *Structuralist Poetics*, 65

[16]Hermann Ebbinghaus, a psychologist noted for his investigation of learning and memory, devised an experiment with nonsense syllables. He found that forgetting the list of syllables occurred rapidly in the first few hours after learning the list and more slowly after a period of time. A further discovery, one germane to our study, was that association aided memory; syllables that most approximated what the learner knew were more easily retained than those with no correspondence. This suggests that it is not indiscriminate sound patterns that are most meaningful (or even euphonious), but those where associations can be made. A nonsense consonant cluster, like one would find in a bad science fiction novel to represent alien speech, is neither meaningful nor pleasing in most cases, but many find the nonsense verse of Lewis Carroll, for example, delightful. See also B. Hrushovski, "The Meaning of Sound Patterns in Poetry," *Poetics Today* 2 (1980), 39-56.

[17]A. Berlin, *The Dynamics of Biblical Parallelism* (Bloomington: Indiana University, 1985), 64-72.

[18]A.R. Millard argues that writing was not uncommon in ancient Israel, therefore, again, the aural aspects of Hebrew literature cannot dominate the discussion without some justification. For Millard's discussion, see "The Practice of Writing in Ancient Israel," *BA* 35 (1972), 195-98, and "The Question of Literacy," *BRev* 3 (1987), 22-31.

[19]R.D. Roberts, *How Poetry Works* (Harmondsworth: Penguin, 1986), 13-7.

[20]See I. Yeivin, *Introduction to the Tiberian Masorah* (Missoula: Scholars, 1980), 47.

[21]Ibid., 48.

[22]See M. Jastrow, *A Dictionary of the Targumim ...* (New York: Judaica, 1975).

[23]Casanowicz, *Paronomasia* , 14-17.

[24]Charlesworth, "Odes," 13; 22.

[25]Henry Peacham in *The Garden of Eloquence* (1577) names and defines 184 rhetorical figures, as reported by H.F. Plett, "Rhetoric," in *Discourse and Literature* , Dijk, T.A. van, ed., (Amsterdam: John Benjamins, 1985), 59-84. Plett suggests that his model may produce even more varieties.

[26]Mahood, *Shakespeare* , 19.

[27]Ibid., 24.

[28]The citations come from Mahood's text; see Ibid., 9, for her sources and method of citation.

[29]Ibid., 26; for more "unspoken" puns, see also D. Fried, "Rhyme Puns," in *On Puns* , 92.

[30]J. Rosenberg, "1 and 2 Samuel," in *The Literary Guide to the Bible* , edited by R. Alter and F. Kermode (Cambridge, Mass.: Belnap, 1987), 139. Rosenberg also observes that the whole scene recalls the purchase of the Cave of Machpelah by Abraham. Allusions in wordplays are often strong, but do not always catch the imagination of commentators.

[31]Mahood, *Shakespeare* , 41.

[32]Ibid., 30.

[33]Ibid., 29.

[34]Ibid., 41.

[35]Ibid., 45.

[36]Ibid., 55.

[37]"the most characteristic feature of modern linguistics ... [is] that each language is regarded as a *system of relations* (more precisely, a set of interrelated systems), the elements of which—sounds, words, etc.—have no validity independently of the relations of equivalence and contrast which hold between them," J. Lyons, *Introduction to Theoretical Linguistics* (Cambridge: Cambridge University, 1968), 50. I would emphasize language in terms of relations and less in terms of a system if by system one thinks of closure. Language is regulative, but not rule-governed; deviation does not stop the "system" from functioning.

[38]Term comes from Nash, *Rhetoric: The Wit of Persuasion* (Oxford: Blackwell, 1989), though I am using it in a slightly different way than he does.

[39]R.B. Chisholm, "Wordplay in the Eighth-Century Prophets," *BibSac* 144 (1981), uses "implicit polysemantic wordplay" for this variety, and "explicit polysemantic wordplay" for a term repeated with different senses, 44-45; he bases his terminology on the work of Ullmann, *Semantics* .

[40]I prefer "paronym" to the often used *figura etymologica* since the latter may carry a misleading implication of shared origins whereas the former term is more general and encompasses either origin or simply words that sound alike (e.g., "pair" and "pear"). A paronym is both pun and paronomasia (thus showing the fluidity of the figure).

[41]Casanowicz, *Paronomasia* , 7.

[42]Ibid., 7.

[43]Driver, "Playing," 121.

[44]Casanowicz, *Paronomasia*, 13.

[45]Driver, "Playing," 122.

[46]Ahl, *Metaformations*, 18.

[47]Ibid., 19.

[48]S.A. Handelman, *The Slayers of Moses* (Albany: SUNY, 1982), 89.

[49]Ibid., xiv.

[50]Frank, "Scriptural Verse." Handelman's approach to rabbinic texts is also found in *Midrash and Literature*, edited by G.H. Hartman and S. Budick (New Haven: Yale University, 1986). For a critique of this approach, see H. Eilberg-Schwartz, "Who's Kidding Whom?: A Serious Reading of Rabbinic Word Plays," *JAAR* 55 (1988), 765-788. A more pointed critique is found in W.S. Green, "Romancing the Tome: Rabbinic Hermeneutics and the Theory of Literature," *Semeia* 40 (1987), 147-68, and J. Neusner, *Wrong Ways and Right Ways in the Study of Formative Judaism* (Atlanta: Scholars Press, 1988), 31-92.

[51]Casanowicz, *Paronomasia*, 4.

[52]Driver, "Playing," 121, 124, 127.

[53]Sasson, "Wordplay," 968.

[54]Glück, "Paronomasia," 78—is "pun" a "lower" form of wordplay and not "elevated diction"?

[55]Black, *Aramaic Approach*, 185; cf. I.H. Eybers, "The Use of Proper Names as a Stylistic Device," *Semitics* 2 (1971-72): The use "probably assisted those who heard the prophecy to remember it better," 82, and again, "In all these cases the pun was probably employed to emphasize the message, to facilitate remembering it and to heighten the effect," 92; and Beitzel, "Divine Name," says that paronomasia heightens the effect of "solemn" pronouncements and "permanently and indelibly" impresses the "proclamation upon the memory of an audience," 6.

[56]T. Rajan, "The Supplement of Reading," *NLH* 17 (1986), 593. Paul de Man's statement is, "Considered as persuasion, rhetoric is performative, but when considered as a system of tropes, it deconstructs its own performance," *Allegories of Reading* (New Haven: Yale University, 1979), 131.

[57]Cf. C. Perelman, *The Realm of Rhetoric* (Notre Dame: University of Notre Dame, 1982): "The aim of argumentation is not to deduce consequences from given premises; it is rather to elicit or increase the adherence of the members of an audience to theses that are presented for their consent," 9, and then, "Argumentation is intended to act upon an audience ... " 11. Noteworthy also is C.C. Arnold's introductory comments to Perelman's work: "What is new in Perelman's analysis is his notice that claims to rationality are embedded in a number of verbal structures that have heretofore been treated as exclusively ornamental or dispositional," ix.

[58]Casanowicz, *Paronomasia*, claims that Greek is more moderate than Latin, German has less than English, but French exceeds them all in the use of wordplay, 13. It would appear, however, that McCartney's ("Proper Names") evidence counters Casanowicz' claim that Greek and Latin have some substantive difference with respect to wordplay; apparently neither Greek nor Latin were lacking in their employment of the device; cf. also Ahl, *Metaformations*.

[59]Driver, "Playing," 122.

[60]Ibid., 124.

Chapter 2

[1]"Sophisticated" as opposed to "*mere* embellishment," "jingling of sounds," and other more or less derogatory epithets used to describe wordplay. Even a "feeble" pun or paronomasia displays some linguistic virtuosity and analytical thinking (drawing analogies between any two items is a move towards abstract thought, at the very least).

[2]L.G. Heller, "Toward a General Typology of the Pun," *Language and Style* 7 (1974), 271-82.

[3]Since Heller argues that one mark performs two potential functions in a text, we must assume that

this formula applies to the genres he mentions as well.

[4]Heller, "Typology," says, "And a knowledge of its dynamic processes offers important insights into the nature of reasoning itself," 271.

[5]Heller makes this remark: "Down through the ages the pun has served as the object of disparaging remarks and 'Oh-no-how-could-you' comments, but this fact has done little to discourage its use, and indeed, many of the greatest writers of all time (e.g., William Shakespeare) have employed the pun with great relish" (271). Many inspectors of puns feel the need to justify their investigation of the trope, which suggests a widespread ambiguous attitude to the device. It should not be surprising that mixed attitudes accompany this trope that celebrates ambiguity (whether of sound or sense).

Obviously the relationship between wordplay and cognition goes well beyond the scope of our purposes here, but some linguists and psychologists follow this avenue of investigation; from the stand-point of psychology, cf., e.g., M.T. Motley, "What I Meant to Say," *Psychology Today* February (1987), 24-28, and the bibliography cited in that journal, 64; several of the essays in *On Puns* (edited by J. Culler) touch on the relationship between psychoanalysis and the pun as well.

[6]Heller, "Typology," 271.

[7]J. Brown, "Eight Types of Puns, " *PMLA* 71 (1956), 14-26.

[8]It is worth noting that the studies by Heller and Brown support the contention that wordplay is not limited to soundplay and that the latter is subordinate to the former in analyzing wordplay. For example, Brown records that some think of pun only in terms of sound: a pun is "a pistol let off in the ear" and has "an ear-kissing smack with it." He objects to this caricature: "Any hearing on the pun must first admit the pun effect, which precedes analysis and shows that we distinguish the pun semantically, not aurally" (14). Thus the phonological fixation of biblical scholars, it seems, is not shared by others who study wordplay; what is required, then, and what I am arguing for, is a view of wordplay where lexical ambiguities and phonological correlations work side-by-side, with semantic analysis being the weightier matter of wordplay.

[9]Brown, "Eight Types," 26.

[10] Ibid., 26.

[11]While Heller is helpful with certain typological distinctions between puns, he does introduce a non-helpful vocabulary—"retentional disambiguation" and the like. This terminology lacks clarity and luster, and we can safely dispose of the incommodious language.

[12]L. G. Kelly, "Punning and the Linguistic Sign," *Linguistics* 66 (1970), 5-11.

[13]Ibid., 10.

[14]Peeters, "Jeu de mots," 127-29.

[15]While wordplay may go *against* the conventions of language, I would hesitate to say that it *breaks* the conventions of language; wordplay stretches and explores the conventions in creative and peculiar ways. Cf. P. Farb, *Word Play: What Happens When People Talk* (NY: Bantam, 1975): "True word play employs linguistic virtuosity while still operating within the general framework of a language's rules," 113.

[16]Peeters, "Jeu de mots," 131.

[17]Ibid., 135; it is also an example of wordplay used to denote reversal with Yahweh as the counter-punster; see the remarks below on Mic 2: 1-4; 6-11.

[18]A. Thau, "Play with Words and Sounds in the Poetry of Max Jacob," *Revue des Lettres Modernes* 336-339 (1973), 125-154.

[19]Cf. M. Greenberg, *Ezekiel 1-20* (NY: Doubleday, 1983), 148, and W. Zimmerli, *Ezekiel 1* (Philadelphia: Fortress, 1979), 195.

[20]A.R. Ceresko, "The Function of Antanaclasis ... in Hebrew Poetry, Especially in the Book of Qoheleth," *CBQ* 44 (1982), 568.

[21]Ibid., 569.

Chapter 3

[1]Casanowicz, *Paronomasia* , 6.

[2]Baum, "Chaucer's Puns," *PMLA* 71 (1956), 227, emphasis added.

[3]Watson, *Poetry,* 237.

[4]Some wordplays are inadvertent; however to say that wordplays are inadvertent does not change the fact that wordplay is "exploiting" the ambiguity of language—an inadvertent wordplay takes advantage to the inherent ambiguity of language on a subconscious level; cf., Motley, "What I Meant to Say": "Almost any time we wish to express a thought, we choose from several roughly equivalent verbal possibilities. Sometimes competition between these choices, or indecision about them, results in a slip of the tongue. This explanation has an intuitive appeal, at least in the case of some errors," 26.

It matters little for our discussion of wordplay whether the trope is consciously employed or not. The connections are present through the varied relationships possible in language use. These associations are largely subjective, but once made, become obvious or at least recognized as possibilities. Moreover, by allowing for "inadvertent" wordplays, we can circumvent the problem of positing authorial intention in every case of wordplay. Inadvertent wordplays recognize the role of the audience in "recognizing" or "making distinct" ambiguities. Thus, wordplays may be found that were "unintentional" or they may go unnoticed. The text, however, initiates the play, whether nascent in the author or exploited by the reader.

[5]S. Ullmann, *Semantics: An Introduction to the Science of Meaning* (Oxford: Blackwell, 1962), 168. One may question whether the "machine" of language really "breaks down," or whether language is simply more than a machine and Ullmann's metaphor breaks down at this point.

[6]Ibid., 188.

[7]Kelly, "Punning," 10.

[8]Guillaume, "Paronomasia," 286.

[9]Driver, "Playing," 121.

[10]Glück, "Paronomasia," 50.

[11]Sasson, "Wordplay," 968.

[12]Driver, "Playing," 121.

[13]In a "Honeymooners" T.V. sketch, Ralph (Jackie Gleason) has been upbraiding Alice (Audrey Meadows) about her stupidity. Alice, an early feminist, retorts by casting doubt on Ralph's intelligence. Ralph (too) quickly counters: "I'm as smart as you're, stupid!" Is that really what Ralph wants to say?

[14]Sister Miriam-Joseph, *Shakespeare's Use of the Arts of Language* , (NY: Hafner, 1966), 171.

[15]Charlesworth,"Odes," 16-17.

[16]Ibid., 20.

[17]Kelly, "Punning": "Especially when, as is characteristic of one sub-type of pun, the sign itself has to be tampered with to carry the load imposed," 10. The problem is focusing on the one sub-type of pun. Indeed, Kelly's earlier example, "Australians are the finest people in the world because they were chosen by the best judges in England," comes about only by the context. The pun hinges on two meanings of "judge" (legal/connoisseur), but the context creates the ambiguity, not the word itself. "Finest" and "best" suggest the meaning "connoisseur" for "judge"; it is only the extra-lexical information that we bring to the sentence that tips off the pun—the "judges" who "choose" the "Australians" were criminal judges [were they judges of criminals or were their judgments "criminal"?]. Kelly acknowledges these points when he discusses this example but seems to ignore it in his concluding comments.

[18]Thau, "Max Jacob," 127.

[19]Baum, "Chaucer," 227.

[20]D.A. Cruse, *Lexical Semantics* (Cambridge: Cambridge University, 1986), 49-68; *passim* ;

Cruse also speaks of non-lexical ambiguity, 66-68.

[21]W. Empson, *Seven Types of Ambiguity* , 3d ed. (NY: New Directions, 1966), 1.

[22]W. Nowottny, *The Language Poets Use* (NY: Oxford University, 1962), 152; see also, G.W. Turner, *Stylistics* (Harmondsworth: Penguin, 1973), 101-103.

[23]Nowottny, *Language* , 147.

[24]Ibid., 149.

[25]Ibid., 152, emphasis added.

[26]Ibid., 156; Mahood, *Shakespeare* , uses a equally delightful phrase for similar purposes: "Augustan cult of correctness," 10.

[27]Baum, "Chaucer," 227.

[28]See A. Hamori, "Notes on Paronomasia in Abu Tammam's Style," *JSS* 12 (1967), 87-88.

Chapter 4

[1]Driver, "Playing," 121; this could lead to the kind of thing Ahl, *Metaformations*, finds where scholars will emend lines since they do not think the original should contain them, 44.

[2]Driver, "Playing," 129, emphasis added.

[3]Sasson, "Wordplay," 970.

[4]Mahood, *Shakespeare* , 17.

[5]Casanowicz, *Paronomasia* , 11.

[6]P.P. Saydon, "Assonance in Hebrew as a Means of Expressing Emphasis," *Bib* 36 (1956), 37.

[7]Ibid., 49.

[8]Guillaume, "Paronomasia," 282.

[9]Chisholm, "Wordplay," 45.

[10]See Eilberg-Schwartz, "Rabbinic Word Plays," 770.

[11]Driver, "Playing," 124.

[12]Guillaume, "Paronomasia," 283.

[13]Ibid., 283.

[14]Ibid., 283.

[15]Watson's examples are found in, *Poetry,* 246.

[16]M.-Joseph, *Shakespeare* , 165, quoting F. Wilson, "Shakespeare and the Diction of Common Life," *Proceeding of the British Academy* 27 (1941), 14.

[17]Vickers, *Classical Rhetoric* , 93-121.

[18]Nowottny, *Language* , 139-40.

[19]Vickers, *Classical Rhetoric* , 121.

Chapter 5

[1]Mahood, *Shakespeare* , 29.

[2]Thau, "Max Jacob," 154.

[3]Ackerley, "Beckett," 19.

[4]Ibid., 20. In Ovid's *Metamorphoses* a similar progression from *chaos* to *caelum* occurs ("Celia" = celestial), which, Ahl, *Metaformations* , argues, is based on a supposed derivation of "caelum" from "chaos" (Varro has *cavum* as a mediating term), 25

[5]Casanowicz, *Paronomasia* , 14.

[6]"Irony" occasional occurs, but one looks nearly in vain for the terms "humor" or "play" in the essays by Driver, Sasson, Glück, and even Watson. Sasson, "Wordplay," does say, "There were also times when Hebrew wordplays expressed a spirit of playfulness" but gives no examples, 968,

and Watson, *Poetry* , says that wordplay may be used to "amuse" but also gives no examples, 245.

[7]Peeters, "Jeu de mots," 129.

[8]It was not always the case that wordplay is disparaged; cf. Sister M.-Joseph, *Shakespeare* , who remarks, "Therefore to play upon the various meanings of a word represented an intellectual exercise, a witty analysis commended and relished by Aristotle, practised by Plato and by the great dramatists of Greece, esteemed and used by Cicero, employed by medieval and Renaissance preachers in their sermons, regarded as rhetorical ornament by Elizabethans, but frequently despised as false or degenerate wit from the eighteenth century to the present day," 164. These remarks require qualification (e.g., Aristotle raised doubts about the use of wordplay), but as a generalization her point is well-taken.

[9]J. Addison, *The Spectator* , May 10, 1711, 229. Further on he says, "But when this distinction [between puns and true wit] was once settled, it was very natural for all Men of Sense to agree in it," 230; this sentiment seems to be a form of cultural chauvinism to be sure.

[10]Ahl, *Metaformations* , 44.

[11]Peeters, "Jeu de mots," 127.

[12]Heller, "Typology," 271.

[13]A. Pope, "God's Revenge *Against* Punning," in *Prose Works* , vol. 1 (Oxford: 1936), 270.

[14]H.W. Fowler, *A Dictionary of Modern English Usage,* (2d Edition, revised by Sir E. Gowers; Oxford: Oxford University, 1965), 492.

[15]See J. Morreall (ed.), *The Philosophy of Laughter and Humor* (Albany: SUNY, 1987), 4-7.

[16]Ibid., 5-6, and more extensively, Morreall, *Taking Laughter Seriously* (Albany: SUNY, 1983), 4-37; see also, Raskin, *Mechanisms of Humor* , 30-41; and see C.P. Wilson, *Jokes. Form, Content, Use, and Function* (London: Academic Press, 1979), 9-19, for a different way of classifying theories of humor.

[17]Morreall, *Philosophy* , 14, quoting from *Poetics,* ch. 5, 1449a.

[18]Ibid., 19, quoting from *Leviathan,* pt. 1, ch. 6, in *English Works,* vol. 3, (ed. Molesworth).

[19]Ibid., 108, quoting from *The Physiology of Laughter.*

[20]Ibid., 65, quoting from *Lectures on the English Comic Writers.*

[21]In addition to the two volumes on humor, Morreall has written, *Analogy and Talking About God* , also published by SUNY.

[22]Morreall, *Laughter* , 39.

[23]Wilson, *Jokes,* 19-31; he also cites "activity" and "excitement" as accompanying feelings, 150-55.

[24]Raskin, *Mechanism* , 99-147.

[25]M. Douglas, "The Social Control of Cognition: Some Factors in Joke Perception," *Man* 3, n.s. (1968), 372.

[26]W. Nash, *The Language of Humour* (NY: Longman, 1985), 126.

[27]Ibid., 10, quoting M. Bishop in *The Penguin Book of Comic and Curious Verse,* (J.M. Cohen, ed.,; London: Penguin Books, 1952).

[28]Nash, *Language* , 127.

[29]Ibid., 128.

[30]Ibid., 127.

[31]Douglas, "Cognition," 373.

[32]Morreall, *Philosophy,* 203.

[33]Nash, *Language,* 137. Cf. also Mahood, *Shakespeare* : "Most of the witty wordplay in Shakespeare is either wanton or aggressive. The liveliest exchanges are between those pairs of lovers who fight their way to the altar, for their wordplay is doubly tendentious in being at once both hostile and seductive," 30.

PART II

Introduction

[1]For example, the investigation of the wordplay in Mic 4: 14 and its relationship to Matt 2: 6 in the present study was published in *JETS* 33 (1990) under the title, "An Even Closer Look at Matt 2: 6 and Its OT Source." The title does not mention wordplay and therefore someone investigating wordplay would not necessarily examine the article or know that its primarily concern is wordplay.

[2]"Micah" will be used generically throughout this study for what we find in the text. An "author" lies behind the text, but whether that author is one person or a group, or whether that author is the historical Micah is not assumed nor argued for in this study.

[3]To which an inveterate punster would add, "The world needs more lerts."

[4]Raskin, *Mechanism* , says that "native speakers are potentially aware of the ambiguity but are typically unable to realize both of the meanings at the same time" because an "obvious" context eliminates any optional ones, 64; see also, M.K.L. Ching, "A Literary and Linguistic Analysis of Compact Verbal Paradox," in *Linguistic Perspectives on Literature* (London: RKP, 1980), 175-81.

[5]Vickers, *Classical Rhetoric* , 111, quoting John Hoskins, *Directions for Speech and Style* (*c.* 1599), italics added.

[6]See Huizinga, *Homo Ludens* , 1-27; he says, "Summing up the formal characteristics of play we might call it a free activity standing quite consciously outside 'ordinary' life as being 'not serious,' but at the same time absorbing the player intensely and utterly. It is an activity connected with no material interest, and no profit can be gained by it. It proceeds within its own proper boundaries of time and space according to fixed rules and in an orderly manner. It promotes the formation of social groupings which tend to surround themselves with secrecy and to stress their difference from the common world by disguise or other means," 13. See also, R Johnston, *The Christian at Play* (Grand Rapids: Eerdmans, 1983), 31-52.

[7]Casanowicz, *Paronomasia* , observes: "Plays upon words are especially frequent in the prophets … with their biting, ironical, or sarcastic force, they are best suited to the prophetic sermons, which adhere closely to the living speech and aim to reach the mind and conscience of the hearer, and to bring home to him directly and vividly a truth or a fact," 42.

[8]Addison, *The Spectator* , 231.

[9]S. Freud, *Jokes and Their Relationship to the Unconscious* (NY: Norton, 1963), 16-89. Terminology is always a problem in discussions of humor, and I may be using "wit" more broadly than Addison would allow; whatever terminology one employs, however, the locus of wit lies in something other than its ability to be translated into another context, linguistic or otherwise.

Chapter 6

[1]A. Cohen (ed.), *The Twelve Prophets* (London: Soncino, 1957), 158-59.

[2]W. Rudolph, *Micha-Nahum-Habakuk-Zephanja* (Gütersloh: Gütersloh Verlagshaus Gerd Mohn, 1975), 48-49.

[3]T.K. Cheyne, *Critica Biblica* (Amsterdam: 1970), 154-55.

[4]The character of the wordplays and the character of the text are not two independent inquiries, but we can separate them for practical purposes and we need not settle the textual questions—something that is unlikely in the present state of the debate in Mican studies—in order to settle the nature of the wordplays that are found in the text as it has been handed down.

[5]J. Wellhausen, *Die kleinen Propheten übersetzt, mit Noten* (Berlin: Reimer, 1892), 134.

[6]J.M.P. Smith (W.H. Hayes and J.A. Brewer), *A Critical and Exegetical Commentary on Micah, Zephaniah, Nahum, Habakkuk, Obadiah, and Joel* (Edinburgh: T&T Clark, 1911), 41.

[7]Rudolph, *Micha* : "Der Abschnitt gehört bekanntlich zu den am schlechtesten erhaltenen des

ganzen AT," 43.

[8]K. Elliger, "Die Heimat des Propheten Micha," *ZDPV* 57 (1934), 81-152.

[9]J.L. Mays, *Micah* (Philadelphia: Westminster, 1976).

[10]S.J. Schwantes, "Micah 1: 10-16," *VT* 14 (1964), 454-61.

[11]A.S. van der Woude, "Micha 1:10-16," in *Hommages à André Dupont-Sommer* (Paris: Adrien-Maisonneuve, 1971), 347-53.

[12]E. Pococke, "A Commentary on Micah," *Theological Works* , vol. 1 (London: 1740), 7.

[13]Schwantes argues that תגילו is the original reading of the Hebrew text, but this understanding depends in some part, at least, upon his reconstruction of בגנח גלה in place of בגת.

[14]Hillers, *Micah* , citing Carmignac, "Notes sur les Pesharim," *RQ* 3 (1962), 505-38, esp 517, who reads בגודלי on a damaged line following a citation of Mic 1: 9b. M. P. Horgan, *Pesharim: Qumran Interpretation of Biblical Books* (Washington, D.C.: CBA, 1979), transcribes the line as] ı . [ ] יבגד . [., and comments that the only clear letters are *bgwd* , 62.

[15]No doubt some influence from 2 Sam 1: 20 is felt (even as some influence can be discerned on the LXX and most other translators or commentators) but the immediate context furnishes enough of an explanation to account for the reading.

[16]D.R. Hillers, *Micah* (Philadelphia: Fortress, 1984), 25.

[17]Ahl, *Transformations* , makes a further point that Latin authors formed "etymological" plays based on these transpositions even with (seemingly) superficial phonetic correspondences between syllables, 44-51, *passim* .

[18]One could posit a text and argue for "intertextuality," but such a contention is difficult to show. More simply, David's lament is part of "cultural literacy," to borrow E.D. Hirsch's (*Cultural Literacy* , Boston: Houghton Mifflin, 1987) words for the shared knowledge that exists in any society.

[19]The translation of עריה at 1: 11 as "her cities" is typical in the sense that the translator will translate a difficult term by a more common term even if the context does not fit the more common term; cf., e.g., "peace" for שלמה ("cloak") at 2: 8. At any rate, the LXX should not be granted a too elevated status with respect to the text—the translator has as many problems with the text as the rest of us have.

[20]Schwantes, "1: 10-16," 455.

[21]Allen, *Micah* , 279.

[22]Pococke, "Micah," characteristically dancing in the middle of the floor, says, "Either sense is good [i.e., the 1st sg. or impv.], and both aim at the same end, whether taken as precept, or as an example," 7.

[23]While there is disagreement over Elliger's argument in its entirety, his contentions that the towns lie in the Shephelah and that each colon contains a single wordplay are generally followed.

[24]Schwantes, "1: 10-16," 456; Mays follows Schwantes in this reading.

[25]Ibid., 456; however, the *hireq compaginis* is regarded as an old genitive case ending according to GKC §90 k-l and with the participial form, GKC §90 m.

[26]Pococke, "Micah," 7.

[27]Schwantes, "1: 10-16," 456.

[28]Ibid., 456, and followed by Mays; cf. Lev 25:9, והעברת שופר.

[29]For example, at Mic 7: 18 there is a change from 2 sg. to 3 sg. (cf. also 2: 11-12); perhaps only trained Semitists write "Classical" Hebrew.

[30]Proximity of the terms or unusual collocation would highlight the alliteration; e.g., if לכם were omitted, then we would find עברי יושבת שפיר עריה־בשה. One could argue that יושבת sets up בשח, but elsewhere in the pericope ישבת does not figure in any paronomastic plays.

[31]See E. Henderson, *The Twelve Minor Prophets* (Grand Rapids: Baker, 1980 [reprint]), 229.

[32]Allen, *Micah* , 280.

[33]Hillers, *Micah* , 26.

[34]Glück, "Paronomasia," makes the interesting suggestion thatt צאנן, in connection with "naked shame" in the previous colon carries a secondary meaning of "prostitute" (יוצאת החוץ), 77; however, this usage comes from rabbinical sources not biblical ones and therefore may be anachronistic.

[35]Pococke, "Micah," 8.

[36]R. Gordis, "A Note on טוב," *JTS* 35 (1934), 186-88. He argues that in Aramaic frequently means "good in quantity"; "very much." This usage clarifies a number of biblical passages; e.g., rather than "I have strengthened thee for good" (Jer 15: 2), Gordis translates, "I will strengthen thee greatly." At Mic 1: 12, he follows Ibn Ezra and Kimchi by taking חלה from חיל, and translates the line, "For the inhabitant of Maroth trembles greatly."

[37]We seem to have an instance of implicit polysemantic wordplay—antanaclasis in our terminology—here; the second טובים is used in a different sense than the first.

[38]BDB places חלה under the root חול, "whirl, dance, writhe."

[39]רע is involved in another wordplay at Mic 2: 1-4 where both "moral evil" and "calamity" play off one another; see discussion in Chapter Seven below.

[40]Commentators do not use the terminology of wordplay when discussing the verse, but they note the opposition between what was expected ("good") and what was received ("evil"); cf., e.g., Eliezer and Calvin for the contrast, but explaining it in vastly different terms (Eliezer says that the Philistines [Maroth] wait anxiously for recompense (לטוב) when evil comes down to Jerusalem, while Calvin says that the inhabitants grieve for the loss of the good when "evil" comes to them from the Lord).

[41]Hillers, *Micah* , 26. The play is certainly "present," but is not as obvious as the other plays, or is more restrained than exploited—"catch me if you can!"

[42]Ibid., 26. Again, perhaps not "significant," but present and part of the rhetorical features of the text. One should not overlook the anagrammatical paronomasia of רע and לשער as well as לשער and ירושלם also in the colon.

[43]Wolff, *Micha* , 31; לכיש plays off not only לרכש, but המרכבה (*rk*) as well.

[44]In Amos 5: 5 Bethel, Gilgal, and Beer-sheba are singled out as cities that Israel is not to put her trust in, and in Amos 8: 14 Ashimah, Dan, and Beer-sheba are cited as cities that one should not swear by since they will "fall and never rise again."

[45]Schwantes, "1:10-16," 458-59.

[46]Schwantes' attempt to "restore" ראשכם to the beginning of the colon—"your chief shall give …"—is no more convincing than the other radical emendations he suggests throughout the pericope.

[47]Mays, *Micah* , 59.

[48]Does a "scribe" (one of Driver's "rabbinic fancies"?) create his own anagrammatical play, אבי substituted for יב(ו)א, making God the express agent of the action?

[49]ירש is used in the sense of dispossessor in Pro 30: 23, "… and the maid when she she dispossesses her mistress."

[50]Pococke, "Micah," 10.

[51]Additionally, the archaeological difficulties are many and we have not attempted to sort those out at all.

[52]D.N. Freedman, "Discourse on Prophetic Discourse," *The Quest for the Kingdom of God* , H.B. Huffman, *et al.* , eds., (Winona Lake: Eisenbrauns, 1983), 141-58, makes a valiant attempt to sort through the syntax of the passage. At one point he says, "The lack of clarity reflects the confusion of battle and destruction," 153, and then later appeals to a psychological explanation, "So we may suggest that the oracle 1: 10-16 was uttered during an ecstatic seizure occasioned by his almost hysterical grief at what he foresaw to be the fate of his beloved country and people" and even offers glossolalia as an analogy, 157. We can at least agree with Professor Freedman that it

is a confused passage; the psychological explanation is unconvincing since a literary explanation can serve equally as well (cf., e.g., Vickers, *Classical Rhetoric* , who argues that rhetorical devices are used to create this sort of emotional response in the reader—a confused text gives an aura of confusion, etc.).

[53]The "texts" are those of every translator and commentator, including Elliger, who posits a single meaning for the pericope, whereas if we accept ambiguity as an essential feature of wordplay (or of texts generally), then we could speak of a "text" with multiple meanings. The various translations and comments are representations of that text, and as representations they can be evaluated for their reasonableness, for the choice of representation—the interpretation conforms to agreed upon rules [philology, literary coherence, theology, or whatever frame of reference that is agreed upon by the particular group that will accept or reject the interpretation] or it does not.

[54]What J. Kugel, *The Idea of Biblical Poetry* (New Haven: Yale University Press, 1981), calls "seconding"; R. Alter, *The Art of Biblical Poetry* (NY: Basic Books, 1985), dubs "how much more so"; and Berlin, *Biblical Parallelism* , "connectedness."

[55]The words are not word pairs, of course, but they are grammatically parallel.

[56]V. Fritz, "Das Wort gegen Samaria Mi 1, 2-7," *ZAW* 86 (1974), 316-31.

[57]J. Carreira, "Kunstsprache und Weisheit bei Micha." *BibZeit* 26 (1982), 57.

[58]The sounds are not noted by Casanowicz as corresponding, and, although the differences between palatals (like *gimel*) and gutturals (like *ayin*) are significant, they are articulated at the palatal-velar area of the mouth, insofar as we can tell. A further possible example of the correspondence of the letters, if not the sounds, in Micah occurs at 2: 1b, עשׂיה, and 2: 2a, וגזלו; see also König, *Stylisk* , who lists Mic 1: 6ab as an instance of alliteration.

[59]Although this study consciously avoids placing an emphasis on reconstructing phonological plays, it is not out of the question to entertain a closer phonological correspondence between these sounds in the light of the wordplays we find and thus seek data that will confirm or deny such a correspondence.

[60]J.M.P. Smith is one of the few commentators who mentions the play; Allen, Mays, Hillers, Wolff are among those who make no explicit mention of the wordplay.

[61]Others, e.g., Mays, *Micah* , argue the opposite: "[אתנן] does not fit the sentence in which it stands or echo 'images/idols,' " 46; and J.M.P. Smith, *Micah* , "[It is] wholly unsuited here to the vb. *burnt* , and the demands of parallelism," 37. The assumption here is that the parallel term or colon should take a particular type of paradigmatic relationship. In point of fact, the parallelism of Hebrew poetry is quite diverse; see, e.g., D.J.A. Clines, "The Poetry of Greater Precision," in *Directions in Biblical Poetry* , ed. by E.R. Follis (Sheffield: JSOT, 1987), 77-100.

[62]Smith, *Micah*, 40.

[63]Driver, "Playing," 123.

[64]Watson, "Allusion, Irony and Wordplay in Mic 1:7," *Bib* 65 (1984), 105.

[65]The understanding that the "hires" are associated with the cult is not strictly required in the Mican passage, but certainly makes sense; cf., e.g., Rudolph.

[66]The story comes to mind of the church treasurer who received a large sum of money from a "questionable" source. "That is the devil's money," a parishioner remarked. To which the treasurer retorted, "Not any more!" The prophet's moral hearing is one octave higher (Abraham Heschel) than the treasurer's; the idol and the money are affined in the prophet's view. Perhaps a linguistic unity exists with the word that we, as modern, non-native speakers of Hebrew, do not apprehend; I am reminded of O. Barfield, *Poetic Diction* (Middleton: Wesleyan University, 1973), who says, "Our sophistication, like Odin's, has cost us an eye; and now it is the language of poets, in so far as they create true metaphors, which must *restore* this unity conceptually, after it has been lost from perception," 87.

[67]We should not overlook, however, the occurrence of "Ephrathah" in 1 Chr 4: 4 where it refers to the descendants of Judah: "These are the sons of Hur, the first-born of Ephrathah, the father of Bethlehem." A point perhaps not lost on the translator of the LXX who renders the initial words

of the colon as, "And you, Bethlehem, of the house (οἶκος) of Ephrathah."

[68]Note the anaphora with להיות used to begin each colon.

[69]It is possible, of course, that the text "originally" read "chiefs" rather than "thousands" but we have no textual witnesses for this reading except Matthew or texts influenced by the Matthean text, Matthew's rendering is more easily explained on theological rather than textual grounds.

[70]The "reading" by Matthew need not be conscious; it works equally well on a subconscious or simply a textual level. Raskin, *Mechanism* , says that native speakers will disambiguate a sentence by "squeezing" out less obvious readings from their perspective, 64.   From Matthew's perspective—Jesus as the greater "ruler"—reading אלופי for אלפי is a more natural reading.

[71]The "scribes" do more than just supply different vowels to this one word; cf. A.J. Petrotta, "A Closer Look at Matt 2:6 and Its Old Testament Sources," *JETS* 28 (1985), 47-52; more recently, see W.D. Davies and D.C. Allison, *The Gospel According to Matthew* , vol. 1 (Edinburgh: T&T Clark, 1988) who say, "The differences [between Micah, LXX, and Matthew] are in fact sufficient to tempt one to speak of an 'interpretation' instead of a 'quotation' of Scripture. The text has been freely altered by Matthew in order to make it best serve his ends," 242.

[72]Gundry, *Matthew* (Grand Rapids: Eerdmans, 1982), 29.

[73]See S.R. Driver, *The Book of Genesis* (London: Methuen, n.d.), who cites the Talmudic tradition that "Shiloh" is a title for the Messiah. Driver, of course, rejects this interpretation of "Shiloh," but does admit that the passage as a whole seems "to contain a Messianic thought," 386.

[74]Gundry, *Matthew* , 29; see also Davies and Allison, *Matthew* .

[75]Eliezer glosses the phrase "his origins" by saying, "These are the ancients who emerged from of old, from the seed of Jesse the Bethlehemite, that is David." Prior to this line of interpretation, many commentators followed the lead of Jerome who interprets these words in the light of John 1: 1; i.e., to Jesus' pre-existence with the Father.

[76]See Allen, *Micah* , who says, "This time can only be the days of David, to which the earlier parts of the verse have been harking," 343.

[77]Hillers, *Micah* , 66.

[78]We should not overlook Mic 7: 20 where the promises made to Abraham and Jacob are "from the days of old (מימי קדם)."

[79]Hillers, *Micah* , 45. Hillers lists "my people"; "he will not answer them"; "there is not response from God"; and the reference to "Jacob and Israel."

[80]Perhaps a correspondence between the speech imagery and the use of נטף in 2: 6-11 should not be overlooked with all the other affinities between the oracles.

[81]Note also the "poetic justice" of the situation and see Chapter Seven below.

[82]Hillers, *Micah* , 46.

[83]Hillers' attempt to link יום ההוא in the second colon with יום in the first colon (over against the MT which separates the cola with an *athnach*), and his reconstruction of the final colon as מים עד ים ומהר עד הר destroys the effect of the cola.

Chapter 7

[1]F. Buechner, *Telling the Truth* (NY: Harper & Row, 1977), says of Jesus' teaching concerning the Kingdom of God: "He does not speak of a reorganization of society as a political possibility or of the doctrine of salvation as a doctrine. He speaks of what it is like to find a diamond ring.... He suggests rather than spells out. He evokes rather than explains. He catches by surprise. He doesn't let the homiletic seams show," 62-63. The words of the prophets are not materially different.

[2]Perelman, *Rhetoric* , 161-62.

[3]V reads, *Quoniam contra Deum est manus eorum,* "Because their hand is against God," which is a very "literal" rendering, and may stem as much from the LXX (διότι οὐκ ἦραν πρὸς τὸν

θεὸν τὰς χείρας αὐτῶν) as from any independently calculated understanding of the words (although note Keil, *Minor Prophets* [Grand Rapids: Eerdmans, 1978, reprint], "For their hand is their god," which he glosses, "Their power passes as a god to them; they know of no higher power than their own arm; whatever they wish it is in their power to do," 439). At Gen 31: 29 and Deut 28: 32 we find examples of אל used in the sense of "strength" or "ability," which fits the present context.

[4]המשפחה alliterates with משכבותם; note the repetition of the initial letters and then the interchange of the labial and guttural, *peh/beth* and *cheth/kaph*.

[5]Allen, *Micah*, notes the "consonance" with מ and שׂ, not just in משכבותם and משפחה, but also with משליך, ימיש, משל, תמישו משם, and.

[6]J.M.P. Smith, *Micah*, 58.

[7]Consider also Ezek 35: 5 where Mount Seir will be cut off because they came against Israel in the time of her calamity (בעת אידם), in the time of her עון קץ which means "punishment" but also "guilt."

[8]Pococke, "Micah," 11, italics added.

[9]Of recent commentators, see Mays, Hillers, and Wolff; and cf. J.M.P. Smith, *Micah*, 54 for earlier commentators.

[10]E.B. Pusey, *The Minor Prophets* (Oxford: 1860).

[11]Rudolph,*Micha*, bases his understanding of נהיה on the work of by J Carmignac ["Precisions apportés au vocabulaire de l'hébreu biblique par la Guerre des fils de Lumière contra les fils de ténèbres," *VT* 5 (1955), 349] who argues that נהיה is used as "lament" in the War Scroll. Hillers cites the more recent works of Y. Yadin [*The Scroll of the War of the Sons of Light against the Sons of Darkness* (London: Oxford University, 1962)] and G. Vermes [*The Dead Sea Scrolls in English* (Baltimore: Penguin, 1965)] to the effect that the occurrence in the War Scroll is really a participle of היה. The form in Mic 2: 4 could still be a fem. form, as Rudolph argues, but this understanding no longer receives support from the extant literature.

[12]Whether a "saying" or a "song," משל is the broadest term used for such literary forms; cf., e.g., G. von Rad, "What we designate by the term 'proverb', sentence' corresponds to the Hebrew *masal*. But the latter has a much wider range of meaning, for it can also designate a maxim, a frequently used figure of speech, even a whole didactic poem" *Wisdom in Israel* (Nashville: Abingdon, 1972), 26, n.4; cf. also, A.R. Johnson, "משל," in *Wisdom in Israel and in the Ancient Near East*, VTSup 3 (Leiden: Brill, 1969), 162-69.

[13]The *waw* introduces the content of the משל, a *waw explicativum*; see GKC §154 *a*, note 1 (b).

[14]Onomatopoeic terms do not always work between languages, even those in the same family; a German rooster says, *kikeri*, not *cock-a-doodle-doo*.

[15]The term was suggested to me by Dr. Ron Sider of Westmont College, Santa Barbara.

[16]We do find this in modern Hebrew; cf. R. Alcalay, *The Complete Hebrew-English Dictionary*, (Jerusalem: Massada, 1975).

[17]One need not accept this belief system to appreciate the patterning or sentiment; see D. Daiches, *God and the Poets* (Oxford: Clarendon, 1984), 212.

[18]Hillers, *Micah*, 34.

[19]Mays, *Micah*, 72.

[20]Allen, *Micah*, 299, n. 78.

[21]KB and BDB do not mention "ecstasy" specifically, only that נטף is associated with "flowing words" and "prophetic discourse."

[22]*Stillo* means to drip, trickle, distil, but, in connection with *voces*, can refer to words "dripping" out.

[23]Hillers, *Micah*, 34.

[24]Keil, *Minor Prophets*, 443.

[25]Hillers feels that the object need not be expressed, and likens נטו to words not coming true, as in

Deut 28: 15.

[26]S.J. Schwantes, *A Critical Study of the Text of Micah* (Unpublished PhD Dissertation, Johns Hopkins University, 1962), 65.

[27]However, the same interchange at 6:14, often appealed to for support by commentators (e.g., Hillers), is less certain; see KB who renders 6:14 as "displace" (see also Holladay, *Lexicon* , "carry off").

[28]Mays, *Micah* , 72.

[29]Hillers, *Micah* , suggests that Micah's words form a threat: "You will create for yourselves prophets who, filled with a lying spirit, will make your blind folly worse," 37.

[30]The idea that the words are used as a structuring device is not new and is implied in the comments of Eliezer of Beaugency who quotes the opening words in his comments on v 11.

[31]In the closing cola we see clearly that a contrast is being made between the prophet and his opponents. If the contrast is not felt when we first read the oracle, the conclusion nudges the reader to reconsider the initial words and the play between them.

[32]The ' *ayin/* ' *aleph* exchange in this passage appears to be insignificant.

Chapter 8

[1]2 Sam 1: 17-27, the lament upon which this lament is ostensibly based, is called a   *qinah* , but contains mostly 2+2 measure and extensive wordplay; cf. H.W. Hertzberg, *I & II Samuel* , (Westminster: Philadelphia, 1964).

[2]Cf. A.J. Obrdlik, "'Gallows Humor'—A Sociological Phenomenon," *The AJS* 47 (1941-42), 709-16. Obrdlik discusses "gallows humour" from the stand-point of the oppressed, specifically the Czechoslovakian invasion by the Nazis in World War II. Nevertheless, his observation that humour is a social phenomenon with a social function is valid and relevant to our discussion.

[3]"Comic catharsis presents us with a fleeting image of man transcending his finitude and, if only for a brief moment, give us the exhilarating idea that perhaps it will be man after all who will be the victor in his struggle with a universe bent on crushing him," P.L. Berger, "Christian Faith and the Social Comedy," *Holy Laughter* , M.C. Hyers, ed. (NY: Seabury, 1969), 127.

[4]Cf., among others, Stählin's articles on θρηνέω and κοπετός in *TDNT* vol. III,148-55 and 830-860 respectively. He says, "In fact, the κοπετός of the prophets shares the twofold character of prophecy, which speaks in the name of God and also declares the future," 840.

[5]Nowottny, *Language* , 155; she goes on to say that "the superimposition itself may be said to have a meaning."

[6]Freud, *Jokes* , 44, emphasis added.

[7]We find an utterance funny when we are pleasantly surprised by seeing the two scripts actualized in a single item. J. Palmer, *Logic* , further argues that one of the scripts will be more implausible than the other, a point that Nash, *Language* , similarly makes when he says that the audience often must discard notions of logic and likelihood in order to appreciate the joke.

[8]Cf. R.R. Wilson, *Prophecy and Society in Ancient Israel* (Philadelphia: Fortress, 1980), 86-88 (general conclusions); 251-52 (conclusions regarding Ephraimite traditions); 294-95 (conclusions regarding Judaean traditions). W Brueggemann, *The Prophetic Imagination* (Philadelphia: Fortress, 1978) says, "The Prophet is engaged in a battle for language, in an effort to create a different epistemology out of which another community might emerge," 59.

[9]Douglas, "Social Control, " 372.

[10]Redfern, *Puns* , 125.

[11]Hillers, *Micah* , 62.

[12]Not necessarily *the* author, but someone who is doing more than simply transcribing a text.

[13]Cf. M. Greenberg, "Ancient Versions for Interpreting the Hebrew Text," VTSup 29 (1978), 131-48.

[14]The translator is not unlike many textual critics: he finds something in the text that does not seem exactly *kosher* , so he searches for an appropriate substitute, one that is at the same time similar to the text before him. Although the verb, ἐμφράσσειν only translates גדר here, the noun φράγμος is frequently employed to translate the root גדר. Moreover, "you shall be enclosed" follows from the "siege" that is laid in the following colon. The Εφραιμ/ἐμφραγμῷ variation is a similar move: E.Z. Melamed ("לתרגום השבעים לספר מיכה," *Eshkolot* 3 (1959), 90-105, argues that Εφραιμ is a confusion with ἐμφραγμῷ; more simply, the latter is a cognate to the verb, and the former reflects a need for a proper noun following "daughter." Whichever way the alteration went, the translator stays close to the text—the variations are minute, not radical reconstructions (a move that any nineteenth-century textual critic might make!)

[15]If we continue our analogy of modern textual critics, Tg is much more radical in his handling of the text to the point of reconstructing the text for the sake of intelligibility.

[16]B. Renaud, *Structure et attaches littéraires de Michée IV-V* (Paris: Gabalda et Cie., 1965), and J.T. Willis, "The Structure of the Book of Micah," *SEA* 34 (1969): 5-42.

[17]D.G. Hagstrom, *The Coherence of the Book of Micah* (Atlanta: Scholars Press, 1988).

[18]Perhaps זמה is a wordplay here: זמה is a technical cultic term, but also a more general term for cunning behavior.

[19]W. McKane, *Jeremiah* , vol. 1 (Edinburgh: T & T Clark, 1986) argues that Jer 5: 7 is best taken in its "well-attested" sense of "gash themselves": "The children of Jerusalem were unfaithful to Yahweh and gave their allegiance to empty idols. Yahweh put them on oath, but, although they had sworn allegiance to him, they gashed themselves at heathen shrines in connections with acts of idolatrous worship" 119. See also R.P. Carroll, *Jeremiah* (Philadelphia: Westminster, 1986), and W.L. Holladay, *Jeremiah* , vol. 1 (Fortress: Philadelphia, 1986).

[20]J.R. Lowell, "Humor, Wit, Fun, and Satire," in *The Function of the Poet and Other Essays* (Boston: Houghton Mifflin, 1893) speaking of Hood's puns, 50.

[21]In English, the same affect is achieved in a phrase such as, "He raged outrageously." One could posit a etymological link between "rage" and "outrageous," but in fact, "rage" comes by way of "rabid" and "outrageous" by way of "oultrage (*ultragium*). The example comes from Cullers, "Phoneme," 3.

[22]Cf. J.T. Willis, "Some Suggestions on the Interpretation of Micah 1: 2," *VT* 18 (1968), 372-79.

[23]Mays, *Micah* , followed by Hagstrom, *Coherence* , argues for a dipartite division, 1: 2 and 6: 1. "Hear" also occurs at 3: 9 and 6: 9, evidently with no structural significance.

[24]RSV reads "Israel" with the LXX for "Bethel" of the MT. Zech 10: 11 and Deut 33: 3 are other examples of "people" refering to Israel and not the world generally.

[25]G.A. Smith, *The Book of the Twelve Prophets* , vol. 1 (London: Hodder and Stoughton, 1906).

[26]In theophanic descriptions, the Lord comes out of his place and has a destructive effect. Hillers cites the study of J. Jeremias, *Theophanie: Die Geschichte einer alttestamentlichen Gattung* (Neukirchen-Vluyn: Neukirchener, 1965).

[27]The recognition of this paronomasia here, then, supports the MT against emendation.

[28]Transposing words is unusual for the translator who invariably follows the word order of his *Vorlage*, which corresponds to the word order of the MT.

[29]The phrase, "Mountains melt like wax before the Lord," is found also at Ps 97: 5, and Isa 34: 3 reads, "The mountains "melt" (נמסו) with their blood." Nowhere else in the OT are valleys "cleft," but at Zech 14: 4 the Mount of Olives will be cleft forming a "great valley" (גיא גדול). We hear an echo of "valley" (בקעה) in the use of "cleft" (יתבקע) in our passage.

[30]The "b" phrase or word, however, is the more obscure of the two and does not delimit the referent, as we see throughout the pericope.

[31]Pococke, "Micah," 2.

[32]Horgan, *Pesharim* , transcribes 1QpMic as ומה במות יהודה ... [מה פשע יעקב]. The interchange of מי and מה reminds me of a Hebrew mnemonic device (inter-lingual wordplay): "Who" is he; "He" is she; what, "ma"? Who, "me"? [הוא is he; היא is she; What, מה? Who, מי?]

[33]Mays, *Micah* , says that the insertion of "high places" here in place of "sin" seems "to make no sense," but he goes on to say that the "subtlety" of the "redactor" is apparent in this shift since his concern is the "offence of the Canaanized cult," 45.

[34]The effect is not unlike that of "unspoken puns" like אלפי and מושל (אלוף), and העמקים and (בקעה) ייתבקעו.

[35]Again, an effect similar to אתנן in Mic 1: 6.

[36]But cf. Pocecke who finds a reference to the leaders and military fortifications—all that is exalted by their own power. Throughout Micah leaders are castigated for abuses of power; cf. Mic 3.

[37]The oracle is not only linked within the book with other oracles, but perhaps even with other books. The words, "Hear peoples, all" (שמעו עמים כלם) are found at 1 Kgs 22: 28 on the lips of Micaiah ben Imlah. Hillers argues that 1 Kgs 22: 28 is an insertion based on mistaken identity, Micaiah ben Imlah for Micah Ha-Morashti. Rather than confusion, we have an allusion or an intertextuality of sorts, a linking, even if done by a redactor.

[38]Since there is this "retrospective redefinition" between the oracles, the ambiguity and universality of this oracle also keeps one from limiting the later oracles to a narrowly confined parochialism. The judgment of God against the nation of Israel is part and parcel of a broader scheme of establishing justice throughout the nations.

[39]G. Köbert, "môrad (Mi 1, 4) Tränke," *Bib* 39 (1958), 82-83, makes an interesting suggestion that מורד refers to a "drinking trough," as in Arabic *maurid* . His suggestion is not widely accepted (cf. Hillers).

[40]Redfern, *Puns* , 40; the "author" of Redfern's quote is Hericlitus, but the sentiment is true of most tendentious humour.

[41]As quoted by F.D. Layman, "Theology and Humor," *Asbury Seminarian* 38 (1983), 3.

Conclusion

[1]J. Sherzer, "'Oh! That's a Pun and I didn't mean it,'" *Semiotica* 22 (1978), 335, quoting E.R. Walsh

[2]L. A. Schökel, *Estudios de Poética Hebrea* (Barcelona: 1963). The chapter heading for Schökel's comments is "Estilística del Material Sonoro," while Watson's chapter heading is "Sound in Hebrew Poetry."

[3]Cf. Peeters, "Jeu de mots," 141-42.

[4]Cf., e.g., Childs, *Exodus* , who says, "The paronomastic formula, which gives the answer its indefinite quality, also testifies that the reality of God will not be different from that made known in his revelation ... God's intention for Moses is an expression of his being God and will be manifest according to his own plan," 76.

[5]One of Redfern's chapters is titled, "The Motions of Puns."

[6]Ullmann, *Style* , uses this phrase when speaking of language generally, but I think it applies especially to wordplay.

APPENDIX I

[1]J. Carreira, "Kunstsprache und Weisheit bei Micha," *BibZeit* 26 (1982), 50-74.

[2]Baum, "Chaucer," 230.

[3]Mic 7 is generally agreed upon by scholars to come from an author/redactor other than Micah; even the conservative scholar Allen, *Micah* , dates Mic 7: 8-20 as post-exilic, 252. However, Carreira's contention that wordplay is absent from Mic 7 is debatable; see Watson, *Poetry* , who

suggests Mic 7: 11 as one example, 249.

[4]Carreira, "Kunstsprache," 64.

[5]Ibid., 53.

[6]Ibid., 64.

[7]במה can mean "back," "height" (mountain ridge), or "(cultic) high place."

[8]Watson, *Poetry*, 225; cf. Ahl, *Metaformations*, who argues that the basic unit of sense in classical Latin "for purposes of play" is the syllable, not the word. Furthermore, Ahl argues that such things as vowel length, doubled consonants, certain spellings (e.g., words with "c" and "g"), do not hinder etymological plays, 54-60. A considerable freedom exists for what constitutes alliterative play, but the examination must be systematic and comprehensive enough to justify one's assertions. Moreover, in Ahl's case, treatises on "linguistics" written by authors contemporary with the works he is examining (e.g., Varro in *Lingua Latina*) give some external validation for his comments.

[9]Holladay, "David's Lament," makes the point that Hebrew only has 22 consonants and therefore "a repetition of consonants and consonant combinations is almost inevitable," 157. However, is the situation really materially different from English which has (only) 26 letters? Certainly there is a degree of inevitability for consonant clusters to repeat in any language with a limited "alphabet" to draw from. What one would need to show that these "consonant combinations" are significant *statistically*.

[10]Casanowicz, *Paronomasia*, 27-28.

[11]A.A. Hill, "Chaucer and the Pun-Hunters: Some Points of Caution," in *On Language: Rhetorica, Phonologica, Syntactica*, edited by C. Duncan-Rose and T. Vennemann (London: Routledge, 1988), 66-78.

[12]This caution is in need of qualification. Wordplay based on bilingualism is suspect only in the sense that one would need to show that bilingualism is an option for the author or during the period in question. Bilingualism may be a tremendous source for creating wordplay since wordplays are based on analogies. The famous wordplay Jesus makes on Peter (כיפא/πετρος) is interesting since it works in both Aramaic and Greek and yet no etymological or phonetic link is evident between the two terms. On bilingualism and wordplay in biblical studies see G.A. Rendsburg, "Bilingual Wordplay in the Bible," *VT* 38 (1988), 354-57, and in classical studies see Ahl, *Metaformations*, 60-63. Hill appeals to a psychological explanation for suspecting bilingual wordplay: "In writing in one's native language, foreign words, even if known, are normally at the outer fringes of consciousness, and are therefore unlikely to appear in puns," 70. I would contend that it is precisely on the "outer fringes of consciousness" that many wordplays exist.

[13]Turner, *Stylistics*, 13.

[14]Ibid., 14; i.e., stylistic choices are "found" in texts and utterances—in the performance of an "author"—but discussions of these choices usually employ value or aesthetic terms—we speak of an author's "competence."

[15]H.G. Widdowson, "Stylistic Analysis and Literary Interpretation," in *Linguistic Perspectives on Literature*, ed. by M.K.L. Ching, *et al.* (London: RKP, 1980), 236.

[16]Simply looking at a dictionary of synonyms is insufficient; even establishing contemporary usage would not guarantee a particular author's awareness of a term. However, contemporary usage and internal coherence provide the necessary preconditions for authorial style.

[17]Carreira, "Kunstsprache," 69.

[18]Ibid., 71.

[19]J.L. Crenshaw, "Education in Ancient Israel," *JBL* 104 (1985), 615.

[20]Kökeritz, "Chaucer," 952. The notion that wordplay is part of the general culture and not tied to a specific segment of society accords with Crenshaw's argument for diversity in Israelite education.

APPENDIX II

[1]Allen, *Micah* , 283-84.

[2]J. Fichtner, "Die Etymologische Ätiologie in den Namengebungen der geschichtlichen Bücher des Alten Testaments," *VT* 6 (1956), 372. citing I Sam 25: 25; cf. also A. Thisleton, "The Supposed Power of Words in the Biblical Writings," *JTS* 25 (1974), 283-99, and S.J. Tambiah, "The Magical Power of Words," *Man* , n.s. 3 (1968), 175-208, for more examples from theology and sociology.

[3]J. Barr, "The Symbolism of Names in the Old Testament," *BJRL* 52 (1969-70), 15.

[4]Tambiah, "Magical Power," 184.

[5]Ibid., 188.

[6]S. Scribner and M. Cole, *The Psychology of Literacy*, (Cambridge, Mass.: Harvard University, 1981).

[7]Ibid., 139. The study was conducted on the Vai people of Liberia.

GLOSSARY

Alliteration: The repetition of consonant clusters, usually at the beginning of the words.

Anagrammatical: The transposition of phonemes between terms.

Anaphora: Subsequent clauses that begin with identical terms.

Antanaclasis: A single term repeated with different senses.

Antonym: Two terms whose meanings contrast.

Assonance: The repetition of vowel sounds.

Chiasm: The inversion of words.

Consonance: The repetition of consonants at the end of words. Rhyme.

Gematria : The numerical equivalent of letters, often used as "codes."

Gradatio: Words that form a "ladder" effect (A-B; B-C; C-D) between clauses.

Homonyn: Two terms that sound similar but have different meanings or morphology.

Hyperbaton: The disruption of normal word order.

Notrikon : Letters of a word considered as acronyms.

Onomatopoeia: Sound imitative lexemes.

Paronomasia: "Soundplay." Wordplays determined by the sound of the letters and syllables.

Paronym: A specialized form of homonym where the terms *may* share the same origin (but need not). Used in place of *figura etymologica* .

Portmanteau: Two terms fused into a single term.

Pun: "Senseplay." Wordplays that are determined by semantic considerations more so than other linguistic considerations.

Repetition: A single term repeated with the same meaning.

Syllepsis: A single term that carries two meanings.

Synonym: Two terms whose meanings overlap.

Trope: General term used for any figure of speech. Most often used as an alternative to "wordplay" in this study.

Wordplay: The comprehensive term used for the trope.

BIBLIOGRAPHY

I. GENERAL WORKS.

Ackerley, C. J. "'In the Beginning was the Pun': Samuel Beckett's *Murphy* " *AUMLA 55* (1981): 15-22.

Addison, J. *The Spectator* , No. 61, May 10, 1711, 228-231.

Ahl, F. *Metaformations* Ithaca: Cornell University, 1985.

Alter, R. *The Art of Biblical Poetry* NY: Basic Books, 1985.

Baker, G.P. and Hacker, P.M.S. *Language, Sense and Nonsense* Oxford: Basil Blackwell, 1984.

Barfield, O. *Poetic Diction: A Study in Meaning* Middletown: Wesleyan University, 1973.

Barr, J. *Comparative Philology and the Text of the Old Testament* Oxford: Oxford University, 1968.

Baum, F. "Chaucer's Puns," *PMLA 71* (1956): 225-46.

Beitzel, B. "Exodus 3:14 and the Divine Name: A Case of Biblical Paronomasia," *TrinJ* (n.s.) 1 (1980): 5-20.

Berger, P.L. "Christian Faith and Social Comedy," in *Holy Laughter* (Hyers, M.C., ed.) NY: Seabury, 1969.

Berlin, A. *The Dynamics of Biblical Parallelism* Bloomington: Indiana University, 1985.

Black, M. *An Aramaic Approach to the Gospels & Acts* (3d edition) Oxford: Oxford University, 1967.

Bloomfield, L. *Language* NY: Holt, Rhinehart & Winston, 1933.

Blyth, R. *Oriental Humor* Tokyo: Hokuseido, 1959.

Böhl, F. "Wortspiele im Alten Testament," *JPOS* 6 (1926): 196-212.

Brown, J. "Eight Types of Puns," *PMLA* 71 (1956): 14-26.

Brueggemann, W. *The Prophetic Imagination* Philadelphia: Fortress, 1978.

Budick, S. (See: Hartman, G.).

Buechner, F. *Telling the Truth: The Gospel as Tragedy, Comedy, and Fairy Tale* NY: Harper & Row, 1977.

Bühlmann, W. and K. Scherer. *Stilfiguren der Bibel: Ein kleines Nachschlagewerk* Fribourg: Schweizerisches Katholisches Bibelwerk, 1973.

Casanowicz, I.M. *Paronomasia in the Old Testament* Boston: Norwood, 1894.

Ceresko, A. R. "The Function of Antanaclasis (*mṣ'* 'to find' // *mṣ'* 'to reach, overtake, grasp') in Hebrew Poetry, Especially in the Book of Qoheleth," *CBQ* 44 (1982): 551-569.

Charlesworth, J. H. "Paronomasia and Assonance in the Syriac Text of the Odes of Solomon," *Semitics* 1 (1970): 12-26.

Ching, M. K. L. "The Relationship Among the Diverse Senses of a Pun," *The Southeastern Conference on Linguistics Bulletin* 2, no. 3 (Fall, 1978): 1-8.

_____ "A Literary and Linguistic Analysis of Compact Verbal Paradox," in *Linguistic Perspectives on Learning* (M.K.L. Ching, *et al.*, eds.), London: RKP, 1980: 175-181.

Chisholm, R.B. "Wordplay in the Eighth-Century Prophets," *BibSac* 144 (1987): 44-52.

Clines, D.J.A. "The Poetry of Greater Precision," in *Directions in Biblical Poetry* (E.R. Follis, ed.) Sheffield: JSOT, 1987: 77-100.

Cole, M. (See: Scribner, S.)

Crenshaw, J.L. "Education in Israel," *JBL* 104 (1985): 601-15.

Cruse, D.A. *Lexical Semantics* Cambridge: Cambridge University, 1986.

Culler, J. (ed) *On Puns: The Foundation of Letters* New York: Blackwell,1988.

Cutler, A. "On Saying what You Mean Without Meaning What You Say," *Proceedings of the Chicago Linguistic Society* 10 (1974): 117-127.

Daiches, D. *God and the Poets* Oxford: Clarendon, 1984.

Davidson, R. *The Courage to Doubt* London: SCM, 1983.

Douglas, M. "The Social Control of Cognition: Some Factors in Joke Perception," *Man* (n.s.) 3 (1968): 361-76.

Driver, G. R. "Playing on Words," *Proceedings of the 4th World Congress of Jewish Studies* (1967): 121-129.

Eilberg-Schwartz, H. "Who's Kidding Whom?: A Serious Reading of Rabbinic Word Plays," *JAAR* 55 (1988): 765-88.

Empson, W. *Seven Types of Ambiguity* (3d edition) NY: New Directions, 1966.

Eybers, I. H. "The Use of Proper Names As a Stylistic Device," *Semitics* 2 (1971-72): 82-92.

Farb, P. *Word Play: What Happens When People Talk* NY: Bantam, 1975.

Fichtner, J. "Die Etymologische Ätiologie in den Namengebungen der geschichtlichen Bücher des Alten Testaments," *VT* 6 (1956): 372-96.

Fordyce, C. J. "Puns on Names in Greek," *CJ* 28 (1932-33): 44-46.

Fraenkel, J. "Paronomasia in Aggadic Narratives" *Scripta Hierosolymitana* 27 (1978): 27-35.

Frank, R. "Some Uses of Paronomasia in Old English Scriptural Verse," *Speculum* 47 (1972): 207-26.

Freud, S. *Jokes and Their Relationship to the Unconscious* NY: Norton, 1963.

Gibson, A. *Biblical Semantic Logic* Oxford: Blackwell, 1981.

Glück, J. J. "Paronomasia in Biblical Literature," *Semitics* 1 (1970): 50-78.

Green, W.S. "Romancing the Tome: Rabbinic Hermeneutics and the Theory of Literature," *Semeia* 40 (1987): 147-68.

Guillaume, A. "Paronomasia in the Old Testament," *JSS* 8-9 (1963-64): 282-290.

Gunn, D.M. "The Anatomy of Divine Comedy: On Reading the Bible as Comedy and Tragedy," *Semeia* 32 (1984): 115-129.

Hacker, P.M.S. (See Baker, G.P.).

Hamori, A. "Notes on Paronomasia in Abu Tammam's Style," *JSS* 12 (1967): 83-90.

_____ *On the Art of Medieval Arabic literature* New Jersey: Princeton University, 1974.

Handelman, S.A. *The Slayers of Moses* Albany: State University of NY, 1982.

Hartman, G. and Budick, S. (eds.) *Midrash and Literature* New Haven: Yale University, 1986.

Havelock, E.A. *The Muse Learns to Write* New Haven: Yale University, 1986.

Heller, L.G. "Toward a General Typology of the Pun," *Language and Style* 7 (1974): 271-282.

Hill, A.A. "Chaucer and the Pun-Hunters: Some Points of Caution," in *On Language: Rhetorica, Phonologica, Syntactica: A Festschrift for R.P. Stockwell* London: Routledge, 1988 (C. Duncan-Rose and T. Vennemann, eds.): 66-78.

Holladay, W. L. "Form and Word-Play in David's Lament Over Saul and Jonathan," *VT* 20 (1970): 153-189.

Hrushovki, B. "The Meaning of Sound Patterns in Poetry," *Poetics Today* 2 (1980): 39-56.

Huizinga, J. *Homo Ludens* Boston: Beacon, 1955 (reprint).

Huncher, M. "How to Play Games With Words: Speech Act Jokes," *Journal Of Literary Semantics* (1980): 20-29.

Jeffers, R.J. and Lehiste, I. "Lexical Change," in *Principles and Methods for Historical Linguistics* Cambridge, Mass.: MIT, 1979: 126-137.

Johnson, Ra. "Jokes, Theories, Anthropology," *Semiotica* 22 (1978): 309-334.

Johnston, R.K. *The Christian at Play* Grand Rapids: Eerdmans, 1983.

Joseph, Sister M. *Shakespeare's Age of the Arts of Language* NY: Hafner, 1966.

Kelly, L. G. "Punning and the Linguistic Sign," *Linguistics* 66 (1970): 5-11.

Kökeritz, H. "Rhetorical Word-Play in Chaucer" *PMLA* 69 (1954): 937-52.

König, E. *Stilistik, Rhetorik, Poetik in Bezug and die biblische Litteratur* Leipzig: 1900.

Kugel, J.L. *The Idea of Biblical Poetry* New Haven: Yale University, 1981.

Layman, F.D. "Theology and Humor," *Asbury Seminarian* 38 (1983): 3-25.

Lehiste, I. (See: Jeffers, R.J.).

Lotman, J. *The Structure of the Artistic Text* Ann Arbor: University of Michigan, 1977.

Lowell, J.R. "Humor, Wit, Fun, and Satire," in *The Function of the Poet and Other Essays* Boston: Houghton Mifflin, 1893: 33-60.

Lyons, J. *Introduction to Theoretical Linguistics* Cambridge: Cambridge University, 1968.

Mahood, M. M. *Shakespeare's Wordplay* London: Methuen, 1957.

McCartney, E. S. "Puns and Plays on Proper Names," *CJ* 14 (1919): 343-58.

Millard, A.R. "The Practice of Writing in Ancient Israel," *BA* 35 (1972): 195-98.

_____ "The Question of Literacy," *BRev* 3 (1987): 22-31.

Milner, G. B. "Homo Ridens: Towards a Semiotic Theory of Humor and Laughter," *Semiotica* 5 (1972): 1-30.

More, P.E. "Thomas Hood," *Shelburne Essays* (7th series) NY: Phaeton, 1967 (reprint): 49-63.

Morreall, J. (ed.). *The Philosophy of Laughter and Humor* Albany: State University of New York, 1987.

Morreall, J. *Taking Laughter Seriously,* Albany: State University of New York, 1983.

Motley, M. T. "What I Meant to Say," *Psychology Today* (February, 1987): 24-28.

Nash, W. *The Language of Humour* NY: Longman, 1985.

_____ *Rhetoric: The Wit of Persuasion* Oxford: Basil Blackwell, 1989.

Neusner, J. *Wrong Ways and Right Ways in the Study of Formative Judaism* Atlanta: Scholars, 1988.

Nowottny, W. *The Language Poets Use* NY: Oxford University, 1962.

Obrdlik, A.J. "'Gallows Humor'—A Sociological Phenomenon," *AJS* 47 (1941-42): 709-16.

Palmer, J. *The Logic of the Absurd,* London: British Film Institute, 1987.

Peeters, L. "Pour une interprétation du jeu de mots," *Semitics* 2 (1971-72): 127-142.

Perelman, C. *The Realm of Rhetoric* Notre Dame: University of Notre Dame, 1982.

Plett, H.F. "Rhetoric," in *Discourse and Literature* (Dijk, T.A. van, ed.) Amsterdam: John Benjamins, 1985: 59-84.

Pope, A. "God's Revenge Against Punning" in *The Prose Works of A. Pope* , vol. 1 (Ault, N., ed.) Oxford: 1936.

Rajan, T. "The Supplement of Reading," *NLH* 17 (1986): 573-594.

Raskin, V. *Semantic Mechanisms of Humor* Dordrecht: D.Reidel (1985).

Redfern, W. *Puns* Oxford: Blackwell, 1984.

Rendsburg, G.A. "Bilingual Wordplay in the Bible" *VT* 38 (1988): 354-57.

Richard, E. "Expressions of Double Meaning and Their Function in the Gospel of John" *NTS* 31 (1985): 96-112.

Robbins, R. "A Prevalence of Paronomasia," *Times Literary Supplement* (May 8, 1981): 522.

Roberts, R.D. *How Poetry Works* Harmondsworth: Penguin, 1986.

Rosenberg, J. "1 and 2 Samuel," in *The Literary Guide to the Bible* (Alter, R. and Kermode, F., eds.) Cambridge, Mass.: Belnap, 1987: 122-45.

Sasson, J.M. "Wordplay in the OT," IDBSup: 968-70.

Saydon, P.P. "Assonance in Hebrew as a Means of Expressing Emphasis," *Bib* 36 (1955): 36-50; 287-304.

Scherer, K. (See: Bühlmann, W.).

Schökel, L.A. *Estudios de Poética Hebrea* , Barcelona: 1963.

Scribner, S. and Cole, M. *The Psychology of Literacy* Cambridge, Mass.: Harvard University, 1981.

Sherzer, J. "Oh! That's a Pun and I Didn't Mean It," *Semiotica* 22 (1978): 335-50.

Spitzer, L. "Pun," *Journal of English and German Philology* 49 (1950): 352-354.

Spolsky, E. "The Limits of Literal Meaning," *NLH* 19 (1988): 419-40.

Strus, A. *Nomen-Omen* Rome: Pontifical Institute, 1978

Sypher, W. (ed.) *Comedy* Baltimore: Johns Hopkins University, 1980.

Thau, A. "Play with Words and Sounds in the Poetry of Max Jacob," *Revue des Lettres Modernes* 336-339 (1973): 125-154.

Turner, G.W. *Stylistics* Harmondsworth: Penguin, 1973.

Ullmann, S. *Language and Style* Oxford: Blackwell, 1964.

_____ *Semantics: An Introduction to the Science of Meaning* Oxford: Blackwell, 1962.

Vickers, B. *Classical Rhetoric in English Poetry* London: MacMillan, 1970.

Voss, A. "Lowell, Hood & The Pun," *Modern Language Notes* 63 (1948): 346-347.

Watson, W. G. E. *Classical Hebrew Poetry* Sheffield: JSOT, 1984.

Weinstock, L. I. "Sound & Meaning in Biblical Hebrew" *JSS* 28 (1983): 49-62.

West, M. "Scatology & Eschatology: The Heroic Dimensions of Thoreau's Wordplay," *PMLA* 89 (1974): 1043-64.

Widdowson, H.G. "Stylistic Analysis and Literary Interpretation," in *Linguistic Perspectives on Learning* (Ching, M.K.L., *et al.*, eds.) London: RKP, 1980: 235-41.

Wilson, C.P. *Jokes: Form, Content, Use, and Function* London: Academic, 1979.

Wilson, R.R. *Prophecy and Society in Ancient Israel* Philadelphia: Fortress, 1980.

Wimsatt, W. K. "Verbal Style: Logical & Counterlogical," *PMLA* 65 (1950): 5-20.

_____ "The Criticism of Comedy," in *Hateful Contraries* University of Kentucky, 1965: 90-107.

Yeivin, I. *Introduction to the Tiberian Masorah* Missoula: Scholars, 1980.

II.   COMMENTARIES GENERALLY AND WORKS PERTAINING TO PASSAGES IN MICAH.

Allen, L.C. *The Books of Joel, Obadiah, Jonah and Micah* Grand Rapids: Eerdmans, 1976.

Allison, D.C. (see: Davies, W. D.).

Barr, J. "The Symbolism of Names in the Old Testament," *BJRL* 52 (1969-70): 11-29.

Barrett, C.K. *The Gospel According to John* , 2d ed., Philadelphia: Westminster, 1978.

Barton, J. "Natural Law and Poetic Justice in the Old Testament," *JTS* 30 (1979): 1-14.

Brown, R. *The Gospel According to John: xiii-xxi* Garden City: Doubleday, 1970.

Carreira, J. "Kunstsprache und Weisheit bei Micha," *BibZeit* 26 (1982): 50-74.

Carroll, R.P. *Jeremiah: A Commentary* Philadelphia: Westminster, 1986.

Cheyne, T.K. *Critica Biblica* Amsterdam: 1970.

Childs, B.S. *The Book of Exodus* Philadelphia: Westminster, 1974.

Clements, R.E. *Isaiah 1-39* Grand Rapids: Eerdmans, 1980.

Cohen, A. (ed.) *The Twelve Prophets* London: Soncino, 1957.

Dahood, M. *Psalms II: 51-100* Garden City: Doubleday,

Davies, W.D. and Allison, D.C. *A Critical and Exegetical Commentary on the Gospel According to St. Matthew* , vol. 1, Edinburgh: T & T Clark, 1988.

Dorhme, E. *A Commentary on the Book of Job* Nashville: Thomas Nelson, 1984.

Driver, S.R. *The Book of Genesis* London: Methuen, n.d.

Eliezer of Beaugency *Kommentar zu Ezekiel und den XII kleinen Propheten* , 2 vols. (S.Poznanski, ed.), Berlin: 1910.

Elliger, K. "Die Heimat des Propheten Micha," *ZDPV* 57 (1934): 81-152.

Freedman, D. N. "Discourse on Prophetic Discourse," in *The Quest for the Kingdom of God: Studies in Honor of George E. Mendenhall* (H.B. Hoffman, *et al.*, eds.) Winona Lake: Eisenbrauns, 1983: 141-58.

Fritz, V. "Das Wort gegen Samaria Mi 1, 2-7," *ZAW* 86 (1974): 316-31.

Gordis, R. "A Note on טוב," *JTS* 35 (1934): 186-88.

Greenberg, M. "Ancient Versions for Interpreting the Hebrew Text," VTSup 29 (1978): 131-48.

_____ *Ezekiel 1-20* Garden City: Doubleday, 1983.

Gundry, R.H. *Matthew: A Commentary on His Literary and Theological Art* Grand Rapids: Eerdmans, 1982.

Hagstrom, D.G. *The Coherence of the Book of Micah* Atlanta: Scholars, 1988.

Hawthorne, G.F. *Philippians* Waco: Word, 1983.

Henderson, E. *The Twelve Minor Prophets* Grand Rapids: Baker, 1980 (reprint).

Hertzberg, H.W. *I & II Samuel* Philadelphia: Westminster, 1964.

Hillers, D R *Micah* Philadelphia: Fortress, 1984.

Holladay, W.L. *Jeremiah 1* Philadelphia: Fortress, 1986.

Horgan, M.P. *Pesharim: Qumran Interpretation of Biblical Books* Wash., D.C.: Catholic Biblical Association, 1979.

Jerome *Commentarioram in Michaeam Prophetam* Basle: 1537.

Johnson, A.R. "מֹשֵׁל," VTSup 3 (1969): 162-69.

Kaiser, O. *Isaiah 13-39: A Commentary* Philadelphia: Westminster, 1974.

Keil, C.F. (and Delitzsch, F.) *Commentary on the Old Testament: Minor Prophets*, vol. 10,

Grand Rapids: Eerdmans, 1978 (reprint).

Kirkpatrick, A.F. *The Book of Psalms* Cambridge: Cambridge University, 1902.

Köbert, G. *"môrad* (Mi 1,4) Tränke," *Bib* 39 (1958): 82-83.

Lichtenstein, M.H. "The Poetry of Poetic Justice: A Comparative Study in Biblical Imagery," *JANES* 5 (1973): 255-65.

Mays, J.L. *Micah: A Commentary* Philadelphia, Westminster, 1976.

McKane, W. *A Critical and Exegetical Commentary on Jeremiah*, vol. 1, Edinburgh: T & T Clark, 1986.

Melamed, E.Z. "לתרגום השבים לספר מיכה," *Eshkolot* 3 (1959): 90-105.

Miqr' ot Gedolot Jerusalem: n.d.

Moriarty, F.L. "Word as Power in the Ancient Near East," in *A Light Unto My Path: Old Testament Studies in Honor of J.M. Myers* (H.N. Bream, *et al.*, eds.) Philadelphia: Temple University, 1974.

Nicholas de Lyra *Postilla Super Totem Bibliam* Nuremberg: 1493.

Petrotta, A.J. "A Closer Look at Matt 2: 6 and Its Old Testament Sources," *JETS* 28 (1985): 47-52.

Pococke, E. "A Commentary on Micah," in *Theological Works* , vol. 1, London: 1740.

Pusey, E.B. *The Minor Prophets* Oxford: 1860.

Rad, von, G. *Wisdom in Israel* Nashville: Abingdon, 1972.

Renaud, B. *Structure et attaches littéraires de Micheé IV-V* Paris: Gabalda et Cie, 1965.

Rosenmüller, E.F.C. *Scholia in Vetus Testamentum* Leipzig: 1788-1835.

Rudolph, W. *Micha-Nahum-Habakuk-Zephanja* Gütersloh: Gütersloher Verlaghaus Gerd Mohn, 1975.

Schnackenburg, R. *The Gospel According to St. John* , vol. 3, London: Burnes & Oates, 1982.

Schwantes, S.J. "Micah 1: 10-16," *VT* 14 (1964): 454-61.

Smith, G.A. *The Book of the Twelve Prophets: Amos, Hosea and Micah* , vol. 1, London: Hodder and Stoughton, 1906.

Smith, J.M.P. (Ward, W.H. and Bewer, J.A.) *A Critical and Exegetical Commentary on Micah, Zephaniah, Nahum, Habakkuk, Obadiah and Joel* Edinburgh: T & T Clark, 1911.

Tambiah, S.J. "The Magical Power of Words," *Man* (n.s.) 3 (1968): 171-208.

Thiselton, A. "The Supposed Power of Words in the Biblical Writings," *JTS* 25 (1974): 283-99.
Vuilleumier, R. (and Keller, C.-A.) *Micheé, Nahoum, Habacuc, Sophonie* Neucâtel: Delachaux

& Niestlé, 1971.

Watson, W.G.E. "Allusion, Irony and Wordplay in Mic 1: 7," *Bib* 65 (1984):103-05.

Wellhausen, J. *Die kleinen Propheten übersetzt, mit Noten* Berlin: Reimer, 1892.

Wildberger, H. *Jesaja* Neukirchen-Vluyn: Neukirchener, 1972.

Willis, J. T. "Some Suggestions on the Interpretation of Micah 1: 2," *VT* 18 (1968): 372-79.

_____ "The Structure of the Book of Micah," *SEA* 34 (1969): 5-42.

Wolff, H.W. *Mit Micha Reden: Prophetie einst und jetzt* München: Chr. Kaiser, 1978.

_____ *Micah the Prophet* (R.D. Gerhke, trans.) Philadelphia: Fortress, 1981.

_____ *Dodekapropheton 4: Micha* Neukirchen-Vluyn: Neukirchener, 1982.

Woude, van der, A.S. "Micha 1: 10-16," in *Hommages à André Dupont-Sommer* Paris: Adrien-Maisonneuve, 1971: 347-53.

Zimmerli, W. *Ezekiel 1* Philadelphia: Fortress, 1979.

III. UNPUBLISHED MATERIAL.

Schwantes, S.J. *A Critical Study of the Text of Micah* Ph.D. Dissertation, Johns Hopkins University, 1962.

Willis, J.T. *The Structure, Setting, and Interrelationships of the Pericopes in the Book of Micah* Ph.D. Dissertation, Vanderbilt University, 1966.

INDEX OF SCRIPTURE REFERENCES